Inside Argentina
from Perón to Menem

1950–2000 FROM AN
AMERICAN POINT OF VIEW

By Laurence W. Levine
with Kathleen Quinn

EDWIN HOUSE PUBLISHING INC.

Inside Argentina from Perón to Menem 1950–2000
From an American Point of View

By Laurence W. Levine with Kathleen Quinn

Published by Edwin House Publishing Inc.
P.O. Box 128, Ojai, California 93024 USA
www.EdwinHousePublishing.com

ISBN 0-9649247-7-3

Book design by Ingrid Bromberg

Printed in the United States of America by McNaughton & Gunn

10 9 8 7 6 5 4 3 2 1

Levine, Laurence W.
    Inside Argentina from Perón to Menem : 1950–2000 from an American
point of view/ by Laurence W. Levine with Kathleen Quinn. --1st ed.
    p.cm.
    Includes index.
    ISBN: 0-9649247-7-3

    1. Argentina--History--1943- 2. Argentina--Economic conditions--1945- 3.
Argentina--Politics and government--1943- 4. Argentina--Relations--United
States. 5. United States--Relations--Argentina. I.Quinn, Kathleen, 1951 Feb. 14-
II. Title.

F2849.L48 2001   982.06
                                     QBI00-1042

TABLE OF CONTENTS

INTRODUCTION

It is encouraging that, after long interruptions, Americans and Argentines are once again genuinely interested in each other. Both share many common experiences in their formation as nations. Fate in the guise of a bountiful nature served as a magnet attracting millions of skilled immigrants to their shores. The creation of strong social institutions in both countries formed literate, creative and vigorous peoples. Both nations appeared destined for leadership roles in the world.

Few doubt the United States has reached high levels of its potential. Argentina is still in the process with signs that significant progress is underway. While the full promise of both countries is still unfulfilled in a world where change is constantly accelerating, each undoubtedly has the potential to continue to alter our world for good or ill.

Argentines as far back as Domingo Sarmiento in the mid-1800s were fascinated by the series of developments leading to the United States becoming a primary world power. Americans in the mid-1900s were fascinated by political events in Argentina that appeared to diminish seriously Argentina's chances of reaching its undoubted potential. By the 1930s, with both nations competitors in agricultural exports and following very different political doctrines, a long period of mutual distrust and estrangement was created. American political aggressiveness and economic protectionism, and Argentina's hostile reaction thereto, were exaggerated during World War II and the years that followed. The resultant mutual distrust and hostility made it seem that two nations that had so much in common were to be permanently estranged.

That is why Mr. Levine's book is so timely and so valuable. It is a first-hand record of the many Americans and Argentines who, over the decades, worked to overcome mutual incomprehension. Readers will find a fascinating account by an American lawyer who, as a very young man, became enmeshed in bilateral events as have few others before or since. Larry Levine, is a very energetic, committed and objective person, has the rare luck of generally turning up at the right place at the right time and making the most of it.

Mr. Levine has dealt with Argentine matters for forty-two years. He has made more than seventy trips to Argentina. He has come to know more Argentines and the details of more situations relating to U.S.-Argentine relations than any American I know, and he is always available for constructive counsel based upon his experience. It is a small wonder he was relied upon for his insights by a long series of American ambassadors to Argentina.

That is how I first met Mr. Levine in 1973. By that year, U.S.-Argentine relations had reached another critically low point. As country director for Argentina in the Department of State, I knew it was important that the new American ambassador to Argentina, Robert C. Hill, be adequately briefed and prepared for his difficult mission. Mr. Levine was the strongest member of the team that briefed Ambassador Hill. For several days, I accompanied the ambassador with Mr. Levine and others as we made the rounds in New York City to those individuals and businesses having the most at stake in Argentina. I was impressed that it was Mr. Levine who asked the most acute questions and made the most penetrating observations. We became and remain fast friends.

By the time I was appointed ambassador to Argentina in 1983, Mr. Levine was the president of the U.S.-Argentine Chamber of Commerce. Again I came to rely on his encyclopedic knowledge of a very complicated country. Especially valuable to me was his background on the situations created by the deep historic mutual mistrust. He knew the key individuals exerting influence and how that influence could be channeled in constructive ways. Above all, I remained convinced of his total commitment to as true a brotherhood between two peoples as it is possible to achieve.

The years since Argentina returned to the path of democratic governance and the increased American appreciation of Argentina's accomplishments and importance have seen almost two decades of unparalleled good relations. Today one can truly say that the historic misconceptions are only vestiges of what they once were.

As today's Americans and Argentines work to draw their great countries even closer together, they can learn much from an extraordinary American who has spent most of his adult life in that very enterprise. He is a truly remarkable fellow.

Ambassador (ret.) Frank V. Ortiz
Santa Fe, New Mexico
August 1, 2000

In this book I relate fifty years of modern Argentine history from a single point of view: that of an American lawyer who was fortunate enough to have been deeply involved with the legal and economic life of Argentina on a day-to-day basis. I give the reader a down-to-earth synopsis of an extraordinarily complex time in U.S.-Argentine relations, the era that began with Juan Perón and ended with Carlos Saul Menem. It is my hope that these detailed, personal recollections will provide a better understanding of a wonderful country that too often has been misunderstood. I don't believe anyone else alive today can tell these stories.

I am not a historian, but since I was an intimate participant in many significant events, I have written this book with the intention of providing historians, journalists and students of Argentine history everywhere with useful information. But this book has a more ambitious mission as well: Even though I am not a historian, I want to explain, in broad terms for the layman, the behavior of Argentina from Perón to Menem. It is not generally understood—not even by some professional historians—that during the years that the world generally refers to as "the Cold War," Argentina was embroiled in a slow-motion civil war that only rarely was fought with organized violence and shooting in the streets. This largely clandestine civil war was fought to determine whether Argentina was to be an agricultural nation or an industrial nation, or both. It was a civil war fundamentally not unlike the civil war fought in the United States one hundred years earlier.

But Argentina's civil war was fought, to a surprising degree, on a purely economic front. Governments rose and fell, presidents and economy ministers were arrested, businessmen and politicians went into exile because of the fierce competition in Argentina to set economic policy either firmly on the side of the established agricultural elite (who traditionally brought Argentina great wealth) or on the side of the emerging industrial classes (who wanted jobs and the opportunities to create new wealth). Argentina's leaders periodically tried to find a third way out of this civil war, but none succeeded. When peaceful politics failed, all sides resorted to criminal acts of bloodshed, and Argentina's civil war was more obvious to see.

It has been customary in certain areas of the press and academia to blame all the problems that have recently plagued Argentina on its military rulers. Those who read this book with the expectation of finding that here will be very disappointed. It is my belief, based on actual facts, that for forty years, each time the military took power (with the exception of the government led by General Leopoldo Galtieri that came to power in 1982), it did so because Argentina's two main political parties, the Radicals and the Peronists, had proved incapable of governing. The military came in as an interim government foreseeing the return of elected government. For many years the military was bitterly divided as to whether Peronists should ever have another chance to be elected, but history shows that the military faction that advocated Peronist rehabilitation most often ruled.

There were only two military governments in my experience that acted, at least in certain areas, with utter bad faith toward the Argentine people: The junta that came to power in 1976 has become famous for the human rights abuses that occurred when it sought to eliminate domestic terror. It also allowed its economic team to change too rapidly the flawed economic system which subsidized industry in an effort to destroy Peronism and the economic sector on which the Peronists subsisted. With similar malfeasance, General Leopoldo Galtieri launched the Malvinas War in 1981, which needs to be analyzed as an attempt to distract Argentines from the economic mess created by his military predecessors, bolstered by a belief that the U.S. would do nothing to stop him and perhaps even help him.

I hope that in this light, readers will find my detailed account of key moments in Argentina's financial and legal history helpful to obtaining a complete understanding of the overall history of Argentina during the Cold War years, and especially as to how Argentina finally found the right road to democracy. As the American lawyer for Argentine Airlines and several key Argentine financial institutions during this period, and as president of the U.S.-Argentine Chamber of Commerce for several years, I was a front-line witness to Argentina's long and unhappy civil war.[1]

Specifically, my book gives the reader a first-hand account of three highly important but seldom-studied events in modern Argentine history: the opening of Banco de la Nación in New York City in 1972 (the first foreign bank of its kind in America), the closing of Banco de Intercambio Regional in 1979 (which I predicted would precipitate a catastrophic collapse of Argentina's financial community, which it did), and the strange American odyssey of the late Argentine financier, David Graiver, whose mysterious death was but the tip of a scandal involving so many powerful interests that the whole truth of the story may never be known.

I also relate my experience with various governments, civilian and military, and reveal facts hitherto unknown about the Malvinas (Falkland) War. The reader will also find many previously untold details about the 1966 coup against President Arturo Illia and the 1976 coup against "Isabelita" Perón, and the juntas led by Generals Onganía, Videla, Viola and Galtieri. This book contains my personal encounters with John F. Kennedy, Lyndon Johnson, Golda Meir, Nikita Khrushchev, many of Argentina's recent economy ministers (Alfredo Gómez Morales, José Gelbard, José Martínez de Hoz and Domingo Cavallo) and United States Ambassadors Robert C. Hill, Raul Castro, Frank Ortiz and Terence Todman of the United States. I have also personally dealt with nearly every Argentine president from Perón to Menem.

I tell this history in the form of a personal memoir not only because I have no pretense to being a historian, but also because my professional involvement with Argentina, which began when I was twenty-eight years old, unexpectedly gave me an interesting personal history. It is not every young lawyer who finds himself face to face with an irate Golda Meir in

1. I joined the U.S.-Argentine Chamber of Commerce as a member in 1958, and worked my way up through experience: I served as as committee chairman, officer, director and, ultimately, president.

her Jerusalem office or who is told jokes by Nikita Khrushchev at the Soviet embassy. And I was very surprised, at the age of 34, when I was asked by President Lyndon Johnson to become the United States ambassador to Argentina. (I surprised him by turning down the offer.)

Not all the surprises were wonderful. In my mature years, after a lifetime of service on behalf of Argentina, I was stunned when the democratically-elected President of Argentina, without explanation, simply failed to show up at an international symposium that had been arranged with a great deal of hard work by his own government and the U.S.-Argentine Chamber of Commerce (of which I was president) to help attract investment to his country. (I was especially stunned since the daughter of the United States president had arranged to be there!) And after helping Argentina open a branch of Banco de la Nación in New York City, and after seeing the bank through several hair-raising crises and preventing its bankruptcy, I was shocked when I was suddenly dismissed as that bank's lawyer by a new Argentine Ministry of Economy that expressed a yen for a more "prestigious" New York law firm. So I have had a lifetime rich in experiences, good and bad, which I have included in this book. I hope the reader will appreciate them as both interesting and an indication of how intimately I have been involved in Argentine affairs.

This book is not intended to hurt anybody. My long experience with Argentina has convinced me that whatever mistakes were made, it was, overwhelmingly, more often a case of misfeasance, not malfeasance, at the root of it. Contrary to widespread belief, almost everyone who led Argentina during the years from Perón to Menem—whether they were military or civilian—wanted to take the country in the direction of prosperity and democracy. But, sadly, nearly every single person who led Argentina during the Cold War years failed to understand the way the world worked.[2] Europe's ruination during World War II meant that it was no longer the preeminent financial leader and banker to the world—and never would be again. Argentina needed to forge a good working rela-

---

2. The outstanding exception, as far as I am concerned, was President Arturo Frondizi, who had the right vision for Argentina. Tragically, his fellow countrymen, including members of his own Radical Party, were not so farsighted and failed to accord him the political support he needed to lead the country forward. I often wonder what Argentina would be today if Frondizi had succeeded in 1962.

tionship with the United States if it was to prosper. But that was a reality that practically all Argentines in political power resisted for nearly forty years, and for an understandable reason: The U.S. had not treated Argentina well because the U.S. did not understand Argentina.

As an American lawyer involved in American politics, I was in a good position to see the very sad and stupid mistakes that my country made in its dealings with Argentina during the forty years of the Cold War. Our almost obsessive fear of communism in the Western Hemisphere caused the U.S. to put demands on Argentine leaders that were impossible for them to meet. Later, as the fear of communism in the U.S. faded, our government failed to appreciate how much an ideological war about socialism still drove politics in Argentina—and once again the U.S. put demands on Argentine leaders they found impossible to meet. U.S.-Argentine relations for forty years were damaged, from both sides, by resentments and misunderstandings born of ignorance.

Although the vast majority of the economic mistakes made during the Cold War years were innocent ones, the consequences were still devastating to Argentina's economy. When economic times got bad in Argentina, the political situation generally got worse. Argentina's cyclical economic and political upheavals prevented it from developing a pool of leaders with experience in international finance.[3] In fact, despite its recent great strides forward, Argentines still struggle to educate themselves about the dynamic and very complicated world of international finance and trade.

In October of 1999 the Argentine people elected Fernando de la Rúa to be their president. He is a quiet and dignified man who has spent almost all of his adult life in the Radical Party, and therefore is widely viewed as well-prepared for the job at hand. The challenges facing him are enormous: the valuation of Argentina's currency, distressingly high unemployment and the viability of Argentina's established businesses in the sometimes frantic global economy. Fortunately, unlike his most

3. Argentina's military governments often did better than its civilian governments at handling Argentina's economy for three simple reasons: (a) the military were in power more regularly and for longer periods of time, and therefore gained crucial experience; (b) Argentina's top military leaders often spent time abroad, and hence they had a better understanding of the actual workings of the world; (c) the military didn't worry about getting re-elected and therefore were unafraid to impose drastic measures when needed.

immediate Radical predecessor, Raúl Alfonsín, President de la Rúa fully grasps the importance of cultivating good relations with the United States. Early in his term as president, he visited the United States and opened up important dialogues between the two governments and the two nations' business communities.

It is my greatest hope that this book will give readers, especially today's generation of young Argentines, a firmer understanding of recent history so that the myths and mistakes of the past get discarded once and for all. The Argentine people are a good people who have much in common with the people of the United States. Somehow, in our efforts to encourage democracy and free trade in Argentina, the U.S. failed to communicate to Argentina just how much we have in common. We, too, are a nation whose forefathers came from other continents; we, too, have had to struggle to create a stock market, our banking system and a modern, industrial society. We didn't do it overnight. Today we are a well-educated, largely middle class and centrist-minded people, and we have many aspirations in common with the vast majority of Argentina's people.

There is no reason why our two countries should not enjoy permanent good relations and every reason why we should. As air travel and computers draw our two nations closer, we have a unique opportunity to see the Western Hemisphere enjoying peace, prosperity and democracy from the North Pole to the South. These are the goals that I have worked for all my life, and I am grateful to the people of Argentina for having allowed me such a marvelous opportunity.

Laurence W. Levine
New York City,
August 2000

ONE

THE EARLY 1950s

How My Enthusiasm for Aviation Led Me to Argentina

Bolivia

Brazil

Paraguay

Salta

Teuco

Chile

Andes Salado Resistencia

San Miguel Corrientes
de Tucumán

Parana
River

Cordoba Santa

San Juan

Rio Cuarto Parana River

Mendoza Rosario

Godoy Cruz

Desaguadero

Moron

Lomas de la Plata
Zamora

ARGENTINA
worldatlas.com

Andes

Colorado

Mar del Plata

Neuquen Bahia Blanca

Salado

San Carlos
de Bariloche

Chubut Trelew

Esquel

Rawson

Comodero
Rivadavia

Caleta
Olivia

Puerto Deseado

Puerto San Julian

Andes

Falkland
Islands

Rio Stanley
Gallegos

Chile

Tierra
del Fuego

Ushuaia Isla de
los Estados

Cape Horn

The author in 1952.

M

y earliest introduction to Argentina had nothing to do with either politics, airlines or banks. It came during my childhood when my father's law firm, Walsh & Levine, had as its client Miguel de Alzaga Unzué, the dashingly handsome and witty Argentine playboy everybody called "Macoco."

Macoco was a particular favorite of New York City's gossip columnists: Scarcely a week went by without the newspapers carrying some juicy tidbit about the glamorous guests Macoco entertained at New York's legendary El Morocco Club, of which he was rumored to be a co-owner.[1] As the incorrigible black sheep of one of Argentina's wealthiest and most respected families, Macoco had been exiled to New York City, where he openly shared his chic, $235 per month apartment at 14 Sutton Place with a beautiful American blonde. In addition to the generous allowance he received from his family, Macoco also had a secret source of income which he owed to his close personal friendship with first Colonel, then General, and ultimately President Juan Domingo Perón.

Macoco had been granted by Perón a license to import two automobiles into Argentina each month. Since no passenger cars were produced domestically in Argentina until the mid-1950s (when the "Siam di Tella 1500" came on the market), possessing this particular import license guaranteed Macoco quite a substantial income for very little work. He spent most of his time and money amusing himself abroad.

1. My father's law partner, Bill Walsh, had put himself through Fordham Law School serving drinks at El Morocco during the Prohibition Era. He met Macoco at the club, which at that time was operating as an illegal "speakeasy" in the basement of the St. Regis Hotel. When Prohibition ended, the club opened its doors legitimately, and until it closed them in the 1960s, El Morocco was regarded as the top watering hole in America, rivaled only by the Stork Club and "21" in New York, and perhaps Chasen's of Hollywood.

Macoco's lifestyle in New York became so colorful that MGM in Hollywood made a movie musical about it, whereupon an incensed Macoco threatened to sue—my father talked him out of it. Although he was not Walsh & Levine's only newsworthy client, Macoco certainly was its most entertaining, and the fact that he came from faraway Argentina only increased his larger-than-life stature in my eyes. One of the more vivid memories of my youth revolves around the sole occasion when, as a boy of thirteen, I was considered sufficiently adult to be taken to El Morocco, where I lunched at Macoco's private table on a Saturday afternoon.

Then one day the papers carried the amazing news that Macoco's gorgeous lady friend had packed up her bags, hopped a TWA flight to Hollywood and married Clark Gable. Macoco was stunned, and it became my father's job over the next few months to fly to and from California in an effort to persuade the lady to return all the expensive jewelry that Macoco had been lavishing on her.[2] In the following years, Macoco's luck took an even worse turn. Upon hearing that the now-widowed Perón had been accused of consorting with underaged girls, Macoco heedlessly shot off an angry letter to his old friend and patron, accusing him of being a sex criminal. Perón swiftly responded by revoking Macoco's auto import license—so swiftly that a Buenos Aries-bound shipment of two Cadillacs was left floating in the Atlantic Ocean. Unable to continue paying for his extravagant life in New York, Macoco returned to Argentina, where his remaining years were seldom as glamorous or fun.

To be truthful, once Macoco was gone from my life, I scarcely thought about Argentina. As a young man looking to the future, I certainly never dreamed I'd be spending most of my adult life deeply involved with the country. I did study Spanish in both high school and college to fulfill foreign language requirements, but only because, after taking Latin for three years, I found Spanish quite a bit easier than French. As a teaching fellow at the Harvard Defense Studies Program in the mid-1950s, the foreign countries that intrigued me were China and Great Britain. Argentina was seldom, if ever, on my mind.

2. A settlement was finally reached whereby Mrs. Gable (better known as Kay Spreckles, the sugar heiress) got to keep some but not all of the precious gems.

As I prepared to graduate from Harvard Law School, I already knew that my biggest passion was politics, but I still wasn't sure I wanted to make a career of it. All I knew for sure was that I wanted a chance to do something interesting and different—something other than simply going to work for a big New York law firm and becoming just another stuffed shirt.

So it was pure good luck that one of my roommates at Harvard was a very nice young man from Louisiana named Frank Coates, Jr., because during our last year at Harvard his father became the executive vice president of Northeast Airlines. I'd been wildly enthusiastic about air travel ever since I was a boy and, as a young man, I began to realize that aviation was turning into the most exciting new industry in the world.[3]

Every era is defined by one industry that comes along and changes everything. For today's generation, telecommunications is that kind of industry, creating millions of new jobs and revolutionizing the way things get done all over the globe. Young people are racing to get into it because they see a chance to help create something, and that was the way I saw aviation in the 1950s. The airline industry wasn't an old industry that was already institutionalized. The people who were developing commercial aviation were former World War II pilots and, while they were older than me, they were still relatively young and open in their outlook.

So I was very glad when, one Saturday afternoon in 1955, the elder Mr. Coates dropped by Harvard to take his son out to lunch and I was invited to come along. Mr. Coates was the very epitome of a Southern gentleman, and he listened politely while I—a brash kid from Brooklyn—told him exactly how I thought Northeast Airlines ought to be run.[4]

---

3. In 1946, when I was fifteen years old, my family became the talk of the neighborhood when I persuaded my father to fly us to Florida for a vacation rather than stay home simply because all the trains were booked. I bought tickets on an unlicensed, charter DC-3 aircraft, which carried twenty-one passengers and was flown by a World War II pilot out of Newark Airport, which at that time was little more than a hayfield. Our flight made one stop to refuel in Virginia, and altogether took eight hours to fly to Miami, as compared to more than twenty-four hours by train, or several days by car.

4. True to its name, Northeast served America's northeast: Boston, New York, Washington and Montreal. But recently it had been granted a temporary license to fly to Miami as well. I told Coates that Northeast could make a lot of money by offering Kosher meals on its Miami flights, especially if Northeast advertised those Kosher meals in the temple bulletins that were distributed by synagogues. Northeast did just that. I was put in charge of advertising the Kosher meals and I further recommended and arranged for catering to be done by the famous Broadway deli restaurant, Lindy's of New York City. (Passengers were also offered the option of eating meals catered from Joe's Stone Crab House in Miami.)

When I was through talking, Coates said he was impressed by my suggestions. In fact, he invited me to come to Northeast's offices at Boston's Logan Airport to meet with the company's new president. James W. Austin turned out to be a very tall and imposing air force colonel from Arkansas who knew the airline business well.[5] He, too, listened to me and when I was done talking, Austin said he'd give me a retainer of $500 a month once I'd finished law school if I'd become Northeast Airlines' lawyer in New York!

I was thrilled to accept, but on one condition: Adlai Stevenson was once again running for president against Dwight Eisenhower and, although I admired Eisenhower, I had my heart set on working for Stevenson's campaign in New York. So I told Coates and Austin I wouldn't say 'yes' until after the November 1956 election. I was already certain that Stevenson was going to lose, but I was an idealist: I felt it was important for me to do what I believed was right, whatever the outcome. Coates and Austin assured me that their offer would still be on the table after the election was over.[6]

When Election Day arrived and all the votes were counted, I was sorry that Stevenson lost, but I wasn't sorry that I wouldn't be going to Washington as part of a victory team. Some instinct told me that once there, the thrill of government could have kept me there permanently. Had Stevenson won, I might have spent my whole life in Washington, dependent on political appointments and connections, and never have practiced law. I wanted to prove to myself that I could practice law and make my own way.[7]

So I very gladly called up Coates and Austin and told them I was ready to start.

5. Together, Coates and Austin had run Capital Airlines, an important regional carrier in the South and Southwest.
6. The Stevenson campaign hired me as its office manager in New York and, to this day, I have never had a more exciting political time in my life. I worked for the smartest and best group of political people I have ever met. Among them were Mrs. Franklin D. Roosevelt, New York Senator Herbert Lehman, Thomas K. Finletter (former secretary of the air force), Cass Canfield, editor of Harper's, and Marietta Tree, one of the Democratic Party's most stalwart benefactors. John Shea, who became a good friend of mine, was the executive director of the New York campaign. Just before his untimely death at the age of forty-two, we worked together to create the Committee for Democratic Voters, which formed the nucleus of what later became the powerful "Reform Democrats" in New York City.
7. I also had two other law offers, one of which I accepted. And I kept an office at my father's law firm of Walsh & Levine.

Members of the staff of the Harvard Defense Studies program.
Professor W. Barton Leach, the head of the program, stands center top.
(The author is at the far right, center row.)

A CHANCE MEETING WITH A GENERAL

Argentina came back into my life in a rather mysterious way in 1959, a few years after I'd begun working for Northeast. I was accompanying James Austin to Las Vegas for a convention of ASTA, the American Society of Travel Agents, but we sat separately, each taking aisle seats in different parts of the aircraft so that Austin in particular could rest and have room to stretch out during the flight. Seated directly across the aisle from me was a very distinguished-looking gentleman who, not long after we were airborne, began looking around the cabin for the whereabouts of the stewardess, clicking the call light over his head.

I leaned across the aisle and asked the gentleman what it was he needed. He seemed not to understand me at first, but then he replied: "Café. Café." I tried out my classroom Spanish: "¿Habla Español?" The gentleman smiled for the first time and said: "¡Sí!" He explained he wanted a cup of coffee with no sugar.

I got up and found a stewardess to bring the gentleman his coffee. When I returned, he introduced himself to me as Brigadier Miguel Moragues, the president of Aerolíneas Argentinas. I told the Brigadier in Spanish that the president of Northeast was also on the flight, and I immediately offered to introduce them to each other. The Brigadier looked puzzled; he wanted to know what "Northeast" was. I explained and Brigadier Moragues apologized profusely for his lack of knowledge, saying that he'd only just been named the president of Argentine Airlines: This was his first trip to America and he'd never run a civilian airline before. He said he'd be very happy to meet Mr. Austin, and he further suggested that we might enjoy meeting his traveling companion, a representative of the International Civilian Aviation Organization who was also seated elsewhere on the plane.[8]

I took Moragues to meet Austin. And when Brigadier Moragues brought round his friend from the ICAO, he turned out to be Ralph Starkey, already an old friend of Austin's from their air force days. After pleasantries were exchanged and Starkey promised to stay in

---

8. The ICAO was created by the United Nations in 1944 to promote international standards for the global air industry. It is based in Montreal, Canada.

touch, everyone returned to their separate seats. When the plane landed in Las Vegas, I said goodbye to Brigadier Moragues and would have
forgotten about him forever—had not Austin called me from Boston
the very next week to say that Brigadier Moragues was now standing
in his office.

"He's here with Starkey," Austin informed me in a voice that always
reminded me of John Wayne. "Seems that Argentine Airlines is on strike
in New York and Moragues doesn't like his American lawyer. I told him
you were in New York and just the person to solve all his problems, and
he remembers how helpful you were on the plane trip to Las Vegas. You
better catch our next shuttle up here."[9]

So I caught the next Northeast shuttle to Boston, walking into Austin's
office about four o'clock. Moragues was still there, looking obviously dis-
tressed. Ralph Starkey was also there to act as Moragues' translator, but
the Brigadier spoke to me directly in Spanish.

He explained that the day-to-day operations of Aerolíneas
Argentinas, Argentina's state-owned national carrier, were run by the
Argentine Air Force. When Argentina's new president, Arturo Frondizi,
was elected a few months before, Moragues, a career air force man, had
been appointed the new president of the airline. Aerolíneas Argentinas
was an international carrier, and what the Brigadier discovered when he
assumed his post was that, for more than a year, Aerolíneas Comet jets
had not been flying in or out of New York City, although they were
scheduled to do so three times a week. The explanation Moragues had
been given in Argentina was that the union was on strike in New York.
But Aerolíneas did not use union workers, Moragues told me. Besides,
to make matters more confusing, the American lawyer for Aerolíneas
had told Moragues that the airline workers' union in New York claimed
to know nothing about a strike at Aerolíneas. The Brigadier had flown
up from Buenos Aires for the sole purpose of solving this mystery and
getting Aerolíneas back up in the air. Obviously he was hoping I could
help out.

---

9. It is widely believed that Eastern Airlines invented shuttle service on the East Coast, but Northeast
was first. A fleet of DC-6 B's flew from Boston to New York for $12, and to Washington for $16.

I had no idea what to do. I knew next to nothing about unions or labor law. But as I looked over Moragues' papers, one thing jumped out at me: The airline workers at New York International Airport at Idlewild were affiliated with the Transport Workers Union of New York.[10] I remembered that when I was the office manager for Adlai Stevenson's campaign, I'd often dealt with a man named Paul O'Dwyer, whose law firm, O'Dwyer & Bernstein, represented that same union.[11] As the brother of William ("Bill") O'Dwyer, the former Mayor of New York City, Paul O'Dwyer was very well-connected and knew just about everything that went on in New York City.

So using Austin's desk phone, I called up information in New York, dialed O'Dwyer & Bernstein, and much to my surprise, I was immediately put through to Paul O'Dwyer himself. Rather timidly, I asked: "Mr. O'Dwyer, do you remember me?"

O'Dwyer's hearty Irish brogue came booming down the line: "Of course, Larry, I remember you!" (This brogue, I soon was to learn, could be turned on and off at will.) When I launched into an explanation of the reason for my call, I was interrupted less than halfway through.

"There isn't any strike, Larry!" O'Dwyer hollared at me. "We don't even have Argentine Airlines on any of our lists! It's too small an airline. They don't fly enough flights. We don't represent the workers at Argentine Airlines and even if we did, no airline is ever on strike for a year!"

I figured that if the lawyer for the Transport Workers Union said there wasn't a strike while the head of the Argentine airline said there was, then something very strange was going on.

"Could you do me a big favor?" I asked O'Dwyer. "Could you meet me tomorrow morning at Argentine Airlines—any time you can do it. Maybe we can find out what this is all about. I honestly don't know any more than you do."

O'Dwyer said he'd love to do it. "How about 10:00 am?"

10. New York's international airport was popularly known as "Idlewild" until it was renamed John F. Kennedy International Airport following the assassination of America's thirty-fifth President.

11. Paul O'Dwyer's considerable contribution to the Stevenson New York campaign was to organize Manhattan's West Side, which included the use of "sound trucks" to blare out Stevenson's message as they slowly traveled up and down the residential streets. Part of my job as office manager was to write checks as needed, and it was through occasionally disbursing funds to help defray Paul O'Dwyer's operations that I got to know him, although not very well.

"Absolutely," I instantly replied. "The office is at 9 Rockefeller Center. The ground floor."

ARGENTINE AIRLINES FLIES AGAIN,
AND I BECOME ITS AMERICAN LAWYER

So Moragues, Starkey and I took the shuttle back to New York to meet the next morning with O'Dwyer at the offices of Aerolíneas Argentinas. I was the first to arrive at 9 Rockefeller Center, where I found two pick-eters marching back and forth outside. Inside, I found a three hundred-pound, red-haired Argentine who introduced himself to me, in quite beautiful English, as Alberto Smart, the civilian manager of Argentine Airlines in New York. Despite the cool Spring morning, Smart was sweat-ing profusely. I could tell he wasn't looking forward to this meeting, although he couldn't have been more gracious.

When Moragues, Starkey and O'Dwyer joined us, Smart escorted us into his well-appointed office, whose magnificent floor-to-ceiling window at ground level provided a perfect view of Rockefeller Center and the two picketers outside. We seated ourselves on the long sofa in front of this window, and Smart squeezed himself in behind his desk. Then I asked Smart in my less beautiful English: "What is this stuff about a strike?"

Without saying a word, Smart opened a bottom drawer in his desk, pulled out a green piece of paper, and handed it over to me. I'd never seen one before, but it was an application to the National Labor Relations Board for certification by a group of employees. I knew just enough about American labor law to figure out that the workers at Argentine Airlines at Idlewild had petitioned the government to form a union— apparently more than a year ago. I wondered why the NLRB had never responded; usually they sent representatives to conduct a vote among the employees once an application to form a union was made.

"Did you mail this application to the NLRB?" I asked Smart, handing the paper to O'Dwyer.

"No," he replied nervously in English. "Now that Perón is gone, the military doesn't like unions."

Smart tried to keep his eyes off Moragues. Obviously he was afraid of losing his job. Fortunately for Smart, Moragues hadn't understood a word of what was being said. But Paul O'Dwyer grasped the politics of the situation perfectly.

"Put this thing away," he told Smart briskly, handing him the application. Then O'Dwyer turned to me: "Larry, do you think we can work out a contract? Why don't we start with the simplest kind of first contract that a union signs?"

I turned to Moragues and asked him, in Spanish: "Brigadier, Mr. O'Dwyer wants to know if you have any objection to working out an agreement today." I didn't use the words "union contract."

Moragues had no objections. O'Dwyer turned to Smart. "Get me the wage list," he said. When the wage list was produced, O'Dwyer's mouth fell open.

"These wages you pay to your employees are higher than anything being paid at our big airlines!" he exclaimed. "The Brigadier can get ready to take the first plane back tonight! We'll gladly sign a contract at these wages for two years, with a three percent increase the second year." I translated the gist of that for Moragues, who replied "Wonderful!"

Then O'Dwyer waved at the two picketers outside the window, motioning to them to come inside. When the two puzzled strikers walked into Smart's office, O'Dwyer got right to the point.

"I've just looked at the wage scale," he told them, his Irish brogue having once again returned. "You boys are getting more than what any of the other airlines pay. It's ridiculous for this airline to be on strike. So it's settled. We're signing a contract today that gives you the same wages. You'll get a three percent increase next year."

One of the two strikers was a short, wiry man with black hair, a black mustache and furious dark eyes. He stepped right up to O'Dwyer. "Who are you?" he demanded menacingly in a noticeable Puerto Rican accent.

Unfazed, O'Dwyer told him, then he asked in return: "Who are you?"

"I am the flight dispatcher of Argentine Airlines and its union representative!" came the angry reply.

O'Dwyer looked down at the wage list in his hand and saw that the flight dispatcher was paid seven dollars an hour—a nice salary in those days.

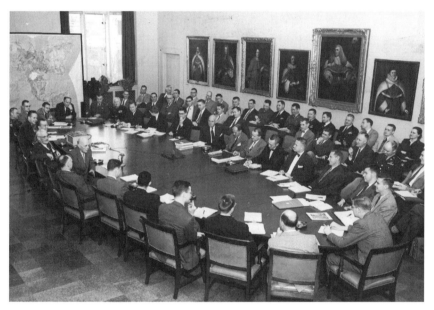

*Members of the Harvard Defense Studies program and the Pentagon review
the budget of the U.S. Air Force in 1955 at Langdell Hall, Harvard
University. (The author is seated at the center of the far side of the table.)*

"You'll have the highest pay in the contract," O'Dwyer assured him.

The flight dispatcher almost spat in his face. "There isn't any contract unless it is approved by the workers—and first by me!"

At that point, Paul O'Dwyer, who in later years became a hero to America's Puerto Rican community for so eloquently arguing before the U.S. Supreme Court that Puerto Ricans had a constitutional right to obtain ballots in Spanish, deployed the tactics of the Irish street brawler he always was deep down inside. O'Dwyer stared right into the flight dispatcher's dark Hispanic eyes and snarled:

"Why an Argentine airline hires a goddam *spic* to be its a flight dispatcher beats the hell out of me. You get out of here!"

But the man didn't budge. He wanted a fight. He shouted right back at O'Dwyer, who bellowed all the louder in return. With the two of them now screaming, the flight dispatcher finally became so enraged he wasn't able to speak at all. He simply stormed out of Smart's office in a furious state, his timid fellow striker scurrying at his heels.

With that settled, O'Dwyer returned to the sofa and produced a copy of a standard union contract from his briefcase. Together, we took Moragues through its terms, line by line: an eight hour workday, half hour for lunch, two weeks vacation the first year, three weeks the second . . . .

I looked up just in time to see the flight dispatcher walk back into the office with the Manhattan Yellow Pages gripped in his hands. I yelled out "Duck!" and, thank goodness, O'Dwyer did. The six-inch thick directory sailed right over his head and crashed through the plate glass window behind us.

O'Dwyer took one look out of what was now the gaping hole of the window frame and at the pieces of shattered glass laying on the sidewalk outside. Then he looked at the flight dispatcher, his face blood red. O'Dwyer got up off the sofa, picked up the man by the shoulders and tossed him right out the window, too!

I stole a quick glance at Moragues. His mouth was hanging open in shock. Smart and Starkey were equally dumbstruck. But no one looked as

12. Years later, after the rent for ground floor space at Rockefeller Plaza became prohibitively expensive, Argentine Airlines moved its offices to the 16th floor.

surprised as the flight dispatcher, who found himself sitting outdoors on the sidewalk. The truth was, the man was the kind of bully who'll only back off when he finally meets a bigger bully. Now thoroughly defeated, he picked himself up off the ground and sullenly disappeared into the crowd that had gathered in Rockefeller Center to gawk at him. The strike was over.[12]

O'Dwyer produced a pen so that Moragues could sign the contract. Then O'Dwyer himself signed and Starkey was asked to sign as a witness. In those days, I always carried my notary stamp, so I stamped the contract and signed it, too.

Once everything was put away, Moragues turned to Alberto Smart and, in Spanish, said: "I want Dr. Levine to be our lawyer." I couldn't have been more pleased. Moragues then very cordially invited me to come to Argentina as soon as it was convenient, courtesy of Aerolíneas, of course. O'Dwyer and I left the office together, and before we parted, I thanked him profusely. O'Dwyer said he was glad he could be of help.[13]

But as I walked past the broken window at Aerolíneas, it suddenly occurred to me that there could be big trouble at the airport that evening when the Aerolíneas Comet jet took off for the first time in a year. The flight dispatcher, after all, held a job with significant responsibilities. He was the only one who would be weighing the plane and balancing the fuel against the cargo and the passengers—most worrisomely, Brigadier Moragues. So I went back into the office and instructed Alberto Smart to go to the airport himself that night to make sure that the plane bearing the Brigadier was double-checked prior to its take-off. Smart agreed to do so, and Brigadier General Moragues did indeed fly safely home.[14]

The next day I drew up a one-page contract, setting my fee at $500 per month, and sent it off to Alberto Smart. In due course, it was signed and returned. What would prove to be my lifelong association with Argentina had now officially begun. There would never be a more interesting or exciting time to become the American lawyer for an Argentine enterprise.

13. O'Dwyer and I remained friends, working on many political issues together, disagreeing on others. Most notably we worked unseccessfully to elect Eugene McCarthy president in 1968, in opposition to the war in Vietnam.

14. Brigadier Miguel Moragues continued to be a friend of mine, long after he'd retired from the presidency of Aerolíneas. In the early 1970s, President Lanusse appointed him governor of the province of Buenos Aires. He is to this day the embodiment of what I consider a good man and a fine military officer.

TWO

IGNORANCE AND ISOLATION BEFORE THE 1950s

How America Developed Its Attitude Toward Argentina

Juan Domingo Perón and his wife, Eva,
enjoying the adulation of the crowd.

A
   s strange as it may seem today, when I took the job of representing Aerolíneas Argentínas in 1958, Aerolíneas was among only a handful of Argentine companies doing business in the United States.[1] That state of affairs was the direct result of the unhappy, often tragic history of relations between the two nations in the twentieth century. While this is not a history book, retelling some that sad story is quite necessary to understand the events that unfold here, and to fully understand the Argentina of today.

Relations between Argentina and the United States have been tense since the very beginning of this century, and it may be that some of that tension was inevitable. Argentina's main exports—wheat and meat—made her a tough competitor for U.S. farmers and ranchers who were looking to sell their products abroad. But it was the worldwide depression of the 1930s that really began the downward spiral in relations between the two countries that wasn't halted until very recently.

During the 1930s, harsh protectionist laws were adopted in the U.S. that imposed special tariffs on Argentine agricultural products and later included a ban on the importation of canned beef from Argentina, one of the backbones of Argentine trade. Mostly designed to help American farmers, these laws helped devastate the Argentine economy.[2] They not only

1. Siam Di Tella, the Argentine licensee of Westinghouse, maintained a small corporate office in New York, and at various times, the Argentine government had a small office for domestic petroleum development in Houston (Yacimeintos Petroliferos Fiscales) and another for shipping in New York. But none of these offices conducted business as Aerolíneas did with the U.S. public.

2. In particular, the 1933 Agricultural Adjustments Act artificially raised the price of U.S. farm goods through government subsidies, and banned the import of any agricultural products that sold under the inflated U.S.-subsidized prices. Even the U.S. Navy was not allowed to import Argentine canned beef for its sailors.

deeply alienated Argentines, these trade barriers set in motion tumultuous political forces inside Argentina, which I believe made fixing the nation's structural economic problem close to impossible for nearly six decades.

During World War II, Argentina got a temporary respite from economic travail because of increased demand in Europe for Argentine exports. Unfortunately, Argentina's relations with the U.S. drastically worsened during that time. Argentina refused to join the Pan American Defense Alliance at the beginning of the war because she was still angry over the special tariffs imposed by the U.S. on Argentine exports and she wanted to be neutral in order to sell her goods to England. During World War I, Argentines had remained neutral to ensure that her boatloads of meat and wheat were not sunk by the Germans while crossing the Atlantic. Now, during World War II, the British pleaded with the Argentines to once again stay neutral and to accept payment for goods in sterling, both of which Argentina did. England might not have survived without the food it got from Argentina, but the U.S. State Department didn't understand the basis of Argentina's neutrality policy and misinterpreted it as a "pro-Nazi" policy.[3] The U.S. government expressed its displeasure by imposing a strict arms embargo on Argentina.

By not allowing Argentine beef to come to the U.S. we alienated Argentina's meat producers and the working class. Then when we stopped all shipments of arms, we alienated the military. All three of these groups ultimately supported Perón.

To make matter worse, the U.S. simultaneously increased arms sales to Brazil, Argentina's bordering neighbor and historic rival. America believed that Brazil's natural resources, not Argentina's, were needed to win the war. These U.S. policies—import restrictions, the arms embargo and the arms sales to Brazil—played right into the hands of Argentina's extreme nationalists, who were strong and often secretly financed by Adolph Hitler. Argentines began looking for ways to assert their independence and national identity in the Western Hemisphere.

---

3. Germany made a strong effort to develop a pro-Nazi government in Argentina and many members of the military were, in fact, pro-Nazi during the war. But the majority were not. Juan Perón in particular was not pro-Nazi, although the U.S. later took just that view of him as he rose to become president of Argentina.

Most significantly, in 1941, the Argentine army was moved to create its General Directorate of Military Manufacturers so as to make Argentina self-sufficient in weaponry—and the military soon extended its reach into manufacturing much further. As the strength and the power of industry grew in Argentina, so did the military.

WHAT THE U.S. CONTRIBUTED TO THE RISE OF PERONISM

The United States bears a great deal of the responsibility for creating the circumstances that brought Col. Juan Domingo Perón and his group to power, and for sending Argentina down the road to isolation. Not only did the U.S. State Department ignore appeals from Argentine moderates (who promised a complete break with Germany in return for lifting the arms embargo), the U.S. cut off credit to Argentina, froze Argentine assets, interfered with her oil supplies and urged her Latin American neighbors to stop trading with her. Worried about border security and in need of manufactured goods, angry Argentines began to see no other course but national self-sufficiency. They rallied behind those leaders who said they could make that happen, and increasingly such talk was heard coming from the military.

Argentina's military was already at the center of wartime manufacturing, since the military was just about the only arm of state government that was organized enough to lead the rush to industrial development. The established political parties of Argentina were so accustomed to working in a basically agrarian culture, they failed to keep up with the changing times.

Industrialization was long overdue in Argentina. As Perón so clearly saw, the future of Argentina could not be built solely upon exports of meat and wheat. As more and more Argentines moved to the cities in search of work in the factories and in small businesses, Perón organized them into his own political power base and pursued his nationalist vision for Argentina, modeled on Mussolini's fascist Italy.[4] Perón consolidated

4. Prior to World War II, Perón had spent time in Italy as a military attaché and he came to the conclusion that Mussolini had handled the 1930s catastrophe of the Great Depression far better than either England or the United States.

his support in the military by letting the various branches of the military oversee manufacturing entities, and by encouraging the military's inherent nationalism and anti-communism. Nationalism won Perón additional support from Argentina's small manufacturers.[5] Anti-communism won him the support of Argentina's powerful Catholic church. Perón's vision became the dominant vision of the future for Argentina.

I am not a historian, and probably only a historian can explain all the myriad forces that helped Perón on his upward climb to full power. But perhaps no one will ever be able to fully explain the force of Juan Perón's political charisma, which exerted such a hold on Argentines. Just like Americans never get over their fascination with the Kennedys, an important segment of Argentine society succumbed to a certain "aura" and star quality in Juan Perón and in his wife, Evita. The Perons possessed the kind of glamour more often associated with movie stars. Only occasionally do politicians, like the Kennedys or Franklin D. Roosevelt, also have that kind of magnetic appeal. Certainly Juan Perón had it, and it played an indispensible role in creating the long-lasting influence he had on his country.

Perón's rise to the top of Argentine politics in the 1940s was watched with suspicion and alarm by the U.S. State Department, whose diplomats harbored an almost a visceral dislike for Perón and his followers. Like foreign ministries everywhere, the U.S. State Department recruits the majority of its members from the nation's established upper class. In the 1940s, the pin-striped, Ivy League diplomats who ran the State Department instinctively shared the elite conservatism and worries of Argentina's oligarchs and traditional professionals. So it was the sentiments of the membership of the Jockey Club, rather than the aspirations of Argentina's emerging industrial working class and its new self-made entrepreneurs, that U.S. ambassadors heard and appreciated. Thus, in fashioning its Latin American policy, Washington relied on "intelligence" from Argentina that said Perón and his followers were Nazis who posed

5. Perón was greatly helped by the brilliant grassroots political skills of José Ber Gelbard, a Polish immigrant of Jewish ancestry, who tirelessly traveled Argentina from north to south, organizing small business owners and manufacturers into a federation of employers (known as the Confederación General Económica, or CGE). As a federation, they supported Perón's industrial plans and were loyal to him. Perón already enjoyed the support of their employees, the rank and file workers and wage-earners who formed the Confederación General del Trabajo, or CGT. Together, these groups gave Perón and his Peronist party a solid majority at the polls.

a grave threat to American interests and regional stability. Argentina's genuine domestic enthusiasm for Perón and his calculated expansion of workers' rights to create a minor form of a workers' democracy were interpreted by the State Department as fearful signs that a rabid lumpen-proletariat was being craftily organized by yet another Hitler.

The American government demonstrated no knowledge of Perón's deep admiration for Italy (and his distaste for Germany, whose culture he found too rigid). Nor did they appreciate that although anti-Semitism existed in Argentina, Perón's own views and his political associations were not anti-Semitic. They paid no attention to the fact that Perón sought out the Jewish community in Argentina to assist in developing his policies and that one of his most important political allies in organizing the industrial sector was José Ber Gelbard, a Jewish immigrant from Poland.

Locked into a one-sided view of the Argentine military as "pro-Nazi," the U.S. simply overlooked Argentina's long history of embracing home-grown "caudillos" (military/political leaders). In addition, the U.S. failed to perceive that there were factions in the military with differing views, and it totally underestimated the depth of Argentina's Catholicism. In 1946, the U.S. State Department capped its errors by openly conducting a clumsy campaign against Juan Perón to defeat him at the polls.[6] This high-handed interference in Argentina's electoral politics not only secured victory for Perón, it confirmed for Argentines their worst fears about post-war America. Viewing us as an immature, crass country that had let power go to its head, proud Argentines of every political stripe turned their backs on the United States. Their suspicion and rejection of us has lasted until contemporary times.

TRAGICALLY, PERÓN MISUNDERSTANDS THE POST-WAR WORLD

In the new, bi-polar Cold War world, Argentina embarked on its long search to find a third position, externally and internally. Her anti-

6. The anti-Perón campaign led by the U.S. ambassador to Argentina, Spruille Braden, was so shame-less, Peronists defined and won the election with the slogan: "¡Perón,sí! ¡Braden, no!" The U.S. later developed second thoughts about its policies toward Argentina and Braden was recalled.

Communist military and largely Catholic populace made an alliance with the Marxist Soviet Union impossible. Yet at the same time, Argentina remembered the 1930s all too well, and she was afraid to open herself to the overbearing United States and its free-wheeling brand of global capitalism. While she was more developed industrially than most of her Latin American neighbors, Argentina still had a financial and social infrastructure that was basically agrarian, which made her feel vulnerable to American corporate domination.

What Argentines really yearned for was to be allied with "mother" Europe and its Christian-Socialist traditions. But this historic and sentimental attachment to Europe blinded Argentines to the fact that World War II had ruined Europe totally. There simply no longer existed a non-Communist alternative to U.S. leadership in the world, either politically or financially.

Further distorting the vision of Argentina's leadership after World War II was its diehard assumption that a war between the Soviet Union and the U.S. was imminent. Argentina thought its best course of action was to quickly achieve industrial self-sufficiency and to maintain a political posture that would allow Argentina to sell food to both sides. When Perón attained full power in 1946, he saw the dilemma facing his nation this way: How fast could Argentina transform herself into an industrial nation without either slipping into the Communist orbit or surrendering independence to the U.S.?

This book is not a defense of Perón, or of Peronism or of any political point of view. Perón did a great many wrong things while he was in power and left Argentina in worse shape than he found it. But Perón's aspirations for Argentina and Argentines should not be condemned. His goal was to bring about vast reform in Argentina, but in a controlled way. He had seen the Great Depression in England and the United States in the 1930s and he had watched Communism rise in response to it. He wanted to develop Argentina's industry before Communism could seize it by force. At the same time, he wanted the country to retain its distinct Argentine identity without overwhelming foreign influence. He wanted social peace for Argentina, which meant providing the unemployed with

work, and workers with decent hours and wages. He wanted social revolution "the Argentine way," and it is easy to see why, especially when you
remember that Perón was a man of his time. Argentines of many differing political views also wanted things to change.

When he came to power, Perón was committed to developing
Argentina into an Italian type of state. He wanted a form of fascism
where the state controlled the banks through a central bank, and where
agriculture and industry were controlled and subsidized through federal
agencies in which the military played a major role. Perón's justification
for state-run development was that sufficient private capital wasn't available at that time, and a lack of trained personnel made it impossible to
simply throw open the doors to unplanned industrial development.
State-organized development was also a politically attractive idea
because, following World War II, Argentina's state treasury reserves were
overflowing with money from food sales to Europe, yet so many of its
people were poor and without work.

Perón mistakenly believed that the Argentine government could subsidize industrial development indefinitely by appropriating the marketing
of agricultural exports. He set things up so that the state could buy meat
and wheat at a low price, then sell it abroad at a profit. (This also gave
him a major source of political patronage, and created graft and corruption.) Economically and politically, Perón laid the foundations of an
impossible situation.

Government spending spawned inflation; government control of agriculture depressed production. And even though Europe had a need to
import industrial products from Argentina as well as food, Perón
designed industrial growth primarily to absorb his domestic unemployed
and to attain self-sufficiency, not to make Argentina an international
industrial competitor. Without the incentive of competition, Argentina
produced overpriced, inferior goods and her factories were inefficient.
They didn't become self-supporting.

Perón could no longer afford to subsidize industry when Argentina's
monetary reserves dried up, especially after the United States crafted the
Marshall Plan in a way that prohibited Europe from using U.S. aid to buy

Argentine products (a payback for Perón's anti-American "arrogance"). Perón's government printed money and inflation grew alarmingly. Industrial growth stagnated. Unemployment rose. Political turmoil ensued.

Perón had tried to do too much too quickly. And he had tried to do too much alone. If there was to be any hope at all for a rapid industrialization of Argentina, large quantities of foreign investment were needed, especially to develop Argentina's oil wealth. But in a country where official industrial policy was designed to serve labor first and foremost, public spending inevitably got out of control, so foreign capital was steering clear.

Besides, Perón had boxed himself in rhetorically and politically. Inspired by him, Argentines had become committed nationalists, so they denounced Perón's modest efforts to obtain foreign investment as betrayal and corruption. When Perón tried to shift course economically, the masses that his policies had enfranchised and lifted from poverty refused to sacrifice their gains. The agricultural oligarchs would not stand for any more confiscation of their wealth. Each branch of the military was now deeply entrenched in industry and they would not be denied their share of the pie, nor would they tolerate any instability because of their fear of communism.

To keep his supporters in line, Perón resorted more and more to personal abuse of power, and he lacked the knowledge and the in-house experts to know what else to do. As economic conditions worsened, many thought getting rid of Perón was the only solution. In response, Perón tried to consolidate his grip on power by encouraging a doctrinaire cult around his person and ideas. In doing so, he completely lost the support of the Catholic church, which now allied itself with the agricultural oligarchy, a group that already despised Perón. When all else failed, Perón used repression, making his enemies only more determined to see him replaced.

By the mid 1950s, in the eyes of many powerful people, it simply wasn't enough to remove Perón to set Argentina aright. Peronism itself and every societal structure it had spawned had to be vanquished and removed—permanently—from the Argentine political panorama. This impossible mission to turn back the industrial clock and destroy all-things-Perón kept Argentina in a state of political chaos for the next three decades. It was an undeclared civil war between the agricultural and industrial sectors of the country, in which the military was divided into two groups. One wanted to eliminate Perón, Peronism and everything that went with Peronism. The other military group wanted to retain the Peronist party and work with it, but only if Perón was replaced with another leader (one, they hoped, from the military). The Peronists were the largest political party in the country, but they too were divided into many groups and factions. But they all had one thing in common: they only wanted Perón as their leader.

A WINDOW OF OPPORTUNITY OPENS: 1955–1962

Perón's downfall came in September of 1955, after a summer of bloody confrontations which pitted Peronists against the supporters of the country's Catholic church. And although Perón's immediate successor, retired General Eduardo Lonardi, promised a society of "neither victors or vanquished," this spirit of reconciliation—and the rule of Lonardi—was short-lived. In less than a year, General Pedro Eugenio Aramburu replaced Lonardi, who shortly died of illness, and Aramburu wasted no time in attempting to crush every element of Peronism that existed in the land. The Peronist Party was outlawed and its assets were seized. When this provoked a rebellion by Perón's remaining loyalists in the military, the near-coup was crushed and the rebels were publicly executed. Aramburu also allowed a constitutional convention which overturned the laws that had enabled Perón to hold the presidency for two consecutive six-year terms; a president could now serve only one six-year term.[7]

But Arumburu had also promised to hold elections and return the presidency to civilian rule. The very interesting result of those elections in February 1958 was the presidency of Arturo Frondizi.

A shrewd and far-sighted civilian politician, Frondizi had organized his

7. Forty years later, Carlos Saúl Menem called another constitutional convention, which once again allowed the president to serve two consecutive terms, but of only four years duration each.

own reformist wing of the Radical Party, solidly trouncing the tradition-alists led by Ricardo Balbín. Frondizi rose in political influence by loudly criticizing Perón, which won him favor with the agrarian oligarchs and gained him legitimacy with significant factions in the military. Yet secret-ly, Frondizi forged a deal with the exiled Perón to win election-day sup-port from the Peronists, who had not been allowed to put a genuine Peronist candidate on the ballot. But Frondizi was not merely ambitious. Frondizi was smart enough to understand that Argentina would never be whole unless the outcast and embittered Peronists had a voice in the political life of the nation, and unless Argentina continued to industrial-ize, despite the wishes of the old-line agricultural oligarchs.

Frondizi wanted development, and he knew that the linchpin of that development would be oil. All around Argentina in the late 1950s and early 1960s, one often heard the phrase: "Meat, wheat and now oil." But to develop oil, Frondizi needed to reverse his own ultranationalist stance and attract U.S. investment.

Opposing Frondizi's interest in rapprochement with the U.S. was his own Radical Party, which had long promoted a European-led model of industrial development and which still remembered with bitterness the U.S. policies of the 1930s and 1940s. The Radical Party was largely made of up small business people, professors, doctors, lawyers and even small farmers. They were mainly uninvolved in large industry (which was dom-inated by the military) and Perón's government-organized corporations. Fearing for their small businesses, the Radicals adhered to the belief that the United States was too big to be allowed to invest in Argentina. In their view, all across Latin America, the U.S. was turning sovereign nations into client states of the north, and the word "imperialism" frequently was used by Argentine critics of the United States. Rank-and-file Radicals took up the cause of defending Argentine independence against U.S. dominance of the hemisphere, even if it meant going against their own elected leader, Frondizi.

But however understandable their motives, the nationalist Radicals were really condemning Argentina to backwardness. It has simply been a hard fact of the latter half of the twentieth century that investors do not send capital anywhere abroad unless the United States goes there first. After World War II, the absolutely necessary pre-condition of Argentina's development was that she have good relations with the United States, whether the Radicals liked it or not, because America had replaced England as the leader of the Western world. So even though Frondizi was a Radical who had come to power by taking stands that were sharply anti-American, Frondizi understood, once he wielded power, that he needed to act differently. He immediately showed himself to be a far-sighted and intelligent politician in his efforts to improve relations with the United States.

But Frondizi had to work very carefully, because the political situation beneath his feet was so precarious. With every step he took he risked his downfall. By cultivating the U.S., Frondizi had the Peronists against him along with the Radicals. The military was solidly in favor of better relations with the U.S., but Frondizi always had to make sure he wasn't perceived as aligned with the military—and he often angered the military by making concessions to the Peronists and the left-leaning members of his own Radical Party. Frondizi couldn't please one group without alienating another, and he needed all of them to succeed. Any one group could at any moment paralyze his government, and I watched with fascination as Frondizi zigzagged, sometimes brilliantly, to keep Argentina moving forward, although each compromise he made cost him dearly.

Coming aboard Argentine Airlines at the time that I did put me in a unique position to observe the progress of U.S.-Argentine relations. One of the more modest but ingenious pro-American steps that Frondizi took was to invite all of the governors of the United States (forty-eight, at that time) to fly to Argentina, courtesy of Aerolíneas Argentinas.[8] It provided a telling example of the shrewdness, both domestic and international, with which Frondizi could operate.

Frondizi simply couldn't invite the president of the United States to Argentina, as much as he might have liked to. Not only would the presi-

8. All the governors accepted Frondizi's invitation, and two Aerolíneas planes were provided to fly them and their wives, en masse, from New York City to Buenos Aires. The diplomatic niceties were handled by the Argentine embassy in Washington, but I was asked to handle the sheer logistics of getting ninety-six very important people, traveling to New York from forty-eight separate state capitols, on board the Aerolíneas aircraft on time. Although no other foreign country had ever attempted before to organize such an "all-the-governors" trip, Argentina's went off without a hitch.

dent not come, but the invitation alone would earn him knives in the back from other Argentine politicians. But by inviting the U.S. governors instead, and arranging for them to visit the six powerful provincial governors of Argentina, Frondizi accomplished two things at once: he both flattered his political rivals at home and got good press for Argentina in every state in the U.S.

Improving the image of Argentina in the United States was absolutely crucial for Frondizi. For many years, the American media had portrayed Argentina as a fascist, even Nazi country, where military men in dark-colored glasses held power with an iron fist. Because of my position with Argentine Airlines, I frequently talked to members of the military and, contrary to popular belief, the great majority sincerely wanted to see the process of democracy established in Argentina. More than one general told me personally that military training was not the right kind of preparation for leading the country politically, and that the military, after Perón, assumed power only as a last resort, when it was obvious the politicians had totally lost control. Sadly, it had been true for at least a generation that the Argentine military was the only sector of government and society that had kept itself well-organized.

But it was also obvious that Argentina's strongly Catholic military saw itself as the ultimate defender of the nation's soul, and throughout the Western world, the spectre of "godless" communism was felt as a very real threat, especially after the Cuban revolution. So the military watched Frondizi like a hawk. They liked Frondizi for drawing closer to the anti-communist U.S. while at the same time they worried that Frondizi and his cabinet were too tolerant of socialist ideas and too protective of labor unions, which they knew were still controlled by the exiled Perón.

Frondizi initially did bend over backwards to make the labor unions and the Peronists happy, but when he appealed to them to make some sacrifices, they staged crippling strikes. Frondizi knew there was a limit to what the military would let him give the Peronists, and when he gave no more, the exiled Juan Perón betrayed Frondizi by publicly withdrawing the support he had secretly pledged before the election. Simultaneously it was made public that the chief architect of Frondizi's

industrial development policy, the brilliant Rogelio Frijerio, had personally visited Perón to forge that secret pre-election deal. The military, who
never liked Frijerio anyway for his alleged leftist leanings, threatened a
coup unless Frijerio was removed as Frondizi's special economic advisor.[9]
To save his administration, Frondizi replaced Frijerio with Álvaro
Alsogaray, the head of the Conservative Party and the kind of agrarian
economist that the army preferred. (Alsogaray eventually became minister of the economy.) While that bought him time politically, Frondizi's
ambitions to develop Argentina industrially seriously suffered, as did his
image abroad as a genuinely independent leader.

Although Americans who knew anything at all about Argentina
admired Frondizi and wanted to see him succeed, American investors
still held back. Investors weren't sure they could have confidence in his
ability to keep his promises. They weren't sure how long his government could last. They weren't sure whoever succeeded him would
share his progressive views about America. Nor were they comfortable
with the military's obvious role in setting economic policy. In America,
the Argentine military still had an image of being pro-Nazi, and with
World War II not far away in memory, nobody in America wanted to be
known as doing business with a fascist country. A lot of people in
America saw Frondizi as Argentina's best hope, but they wondered if
Argentines saw it, too.

I BECOME A STUDENT OF ARGENTINA, STARTING WITH QUEBRACHO

There were, however, some American corporations who were already
quietly doing business in Argentina, and I got to know them well when I
joined the U.S.-Argentine Chamber of Commerce, which has been in
existence since 1919. In those years, the Chamber was made up of
approximately sixty American companies, very large ones (such as the

9. The army was also deeply uncomfortable about Frijerio's alleged ties to the left. He ran a newspaper
in Argentina that was accused of being communist. He was repeatedly denied entry to the U.S. on the
grounds he was a communist, a situation that was not rectified until Raúl Castro, the U.S. ambassador
to Argentina during the Carter administration, assisted Frijerio in obtaining a visa.

Bank of Boston and St. Joe's Mining) and small ones involved in things like leather or wine importation. Because of Argentina's extremely poor reputation at that time, the U.S.-Argentine Chamber kept a very low profile. Its activities mostly consisted of private monthly lunches featuring speakers, who tried to keep us abreast of the ever-changing economic situation in Argentina.

But I wasn't only interested in business and economics. I wanted to know everything I could about Argentina. I made a point of reading the three Argentine newspapers that arrived in the offices of Argentine Airlines (one day late) each morning. I subscribed to Argentina's wonderful bi-lingual journal of politics, the *Review of the River Plate*, and even began writing for it in the late 1950s.[10] And through a bit of luck, I was able to become intimately acquainted with the very small circle of Argentines who were living in New York City at that time, who shared with me all the latest political gossip.

Before hiring me, Brigadier Moragues had instructed Alberto Smart to check up on my background and I later learned that his first call was to Alberto Severgnini, perhaps the most prominent Argentine then living in New York. Alberto Severgnini was a hard-working, self-made man and an extremely good lawyer. His law firm in Buenos Aires was and still is one of Argentina's most respected.[11] Modest and sensitive, he was so low-key in manner that he probably would have gone totally unnoticed in New York City were it not for the fact that two of his clients were the very formidable Aristotle Onassis[12] and Argentina's rich and powerful Di Tella family.

In the late 1950s, the Onassis shipping empire circled the globe and Siam Di Tella was Argentina's biggest manufacturing entity, with its brand name appearing on every refrigerator and washing machine made and sold in Argentina. Di Tella was the licensee of Westinghouse and, in 1958,

---

10. Archibold P. Norman was the editor of the *Review of the River Plate* at that time, and he asked me to write a monthly article about the political situation in the U.S., especially as it might affect Argentina. I continued writing for the *Review* until 1991. (I also wrote articles about aviation for the publication *Revista Aeronautica* in Argentina.)

11. Severgnini, Robiola, Larrechea, Grinberg & Quijano.

12. It is often forgotten that Onassis began his career as a telephone operator in the Plaza Hotel in Buenos Aires. In his later years Onassis admitted to me that he first learned how to make money in international trade by surreptitiously listening in on the telephone calls made by businessmen staying at the hotel.

it also had just been licensed by Morris Hillman to produce the nation's first automobile. To this day, Argentines remember the "Siam Taxi" as among the best cars ever made in automotive history.[13]

Alberto Severgnini maintained an office in the Chrysler Building in New York and an impressive apartment on Park Avenue in order to watch over the American business doings of Di Tella and Onassis.[14] But he also represented other, lesser known Argentine clients in America, some of whom did business with my father. I had met Severgnini at my father's offices and occasionally accompanied the two of them to business lunches, which is why Severgnini vouched for my good background when Aerolíneas asked. So I was delighted when, in less than a week, I got an opportunity to repay Severgnini's favor.

Severgnini had called me with an urgent request. At the time, he and my father were jointly representing the defendants in an extremely complex, private anti-trust suit that involved the production and distribution of tanino. Tanino, which tans leather in one third the time required by other natural tanning agents, is extracted from the South American quebracho tree, but it was marketed through British and American companies—making the suit enormously cumbersome to litigate. There were fourteen defendants, each with their own set of lawyers, and evidence to be gathered on three different continents.[15]

And now disaster had struck. One of the many young lawyers involved in what Severgnini called "the Quebracho Case" had just flown on an Aerolíneas flight from Buenos Aires to New York, transporting a thick file of crucial, irreplaceable legal documents—which he had left on the plane in his briefcase! Calls to the airport had turned up nothing. Severgnini asked me: Could I possibly locate it?

13. Although there are very few Siam Taxis in existence today, those that remain are still running after nearly forty years of service. The licensing agreement to build the car was one of the very first legal arrangements I helped see to completion as a young lawyer.
14. Severgnini kept a collection of prized European art in his New York apartment, which he had purchased in the South of France during the winters he spent there with Onassis. He once asked me to take care of selling the collection once he and his wife had died, but he failed to specify that in his will. The Severgninis died childless, and the surviving relatives never contacted me. I've never known what happened to Severgninis' art collection, which was of museum quality.
15. In the Federal Court of the Southern District of New York, the suit was formally known as *International Products Corporation v. Forrestal, Land, Timber and Railways Co., Ltd. et al*, Civil Action 132-141 of 1957. Followed by *River Plate Corp. v. Forrestal, Land, Timber and Railways Co., Ltd.*, 60 Civ 483. My father represented the De Breuers of England and Argentina, who bought and sold quebracho.

I told Severgnini I would certainly try and immediately called Alberto Smart. He quickly ascertained that a stewardess had discovered the briefcase in a carry-on luggage compartment, and she brought it to the Aerolíneas office at the airport. When I called back Severgnini with the good news, he invited me to lunch on the spot.[16] And the next time Severgnini came by my father's office to discuss "the Quebracho Case", he specifically asked for my opinion.

That case was at a delicate stage. Although the large British and American companies involved in the suit were preparing for trial, our much smaller Argentine clients desperately wanted to settle. And we had heard rumors that at least one of the other smaller parties to the suit wanted to settle, too.[17] My opinion, since Severgnini asked, was that we should float a story to the press suggesting that our clients—the River Plate Corporation—had been offered a settlement by one of the parties and was inclined to accept—without saying which party it was. I was betting that if the story ever saw print, our major co-defendants in London and New York might read it and get curious.

"Who knows?" I told Severgnini. "Maybe you'll get a telephone call." We'd need at least one large party in the suit to be on our side to make a settlement work, and this was a subtle way of starting a conversation.

So I drafted a story, and made a particular effort to give it to the *Financial Times* of London, since it was the only paper I could think of that was sure to be read in both London and New York. The *Financial Times* did publish it and sure enough, our major co-defendants in Great Britain and America got in touch with Severgnini and, ultimately, the case was settled very favorably.

So, in very short order, I was a hero twice over in Severgnini's eyes. He began taking a personal interest in this young lawyer who now represented his country's national carrier and who had twice been so helpful

16. We ate at the exclusive Metropolitan Club which, like most businessman's clubs of that era, ordinarily was not welcoming to Catholics or Jews. But an exception was made for the financially and politically well-connected, like Mr. Severgnini and his guests.

17. Among the very first things I learned as lawyer representing Argentine clients is that Argentines do not like lawsuits. While it's true that no one does, Argentines in particular don't like them because if there is a little bit of blood, it usually turns into a bloodbath. Argentine business at that time involved so many special rules and regulations that Argentines never wanted their business practices examined by adversaries in a courtroom.

to him.[18] He invited me into his home to meet his family, and introduced me to his Argentine friends in New York. They were sophisticated, professional people, almost twice my age, and I was fascinated by their discussions of Argentine politics and their attitudes toward America.

In those years, Argentines displayed both a superiority and an inferiority complex about America. In public, and especially among their South American friends, Argentines looked down on the U.S. as an upstart, an offshoot of Europe, and they said they much preferred Great Britain as an English-speaking nation. At best Argentines would speak of Americans as if we were a bunch of bratty kids, always pushing to get ahead. At worst, we were a bunch of gangsters, with a business culture that reminded them of the Mafia. Since the 1930s, there had been precious little interchange between Argentina and the United States, and the ignorance and suspicion of American ways harbored by Argentines was profound.

Yet once they knew you very well, Argentines would tell you in private how much they admired the U.S. They envied the U.S. for its efficiency and modernity. They were jealous that America had made itself the richest country in the world, and they wondered why Argentina, with similar riches and talented people, had become mired in so many problems. It wasn't fashionable to admit it, but many Argentines wanted a closer relationship with the United States, where life was so energetic and things seemed to work so well. But politically they resisted it because they were afraid of us.

For all their complexities and the misunderstandings that separated our two countries, it was hard not to like the Argentines. They were so

18. There was one final incident that forever sealed my high standing with Severgnini. As the lawyer for Northeast Airlines, I made frequent trips to Washington, D.C., where I stayed at the Jefferson Hotel, which also rented a suite to Senator John F. Kennedy of Massachusetts. One evening in New York City, while dining with Severgnini at the Metropolitan Club, I bumped into Senator Kennedy in the men's room, where he asked me for a personal favor: Apparently he had a more interesting date waiting elsewhere, but he couldn't break free of his dinner companion: his father. Kennedy had noticed that Severgnini and I were drinking our coffee and about to leave, so he asked if, when I left the club, would I please stop by his table and announce: "Senator, you have another appointment." Kennedy planned to then introduce us to his father, and exit with us. To my own surprise, I readily agreed to this ruse and returned to my table, disclosing nothing to Severgnini. As we left a few minutes later, I stopped by the Kennedys' table and (with shaking knees) said my line. The Senator hastily introduced us to his father, then just as hastily rose to accompany us out the door. The Senator gave us a lift in his waiting limousine and, after dropping off Severgnini at his Fifth Avenue apartment, the Senator asked if I'd like to join him and his friend for a drink at the Carlyle Hotel. I declined and before he left the limousine, the Senator told his chauffeur to drive me home. Kennedy was already considered a serious candidate for president, and Severgnini became convinced, no matter what I said, that I moved among the most powerful circles on earth.

well-educated and well-mannered. They were interested in so many things. Once they learned I could be trusted, they opened their hearts to me about their country. Everything they told me about Argentina made me eager to see it for myself. I especially wanted to learn more about Argentina's political leaders. Argentines in America spoke of Frondizi with hesitant excitement, allowing themselves a fragile hope that new opportunities were being created in their native land. So when the winter ended in the southern hemisphere, I let Brigadier Moragues know that I was accepting his invitation, and booked my flight on Aerolíneas Argentinas.

THREE

LESSONS
LEARNED IN
THE 1960s

*President Arturo Frondizi (fourth from left) reviews an Independence Day parade
in Buenos Aires, one of the happier days of his presidency.*

Brigadier Moragues was delighted to hear I was coming to Buenos Aires. He promised me a dinner at the military officers' club, the Círculo de Armas, across the square from the Plaza Hotel, where I decided to stay at his recommendation. Severgnini was also keen on my having a pleasant time in Buenos Aires, and arranged to have the young son of one of his law partners meet me at the airport.

On the evening of my departure from Idlewild, I was surprised to run into Severgnini at the Aerolíneas terminal. As it turned out, he was seeing off another of his Argentine law partners who'd been visiting New York. Severgnini introduced me to Juan Francisco de Larrechea, who recently had been named president of Argentina's state-run Banco Industrial.[1] When we discovered that our seats were at opposite ends of the airplane, Larrechea gave me his card and suggested I pay him a visit at the bank in Buenos Aires as soon as I found it convenient.

Aboard the flight I found myself seated next to a middle-aged Argentine who gave no indication of wanting to talk. But I broke the ice by introducing myself as the American lawyer for Argentine Airlines. In response he told me that he was an "expediter," and when I inquired further, he reluctantly revealed that he worked full-time for Argentina's state-owned telephone company but, in his spare time, he obtained telephone lines for people who couldn't get them through ordinary means. Argentina's phone system, he explained, had been built by ITT before World War II. At one time it was ranked the best in South America, but

1. In 1958, there were three large federal banks in Argentina. The largest and oldest was Banco de la Nación, which was formed to assist the agricultural industry in Argentina. Banco Industrial, as the name implies, promoted industrial development, and Banco Hipotecario was the national home mortgage bank.

when Perón expropriated the phone company it became a terrible mess. For instance, now when somebody needed a new phone, there could be up to a ten-year wait—sometimes even as long as thirty years!—unless that somebody had between $5,000 and $10,000, and knew a good "expediter."

With a little bit of prying, I found out that expediters read the obituary notices and visited funeral parlors to find out who had died—and since burial in Argentina is very quick, an expediter needed to be on his toes. If the deceased had left behind an active phone line, the expediter would quickly buy the line and sell it to his "client." An expediter also had to be good at moving wires and getting the paperwork done.

It didn't sound legal, but I didn't mention that. I had come to Argentina to learn all about it, and this was a fascinating introductory lesson. When the plane landed in Ezeiza Airport in Buenos Aires, the expediter and I exchanged cards and we wished each other the best of luck.

As I moved down the aisle to leave the aircraft, I noticed that Larrechea was carrying a little cardboard box that contained a brand new transistor radio. They were now quite novel in the world at that time and he'd bought it for only a few dollars in New York. I realized that if Larrechea declared the radio to Argentine customs, the duty fees would be painful. Argentina had no electronics industry as yet, and transistor radios were worth a fortune. The duties he would have to pay were many times the little plastic radio's value.

I instantly offered to carry the radio through customs for him. "I'm the lawyer for Aerolíneas," I pointed out to Larrechea. "The officials won't charge me or take it away. I'll say it's for my personal use, which isn't far from true. I love listening to the radio!"

Very hesitant at first, Larrechea finally yielded to my insistence when I told him I'd pay the duty if need be and get repayment from him. I took the radio from him and promised I'd bring it by his office the following day.

But as we descended the stairs of the airplane, a surprising thing happened: a small military band that was waiting on the tarmac suddenly struck up a rousing fanfare. President Frondizi, it turned out, had come to the airport to welcome Larrechea home. The esteemed president of the Banco Industrial was escorted ceremoniously to a waiting limousine, which then sped out of the airport, bypassing customs completely.

I, on the other hand, was treated far differently. As I passed through customs, a sharp-eyed inspector pounced on the little box I was carrying. It didn't matter to him one bit that I was the lawyer for his nation's airline. He demanded to know exactly what I had in mind transporting a new transistor radio into Argentina. When I claimed I needed a radio to listen to the news in my hotel room, I was informed that Argentina was modern country with a radio in every hotel room. For some reason, I began arguing that couldn't possibly be true (I discovered within the hour it was). I think it was only by somehow persuading the official that this radio picked up stations from the U.S. (which it didn't) that I was able to regain possession of the radio, and the rest of my luggage, without paying duty. And perhaps the fact that I made every effort to speak Spanish to the inspector won me some respect.

Patiently waiting for me on the other side of customs was Héctor Grinberg, the son of Mauricio Grinberg, a partner in Severgnini's law firm. He personally drove me to the Plaza Hotel because taxis, in those days, were virtually non-existent in Buenos Aires on a Sunday. As we traveled through town, I was immediately struck by the cleanliness of the city streets and the well-dressed women I saw everywhere. Buenos Aires looked modern and prosperous, like a thriving European capital. But all those impressions were at the same time contradicted by the absence of modern glass buildings and the presence of so many old-cars on the road. Frondizi had only just begun to create Argentina's domestic auto industry, so the only cars available in the country were American-made imports, mostly makes and models of Dodges, Chevrolets and Buicks that I hadn't seen since my childhood. The younger professionals, like Héctor, drove shiny new imports, but most Argentines were making do with cars that dated back to the 1930s and 40s, obviously kept in excellent repair. All these antique American cars gave Buenos Aires a romantic look, but they also made absolutely plain how distant Argentina was from the rest of the Western world, in miles and in experience.

Héctor spoke perfect English, and he invited me to dine with him and his friends that evening. I instantly accepted, glad for the chance to meet Argentines my own age. He promised he'd be back in time to pick me up for dinner, but neglected to mention that nobody eats dinner in Argentina until after nine-thirty at night. I survived until his return by eating an entire tray of ham and cheese sandwiches that was served with tea at the hotel. I eventually did have a wonderful evening with Héctor and his English-speaking friends, devouring gigantic steaks and talking far into the night about life and politics in our respective countries.

Like the older generation I had met in New York City, I was surprised that these young men and women, the well-educated children of Buenos Aires professionals, knew next to nothing about the United States. They'd all seen American movies,[2] they loved American cars, they drank Johnnie Walker scotch, and they envied the wealth of the United States. But they'd been brought up to believe that the United States was a fast, crude, unfinished place, far inferior to Europe, where they went for vacations, higher education, to learn business, and even just to shop. (The society women of Buenos Aires used to boast of going to Paris just to have their hair done.) And during the 1950's, the intellectual youth of Argentina, not unlike many Americans their own age, echoed the opinions of European intellectuals of the left, reviling "imperialist" America for its atom bombs and its racial strife.

Still, a young American traveling in Argentina was a rarity, and Héctor and his friends personally treated me very nicely. They insisted on taking me to the fashionable nightclubs that ringed Buenos Aires. Television barely existed in Argentina in those days, so all the young people spent their evenings out of the house, strolling up and down the avenues or inside smoky nightclubs, dancing the tango to long-playing records. I was a wide-eyed, first time visitor, and I fast became a bleary-eyed one. A night out in the middle of the workweek was simply not done in America, and it was four in the morning before Héctor finally dropped

---

2. In the era before television, American movies were the most popular movies in Argentina, even though the country had its own thriving domestic movie industry. Argentines used to go to the movies three times a week, and studies at the time revealed that the greatest user per person of American movies was Argentina.

*The author in 1961 during his first visit to Jerusalem,
where he met with Golda Meir.*

me off at my hotel.[3] I was determined, however, to return Larrechea's radio to him as promised. So after a short nap, I was outside the ornate entrance to the Banco Industrial, waiting for it to open.

Alas, no one had told me that government banks in Argentina (in those days) didn't open until noon. When I finally was allowed to take the elevator to Larrechea's office on the top floor, I was ushered into a room so large that it would have helped to have roller skates to get from one side to the other. Across what seemed like miles of floor, Larrechea was sitting behind his desk, looking truly happy to see both me and his little radio. He explained, once I got within earshot, that this executive suite formerly had been used by Eva Perón to distribute the largesse of her Foundation. It wasn't hard to imagine what a dramatic figure Mrs. Perón must have cut there, regally bestowing gifts upon needy Argentines who were obliged to walk that final dozen yards to reach out to her for help.

Larrechea treated me to lunch at a wonderful restaurant, where we were joined by distinguished friends of his, including highly placed ministers in Frondizi's administration. The lunchtime conversation, which I just barely followed in Spanish, centered around the fact that one of these ministers was getting married on Sunday and he was absolutely frantic: He'd been unable to get a telephone installed in the apartment that he'd soon be moving into with his bride!

I interrupted to say that maybe I could get him a telephone. Everyone at the table turned to stare at me. Then they laughed, and the affianced minister tried to set me straight. "You just arrived here. If I, who am a government minister, cannot obtain a phone, how could you?"

Slowly, in my struggling Spanish, I told to them about the long conversation I'd had on the plane with the expediter. I even passed around his card. The gentlemen at the table looked at one another. Then the minister slipped me the address of his new apartment.

That night, I called the expediter. I suggested I might have a job for him and invited him to come to breakfast at the Plaza. The following morning at the hotel restaurant, I simply gave him the address of the

---

3. Héctor Grinberg remained in the Severgnini law firm and is now a senior partner. He has also remained a friend of mine to this day.

apartment and said that I wanted a phone there no later than Saturday. The expediter said he needed a day to check out the feasibility and get back to me with the information. Since he knew better than to discuss business on an Argentine telephone, the expediter suggested we meet again for breakfast the following day.

Over a second pricey breakfast at the Plaza Hotel (which I paid for), the expediter reported a few difficulties: this apartment not only was in a new building, it was in a new district that had yet to install many telephone lines. But he thought he could do it—if the price was right. I said I'd have to think about it.

I hurried the news over to the bridegroom. He got very excited. Could I arrange for the expediter to come for a meeting at a friend's place?

I paid for yet a third breakfast. The expediter had no problem going to a meeting until I happened to mention who the phone was for. Then the expediter turned dead white.

"Do you want me to spend the rest of my life in jail?" he gasped. "I can't sell a phone line to a government minister!"

I assured the expediter that he faced no such threat. The minister could be trusted. In fact, I was sure some very important people in Argentina would regard the expediter as a great friend for helping this desperate bridegroom. He really needed the phone.

It took all my powers of persuasion, but I finally got the expediter to promise he'd keep the appointment. I wasn't at the meeting, but I later learned that when all was said and done, the newlyweds began their married life with a telephone in their new apartment.

While in Argentina, I ran another personal errand, this one on my father's behalf. I paid a visit to Macoco, who I found living in a dilapidated building in downtown Buenos Aires, quite unlike his glamorous surroundings on Sutton Place in New York. Since the 1940s, my father had kept locked in his safe at Walsh & Levine all of Macoco's correspondence with Juan Perón; now I was returning it to him. My father had instructed that no copies of the correspondence ever be made, but I read all the letters before handing them over. Most of them contained nothing but lighthearted chitchat, with Macoco occasionally complaining about the crimp that wartime rationing had put into his lifestyle in the U.S. Perón's brief letters of reply were equally light and friendly, although sometimes he dwelled on conditions in Argentina, lamenting rising unemployment and discussing the need for better, universal education.

My stay in Buenos Aires was capped with dinner at the Círculo de Armas, organized by Brigadier Moragues and attended by the top brass of all three branches of the military. They listened to Brigadier Moragues extol my success in ending the Aerolíneas strike, and toasted me. I realized that although I had come to Argentina just to take a look around, I was leaving with the reputation of being an American friend. I can't say that I was displeased. I liked Argentina, and I liked the Argentine people. I knew I would be happy to acquire more Argentine business and more opportunities to return.

1961: AEROLÍNEAS ARGENTINAS AND I
(AND GOLDA MEIR)

Severgnini's law firm in Buenos Aires did, in fact, refer a number of clients to me in New York, mostly Argentines who did business with U.S. companies or who had personal problems here. I also drew up wills, trusts and lease agreements, and once I found myself in the middle of a scandalous divorce that rocked Buenos Aires high society.

But most of my lawyering was for Argentine Airlines, which, during the 1960s, had an excellent professional staff that opened offices in Miami and Los Angeles, and expanded its business around the world.[4] Much of the legal work I did was routine, but during the Frondizi administration, I was surprised by a phone call requesting that I fly to Tel Aviv to witness the signing of an agreement between Israel and Argentina that would initiate air service between the two countries.

The request came with no explanation as to why I was being asked to go. But I talked to enough people in Argentina to know that the deal was controversial, perhaps too controversial to permit a military officer from the air force to attend the signing in Tel Aviv. Argentines of Arab descent

4. Aerolíneas flew twice a week to London, and from there to Paris, Frankfurt and Madrid.

(of which there were about five hundred thousand or more) had protest-ed the deal, claiming that flying the national carrier to Tel Aviv gave legit-imacy to the state of Israel, which many of them bitterly opposed. There was a scattering of opposition from some of the military as well.

Frondizi, however, was very eager to shed Argentina's bad reputa-tion as a haven for Nazis and a fascist state.[5] He saw more benefits to the deal than liabilities. And the managers of Aerolíneas thought it would be marvelous for business. Argentine Jews numbered about five hundred thousand, and Israel was a source of pride for most, if not all of them. Many were very interested in traveling there, but they were flying other airlines to do it. And just as a United States politician is always well advised to embrace "the three I's: Ireland, Italy and Israel" in order to win votes in America's largest ethnic communities, Frondizi thought it was good politics to woo Jewish voters in Argentina and keep them on his side.

I couldn't help but wonder if Aerolíneas wanted me to go to the signing because of my Jewish name. But I also took it as a sign that Brigadier Moragues trusted me with sensitive situations, and I didn't ask any questions.

Aerolíneas booked me on an El Al flight that had a brief stopover in Paris. As I settled into my first class seat after boarding in New York, I noticed Golda Meir entering the cabin and also taking a seat in first class. I had met Mrs. Meir very briefly during the Stevenson campaign in 1956, when she visited campaign headquarters. At that time she had been Israel's minister of labor; now she was its foreign minister.

Once we were airborne, I went over to Mrs. Meir and re-introduced myself. I told her I was going to Israel for three days, principally for the signing of the agreement between El Al and Aerolíneas.

"Ah, thank God it's finally happening," she told me in her surprising-ly deep voice. "It's wonderful for the two countries."

Apparently the idea for the flights had originated with Mrs. Meir quite some time before. I learned from her that there had been opposition in

5. It was during the Frondizi adminstration that Adolf Eichmann was captured in Argentina and taken to Israel to stand trial, and I was later told by José Ber Gelbard that Frondizi secretly approved Eichmann's capture.

Israel to the deal as well, largely because of Argentina's reputation for anti-Semitism, but in the end an agreement was reached whereby each country would schedule two flights a week to each other's capitals.

When our plane stopped to refuel in Paris, Mrs. Meir asked me for a favor. Since she wouldn't be leaving the plane, she wondered if I would buy her a copy of the *International Herald Tribune*. I gladly did, and when I gave her the newspaper, she handed me her card and said: "If you're ever in Jerusalem, call me." I thought she was very nice to do that and I promised her I would.

Once in Tel Aviv, I went directly from my hotel to the Argentine consulate's office. When I announced myself to the consul general and stated the purpose of my visit, it was obvious that he wasn't at all happy I'd showed up. His curt greeting was: "This is a government matter and we don't need anybody from Aerolíneas." Then he disappeared into a nearby office without so much as inviting me to sit down.

I took a seat in the waiting room. Despite not being treated very courteously, I resolved not to complain. Aerolíneas hadn't sent me there to pick a quarrel with Frondizi's Foreign Ministry, and it seemed to me the consul general's feelings were understandable. Foreign service people are a stiff group and they never like outsiders coming in.

I heard voices coming from the other room, where I assumed the signing was about to take place. Suddenly the door opened and one of the consul staff appeared.

"There will be no signing," he announced to me sourly.

Before he had time to leave, I asked him why.

"The Israelis now insist that El Al must have a third flight each week," he answered. "They claim it doesn't pay them to fly just two flights. But they won't let Aerolíneas fly here more than twice!"

I didn't dare ask any more questions. I hadn't been in on any of the negotiations. I hadn't been invited into the signing room. The Argentine staffer wasn't getting any friendlier. I simply thanked him and left the consulate, and went back to my hotel.

With no other business on my agenda, I decided to rent a car and driver, which was very inexpensive, and take a tour of Israel. Since it's a small country, you can see a great deal in three days. I wound up in Jerusalem the day before I was scheduled to fly home, and thought to give Golda Meir a call, just to say hello.

Much to my shock, she immediately invited me to come visit her at the Foreign Ministry. When I walked in her door, the first thing she wanted to hear was how I liked Israel. I replied that I was fascinated, and she listened with interest as I told her about all the things I'd seen.

Then she asked me how the signing went. I was surprised she didn't know. When I informed her that Israel hadn't signed the agreement, her jaw just dropped. She demanded to know what had happened. I had to say that I didn't really know because I never got into the signing room, but I repeated what the Argentine consul general had told me. Mrs. Meir shook her head in denial.

"I don't believe that," she said, her temper rising. "It's impossible! We had agreed to equal flights!"

I could only reply, "That's what he told me."

Mrs. Meir now looked fit to be tied.

"Do you know how hard I worked to get that?" she snapped. Then she snatched up the telephone and within a moment, she was yelling and screaming over the line in Hebrew, her face bright red. I don't speak Hebrew, but I suspected she was speaking to the Israeli who'd been sent to the signing. In the middle of her tirade, Mrs. Meir happened to look over my way and noticed me still sitting there.

"Do me a favor," she asked me nicely in English. "Please wait outside."

So I went outside and picked up a magazine, while Mrs. Meir resumed screaming in Hebrew. Then I heard the phone slam down. I waited. I wasn't invited back in. I kept on reading and, twenty minutes later, a man without a tie sailed right past me and through her office door. I heard a shouting match in Hebrew, until the same man burst out of the office, slamming Mrs. Meir's door. As the man passed my chair, he paused and gave me a terrible look.

He was only gone a moment when Mrs. Meir re-opened the door to her office.

"You've just seen a ex-employee of the ministry," she said to me grimly.

I wasn't sure I should say anything. She still looked very upset. But rather timidly, I asked her what had gone wrong with the signing.

"You were quite right," she told me. "We asked for an extra flight. He had no right to do that."

I said nothing.

"When you get back," she urged me, "please do me a great favor. Tell the people at Argentine Airlines that I apologize. Please explain that the government of Israel is very upset. We did not plan to do that at the closing. We planned to sign."

I told her I would of course convey the message.

"I will make you a prediction," said Mrs. Meir. "We won't get a signature on this during my term as foreign minister. " She shook her head sadly. "It should have gone through," she said. "It would have been wonderful."

Mrs. Meir was right. She didn't get a signature on the deal during her term as foreign minister, nor did she get one during her term as prime minister. In fact, to this day, El Al doesn't fly to Argentina, and Aerolíneas doesn't fly to Israel. Like so many things in the Frondizi years, a small window of opportunity was opened, and when it shut, it stayed closed for a very long time. Mrs. Meir was also correct in her feeling that a reciprocal arrangement between the two countries would be a wonderful thing for both of them. And it still would still be.

EXPLAINING ARGENTINA TO NIKITA KHRUSHCHEV

That was my first taste of finding myself in the middle of Argentine foreign affairs, and I had to admit to myself that I rather liked it. But the only other comparable event around that time was an accidental meeting I had with Nikita Khrushchev in the summer of 1961 that led the way to greater trade between the Soviet Union and Argentina.

The Soviet premier was in New York to speak at the United Nations, where he delivered his famous "We will bury you" speech, while banging his shoe on a lectern. On a miserably hot Sunday, an acquaintance of mine who was a television reporter, Lisa Howard, called to say she'd been invited to a fancy cocktail party at the Soviet embassy, hosted by Khrushchev. Would I like to come along? Despite the terrible heat and the fact I didn't like her very much, I told her I'd love to.

In those days, the Soviet Embassy was located at the corner of 68th Street and Park Avenue in a nineteenth century mansion that had very little in the way of air conditioning. When we arrived at the scheduled hour, just before seven in the evening, we were packed tight in a room with several hundred sweating guests—and Nikita Khrushchev was nowhere in sight. Seven o'clock passed, as did eight, and still no sign of the Soviet leader. At eight-thirty, quite a few of the partygoers finally gave up and headed off in search of cooler air and dinner. It was well past nine o'clock when a perspiring Khrushchev finally hurried into the embassy reception room and began shaking hands.

Among those entering with the premier was one of his translators, a young man named Alexander Troianofsky, who I knew had been a student at Swarthmore college the same years as my brother Jay. I used this slight connection to break the ice with Troianofsky when he drifted my way.

The fatigued-looking translator brightened immediately when I mentioned my brother's name, and he asked me to please send his regards. I said I would and then I asked Troianofsky what had delayed the premier's arrival for so long. Troianofsky, rolling his eyes, pulled me a little bit aside.

"We were in Lloyd's Harbor," he informed me quietly, referring to the seaside town on Long Island where Soviet ambassadors traditionally maintained a summer residence. "We drove out there Thursday morning, and naturally we got stuck in bad traffic, this being such a hot weekend." But Khrushchev believed that the only reason for the jam was that all the cars had been sent there on purpose by the U.S. State Department to cause a traffic tie-up. "'There aren't this many cars in New York City!'" Khrushchev reportedly kept insisting. "'They want to fool me into believing that Americans are so rich they all own cars!'" Troianofsky smiled at me and shook his head at me. "He wouldn't even believe his own ambassador when he tried to explain that Americans, whether they are rich or not, can afford to buy a car!"

So on his return trip to the city, Khrushchev was determined he wouldn't get caught in another Potemkin traffic jam. He refused to leave Lloyd's Harbor early Sunday afternoon as officially scheduled, and instead postponed his departure until 6:00 pm. By that time, Khrushchev reasoned, all those cars sent by the State Department to clog up the Long Island Expressway would be back in their government garages. Nobody could persuade Khrushchev that the longer he waited to return to the city, the worse traffic would get.

"It took us three hours to crawl back here," Troianofsky moaned to me. "And the whole way, the premier didn't say a word. He knows now the traffic was real." Troianofsky concluded with a smile: "Russia will never be the same again now that Khrushchev understands America."[6]

The party all around us was breaking up, but Khrushchev began motioning to those of us who remained to join him in a smaller room nearby. My companion for the evening being a television reporter, she was eager to stay. I followed Troianofsky into the room and found a seat at a large round table.

Neither the heat nor the long drive had flagged Khrushchev's energy or his curiosity. He circled the table making jokes and small talk, asking people what line of business they were in. When he got to me, I told him I was a lawyer, and he threw up his hands in dismay.

"What is wrong with America that she has so many lawyers?" he barked in Russian, which was translated by Troianofsky. Everyone laughed, and Khrushchev next wanted to know whom I worked for. I thought for a moment and wondered if Khrushchev understood what a law firm was. Then I simply told him I worked for Argentine Airlines.

"You know something about Argentina?" he eagerly asked.

"Well, I think so," I replied.

"No one in my country knows anything about Argentina!" he exploded. "Not even in the Foreign Ministry! We want to buy wheat from them. We get nowhere! The Argentine system is impossible!" Then Khrushchev laughed.

---

6. Troianofsky also told me that Khrushchev had gone to Macy's while in New York and bought one of every mechanical device he saw. At that time, the Russians only had one commercial ship crossing the Atlantic and its only port of call in North America was Montreal. Khrushchev ordered the ship, the *Batory*, to come to New York to transport all this booty back to the Soviet Union.

"There is this Russian joke," he told the group. "We say that when three Englishmen get together, they will drink tea. When three Frenchmen get together, they will make love. When three Italians get together, they will drink wine. When three Russians get together, they will build a dam for the state. But when three Argentines get together, they start five political parties!"

I don't think anyone else at the table got the joke, but Khrushchev and I laughed very hard.

"Listen," Khrushchev said to me urgently, "I want you to come back here tomorrow and talk to my trade people. Teach them about Argentina. We've been trying for months to buy wheat and nothing happens!"

I promised the premier I'd be back the next morning, and as the party ended, a Russian official appeared at my side to give me his card. At the very same table the next day, I sat with three members of the Soviet Ministry of Trade and gave them a tutorial on the Argentine government. Once I sorted out the difference between the Banco de la Nación, the Banco Hipotecario and the Banco Industrial, their eyes lit up with understanding. I offered to send their cards down to Juan Francisco de Larrechea, the president of the Banco Industrial in Argentina, with a note requesting that the appropriate loan officers get in touch. They were delighted and so was I. I sent the information down to Argentina right away, as promised, but things in Argentina moved slowly in those days—even though the Argentine government very much needed an economic boost during the Frondizi years.

In the end, there is no telling what could have helped Frondizi survive. I watched the Frondizi government and thought it was working very well, yet I kept hearing of problems. It was obvious to me that the people in the Frondizi administration, many of whom I got to know well, didn't know enough about the U.S. to bring progress to Argentina, yet I must say they were some of the smartest people I've met to date in any Argentine government. They were bright young people. They wanted to do something. They wanted to get the country moving in the best interests of Argentina. And yet they couldn't. Every time they tried, they were smacked down.

1962: FRONDIZI FALLS,
AND THE WINDOW OF OPPORTUNITY CLOSES

I was particularly disturbed that when Frondizi attempted to bring oil investment into Argentina he couldn't get it past the Argentine congress, that he was forced to do it instead by executive decree. Frondizi was absolutely correct to see that domestic oil production was essential for Argentina's economic development, and there simply was not enough capital and expertise in the country to develop the resources on its own. I actually met with Frondizi while he was president and spoke to him about this, and I know for a fact the he believed, almost to the point of obsession, that what Argentina need was "meat, wheat and *oil*." Oil was the key to turning Argentina around. Frondizi saw that once Argentina was an oil producer, not an importer, the balance of payments would change and a domestic automobile industry could also be developed. And he was right.

There was no other choice but to encourage American investment in Argentina oil production, yet almost from day one of Frondizi's administration, the Radicals fought against it and the Peronists fought against it, too. But Frondizi was a leader. When he saw that if he brought his plan to develop oil production to the Argentine Congress it would be defeated, he signed a perfectly legal executive decree to get things moving. Yet the minute the Radicals found themselves elected to power again a few years later, the first thing their new president, Arturo Illia, did was annul Frondizi's oil contracts and nationalize oil production—on the ground that it hadn't been approved by Congress![7] That one move ultimately cost the Argentines billions— in reparations, international bad will, lost development and by scaring away other investment. It was one of the worst mistakes ever made in modern day Argentina, and let it be noted that it was made by a

---

7. During the 1970s, I met Arturo Illia in Houston where his wife was receiving medical treatment. I told him then that Argentina should have followed the example of Saudi Arabia in negotiating to buy out the foreign oil companies it no longer wanted on its soil rather than simply seizing them. The Saudi's shrewd behavior earned them abundant good will from the international community and was ultimately a more cost-effective way of getting the same result. Illia agreed that he had made a mistake and asked why I hadn't given my advice to him at the time. I explained I didn't know him then, and added: "But even if I had, I doubt you wouldn't have listened to me tell you something different from what your advisers were telling you was good politically."

Radical, not a Peronist.[8]

But Frondizi, too, made mistakes. He thought he could win over the Peronists with liberal concessions, but finally they weren't capable of compromise. And he thought he could somehow reconcile Argentines with the United States, but there was too much mistrust. And while he tried to be a friend of the United States, he couldn't afford to go along with everything Washington asked for. Frondizi also didn't fully appreciate that the United States, from its point of view, couldn't afford to cut him slack at the height of the Cold War. But in the end, Frondizi's biggest mistake was to believe that he could act as if he were the leader of a fully functioning democracy.

It was particularly sad for an American during those years to watch all the misunderstanding between Argentina and the U.S. with respect to Fidel Castro in Cuba. Frondizi didn't have the backing of the people to do something so strong as to cut off relations with Cuba, and he had no inclination to make an enemy of Castro, yet that is what America expected him to do. By any measure, Frondizi was actually the best president of Argentina that America could have ever hoped for, and the Kennedy administration recognized this and tried to make Argentina a showcase for its anti-Communist oriented program of aid for Latin America called the "Alliance for Progress." But the Kennedy administration also tried to push Frondizi into taking public stances he couldn't afford to take, especially if he was to attain his dream of reconciling the Peronists and the rest of the nation.

The military in Argentina despised Fidel Castro and were terrified of communism, and they pushed Frondizi to join the United States in isolating Cuba. But working people in Argentina, almost all of who were Peronists, rather admired Castro because he stood up to the United States. It was also the case that Che Guevara, Cuba's revolutionary hero, was born in Argentina, and no one should have expected that tie to be forgotten. Many ordinary Argentines felt close to the Cubans as fellow Latin Americans, and there was a fair amount of trade between the two

8. Not that Peronists never made mistakes when they got the chance: In 1971, General Lanusse invited American banks to invest in Argentina, and when he was succeeded by an elected Peronist, Héctor Campora, in 1974, the first thing Campora did was nationalize all the private banks that had opened under previous military governments because their licenses hadn't been issued by Congress!

nations. Frondizi needed the support of Peronists if he was going to continue to win elections. And he scored points with them by not slapping around Cuba like the United States wanted him to do.

But he didn't score points with the military every time he went against the U.S., and finally Frondizi found himself caught between the Peronists and the military, while getting no help from the Radicals at all.

Four years into his presidential terms, and with only two more years remaining to it, Frondizi was urged by two of his advisors, Alfredo Vítolo and Rogelio Frijerio, to go ahead and hold national elections for Congress and the provincial governorships. The theory was that the public was so admiring of Frondizi's accomplishments that his wing of the Radical Party would surely win, and it would give him a stronger hand in pushing the rest of his agenda.

Frondizi allowed the formation of a new opposition political party, confident that he would be rewarded with Peronist support at the ballot box.[9] However, the Peronists banded together to join the new "Unión Popular" and ran full slates of candidates for Congress and governorships. When obviously Peronist candidates actually won several key provincial elections by healthy margins, panic set in. The chaos that ensued set the tone for Argentine politics for the next thirty years.

Frondizi had to declare a bank holiday to stop a financial disaster. Facing calls for his resignation and a threat by the military to depose him if he failed to annul the elections, the president hurriedly tried to form a coalition cabinet with the military and the traditionalist wing of the Radical Party, still headed by Ricardo Balbin, who had so long been Frondizi's chief political rival. But Balbin refused to join the coalition, and the Peronists called for a national strike. In the midst of the crisis, Frondizi got a brief reprieve when Argentines of all political colors temporarily laid aside their differences and lined the streets of Buenos Aires to welcome Prince Philip of Great Britain to town.

On March 24, the head of the Conservative Party, the man who had

9. I heard from a member of the Argentine Air Force that the air force hired an American polling firm to find out how people were going to vote in Argentina, and the polling predicted that Frondizi was going to lose and the Peronists would win. Frondizi, however, really believed he could defeat the Peronists in an election and simply wouldn't listen to anybody.

replaced Juan Perón as president, General Pedro E. Aramburu, stepped in to mediate the crisis. Aramburu told Frondizi to resign. Frondizi refused. At dawn on March 29, the military arrested Frondizi. Twenty-four hours later, the president of the Senate, José María Guido, was sworn in to replace him.[10] Prince Philip left town without meeting Argentina's new head of state.

I am told that the Radicals were simply too angry with Frondizi for his pro-U.S. stands to save him. To this day, there are people in the military who believe that if the Radicals had said out loud that they wanted Frondizi to stay in power, it would have stopped the coup. But they claim the Radicals ultimately preferred military rule to a government led by Frondizi.

Personally, I don't know. But I became convinced when I saw Frondizi removed from office in March of 1962 that the next political party to rule Argentina successfully could only be the Peronists, and for them to be able to rule successfully, the Peronists would need at least twenty years, or another generation, to develop leaders who understood the new post-World War II era. I wasn't wrong, but I had to wait longer than twenty years to see it happen.

10. I was also told another intriguing story about the coup, of which I have no proof. I was told that long before the coup, President Frondizi arranged to meet secretly with the Peronist leadership at the Casa Rosada and then, at the last minute, sent his vice president to chair the meeting. Frondizi then notified the military that the vice president was secretly meeting with Peronists, and the horrified military forced the vice president out of office. Thus, when Frondizi was removed by the military, it was unclear legally who should be installed as president. As the military brooded over the problem in a closed session, leaders of the Radical Party rushed the president of the Senate, José María Guido, through a swearing-in ceremony. The military reluctantly accepted the result as legal.

FOUR

ARGENTINA GROPES FOR STABILITY IN THE 1960s

with Presidents Guido and Illia—and a coup

President Arturo Illia among well wishers.

From the beginning of my career as a lawyer representing Argentine interests, I made it a rule not to side with any one political party in the country or with any faction of the military. I didn't think it was right for me to become a political player in Argentina. And besides, from a purely practical point of view, it was obvious to me that governments come and go, especially in Argentina during this period of time, and that I would be unable to do my work for Argentine Airlines and other Argentine clients unless everyone I came in contact with knew that I would deal straight with them and could be trusted.

It was a good rule and I'm glad I never wavered from it, especially during the 1960s. The administration of José María Guido was in reality controlled by the military, which in itself was very divided about which direction Argentina should take. Many in the military had wanted Frondizi to stay. Many had wanted a rapprochement with Perón. Many were rabidly anti-Perón and anything that smacked of Peronism. And the Peronists, who were now political outcasts, were also divided among themselves.

The army divided into "Red" and "Blue" camps that fought pitched battles in the streets of Buenos Aires. A victory of sorts was secured by the "Blue" camp, who favored moving steadily in the direction of free elections. These elections were to allow candidates with Peronist sympathies and ideas to appear on the ballot alongside candidates from the other established parties—although the Peronist Party itself was once again officially outlawed and Perón was still not allowed back in the country during the campaign.

But two days before the scheduled election to replace Guido in July of 1963, Perón issued an order from Spain that all good Peronists in Argentina should hand in a blank ballot to show the strength of their numbers. When the votes were counted, the new president was declared to be an anti-Frondizi Radical named Arturo Illia, who won with only twenty-four percent of the vote.

A doctor by trade, Illia came to power with no national or international experience in politics. He was from the old school of Argentine Radicals who thought that the U.S. was controlled by industrial giants, and Argentina would be crushed if she got close to the U.S. Illia was a good, honest man, but a very bad president. The patient, visionary work done by Frondizi to improve U.S.-Argentine relations was "radically" reversed by Illia. As I mentioned in the previous chapter, among the first and very worst things that Illia did upon assuming office was to annul the oil contracts Frondizi had signed with American corporations and nationalize Argentina's oil production, all because Frondizi had resorted to using an executive decree to do what was right for the country after the Congress failed to find the political courage to do it.

I watched Illia take over a country that was in disastrous economic condition. Fifty percent of industry in the country was dead. Argentina stumbled along from one crisis to the next. The largest labor organization, the CGT, embarked upon an escalating program of disturbances and strikes, and at the peak of the chaos, Juan Perón attempted a return from exile in Spain. He was turned away in Brazil, leaving his party to divide into factions. The military, too, was divided into factions. The Radicals were divided as well. As I listened to Radicals, Conservatives, Peronists, and military men talk about their national situation, I heard each one of them speaking a piece of the truth, but none seemed to grasp the whole picture. Each was stuck in their ways, and it was inevitable that all would behave in the way that they did, tearing the country apart without meaning to.

It was going to take a very special leader and a very special set of circumstances for Argentina to find a way out of her difficulties, just as it took special leaders and circumstances to bring an end to the global Cold War. I was always hoping that Argentina was just about to turn the corner, but so often she turned out to be merely going in circles. None of the traditional political players in Argentina seemed to understand that the world had changed drastically since World War II.

So when I say that privately I became convinced that Argentina would not be successful in solving her problems until the Peronists were capable of putting forth a leader who could develop good relations with the United States, that doesn't mean that I was working for Peronists. But I did work hard on behalf of Argentina, giving my clients my best advice and promoting the economic interests of Argentina whenever and wherever I could.

HOW I PREDICTED A COUP IN
ARGENTINA WITHOUT MEANING TO

In 1966, Brigadier Roberto Baltar was the president of Aerolíneas Argentinas. Baltar was a quiet, proud air force man who wanted to take his country's national carrier into the next phase of modern air travel. He set about upgrading Argentina's outmoded fleet of gas-guzzling Comet jets with newer, more powerful aircraft, planning to make Aerolíneas the fastest-growing airline in Latin America. He looked into buying either British-made VC-10s from Vickers or the Boeing 707s made in America.

Argentina's long history of friendly trade relations with England argued in favor purchasing British planes, and a group of air force generals went so far as to fly to London to buy the VC-10s. But scarcely had they landed at Heathrow Airport when they were instructed to get back on the plane: a last-minute decision had been made in Buenos Aires to buy America's Boeings instead. Unlike the rest of the Argentine military in those days, air force generals tended to be pro-United States. Almost all of them had been trained in America and they admired American technology. Once the decision was made to buy six American jets, it became my job to help Aerolíneas obtain a big enough loan from the Export-Import Bank in Washington to do it.

The first hurdle to overcome was that, under the Illia government, the national economy was in chaos, and Aerolíneas, of course, was still owned by the state. Argentina's balance of trade was terrible and, from the standpoint of a lender, her credit standing could not have been worse, especially since President Illia had only recently confiscated all the foreign oil companies and their equipment. But I worked very hard to demonstrate to the bank that a loan to Argentina, perhaps especially one coming on the heels of the oil nationalization, would be a positive step forward for both the U.S. and Argentina because it would help stabilize U.S.-Argentine relations. Fortunately, I was well acquainted with one of the directors of the bank, a man named Hobart Taylor, who had once been Lyndon Johnson's secretary. For many years I had been keeping Taylor abreast of Argentine affairs, and I had won his trust.

Perhaps my biggest headache was providing in timely fashion the reams of documents and paperwork that every U.S. government agency requires in its transactions. I did provide extensive documentation on Aerolíneas and Argentina's recent financial history, but it seemed to take forever to get the material sent up from Buenos Aires.

The Boeing Corporation, of course, was very eager to close this sale. Although headquartered in Seattle, Boeing kept a large office on "K" Street in Washington, D.C. (right near the Ex-Im Bank), solely for the purpose of selling aircraft to foreign governments. Boeing's head salesman there, a hearty man named Bob Murphy, helped me enormously. In the end, the two of us managed to persuade the bank that a loan to Aerolíneas, for ninety percent of the purchase price of six Boeing 707s, was not only good business but good politics, too. Everything was approved and the preliminary papers were signed.

All that was now needed to close on the deal was for Aerolíneas to send up its representatives from Buenos Aires and for Boeing to send its chief officers in from Seattle. Then everyone could sit down in Washington with the Ex-Im directors and sign the final loan papers on the dotted line.

A closing was arranged, but when the date grew near, Aerolíneas asked for a postponement. Boeing actually had the planes ready for delivery, but it and the bank agreed to my request for a postponement, and another date for a closing was set. Then Aerolíneas cancelled again at the

Ambassador Rafael Vázquez, one of Argentina's most dedicated public servants.

last minute. I once again rescheduled, but the airline cancelled again. And again. I got no explanation from Aerolíneas for these repeated delays, but privately I could guess: In Argentina, where the guerillas were beginning to organize and inflation was running out of control, the Illia government was so disorganized that Brigadier Baltar was now having trouble getting final approval for the deal.

Still, I kept scheduling closings and Aerolíneas kept cancelling them until, finally, the lawyer who was handling the loan for the Ex-Im Bank, a lovely man named Marvin Solomon, said to me: "Larry, how about we just forget about this until you're sure the Argentines can make the time?" I couldn't really argue. All I could do was call Murphy at Boeing to apologize yet again, and tell him I'd definitely be back in touch some-time soon.

It turned out not to be soon at all. Months went by with not a peep from Buenos Aires. Then late in June of 1966, on a Sunday evening which I'd planned to spend quietly at home, I received a telephone call from Brigadier Baltar. He announced to me that he was boarding the next Aerolíneas flight to Miami and that he planned to be in Washington the following day, Monday. He told me to arrange for a closing of the loan at the Ex-Im Bank for late Monday afternoon.

For a moment I thought I hadn't heard him correctly. But I had.

"Brigadier Baltar," I told him, "you can't have a closing tomorrow afternoon for two reasons. Number one, it's been so long that I don't know what the status of the loan is at the Ex-Im Bank. I don't know how long it takes them to prepare for a closing or if the money is even there! And, two, Boeing's chief officers are in Seattle. They need at least one business day's notice to get themselves to Washington, D.C."

Like most brigadiers, Brigadier Baltar was not accustomed to being argued with.

"You must try your best to do it," he replied, and then he hung up the phone.

I hung up too. Then my phone rang again. This time it was the civilian financial manager of Aerolíneas, Carlos Scherpa, who worked directly under Brigadier Baltar. I often dealt with Scherpa on Aerolíneas matters and I admired him. He was an intelligent, likeable man but right now he was a nervous wreck.

"I'm coming up tonight. Meet me in Washington tomorrow," he blurted out. "This is terribly urgent. You have to arrange to close the loan immediately. We'll be staying at the Washington Hilton."

Since I was their lawyer, I knew I had to be there. I still had time to catch the Sunday 9:00 pm shuttle to Washington, so I flew down right way and got myself into a room that night at the Washington Hilton. The very first thing Monday morning, I was standing in Murphy's office at Boeing to ask if we could close on the loan that afternoon. Murphy was glad to start his day with a laugh.

"They want a closing today?" he asked incredulously. "You know we can't have it today. I've got to bring in people from Seattle, and it's still only 6:00 am out there."

I assured him that this time Aerolíneas really did want to close. Murphy simply sat there and thought for a few moments. Boeing flew a corporate jet to Washington every day, although it wouldn't arrive until quite late in the afternoon. The sale of six 707s meant a big deal for Boeing, and of course his bosses would like the contract closed. He looked at his watch.

"We can't call anybody in Seattle for another hour or so," Murphy informed me. "But if they can get on the plane today maybe—maybe—we can have closing tomorrow. Why don't you go get some coffee and come back later?"

I told him I better run over to the Ex-Im Bank and see Marvin Solomon to let him know what was up. Murphy agreed that was a good idea. On my way out the door, he asked: "Why are the Argentines in such a rush all of a sudden?"

"Well, this is just my personal opinion," I told him, "but it looks to me like maybe the government of Argentina is going to change. And that somebody really wants this closed before it changes."

"Oh really?" Murphy said. I didn't elaborate further. He already knew that this deal needed to be closed before the normal six percent commissions would get paid out in Argentina by Boeing. Those who had put the deal together wouldn't want to take any chances that a future government might close the deal and get the credit—and the commissions.

Over at the Ex-Im Bank, Marvin Solomon was stunned but happy when I asked him to reopen the loan so that Argentine Airlines could close it that afternoon.

"I don't even know where the file is," said Solomon, who handled all the air carrier loans for the Ex-Im Bank. He started turning his office upside down. "But even if I have the file, Larry, we can't have a closing today. First of all, I have to set it up with the closing room. Then I have to find out who from the bank is available to sign." Solomon was a first rate professional who knew the workings of the Ex-Im Bank very well. In addition, he was a delightful person.

"By the way, what's Argentina's hurry all of a sudden?" he asked as he continued to search his files.

"Personally, I think the government of Argentina is going to change," I told him, "and they want this signed before it changes."

Solomon finally found the file.

"Give me a little time," he asked of me. "I'll try to get it through for tomorrow."

I hurried back over to Boeing. I found Murphy was all smiles.

"Larry, we're getting this thing on the road. My people will be on the plane today when it leaves Seattle. We can sign tomorrow."

I immediately called back Solomon to tell him Boeing's people were on their way. Solomon said he was still trying to work things out at the Bank, and suggested that I call him again before lunch.

It was now about eleven am. I didn't know exactly when Baltar and Scherpa would be arriving in Washington, so I left messages for them at the Washington Hilton saying that there might be a closing tomorrow afternoon, and I would confirm that as soon as possible. That was all I could do for now. Then I decided to call Senator Vance Hartke of Indiana, whom I knew through a mutual friend, the economist Eliot Janeway. We'd often found ourselves at the same dinners in New York, and Hartke (who had a marvelous voice) always said: "Why don't you call me when you're in Washington? Stop off at the office and we'll have lunch."

So when I reached Senator Hartke we made a lunch date for one o'clock. Around half past twelve, I checked back with Solomon at the Ex-Im and learned that the closing for Argentine Airlines was now definitely set for 2:00 pm Tuesday, the following afternoon. Overjoyed, I called Murphy at Boeing.

"Oh Larry," Murphy said ominously but humorously the minute he heard my voice. "You better go into hiding. I just got a call from Mr. Martin, the American ambassador to Argentina. He's looking for you."

Murphy started laughing, but I was bewildered.

"You should have heard him!" Murphy continued. "He wanted to know: 'Who is this man Levine who's supposedly the lawyer for Argentine Airlines? He's committing a felony!'" And then Murphy laughed even harder, but I wasn't sure it was funny.

"Which law did I break?" I asked nervously.

"Sounds like, according to some Federal code, you're not supposed to go around telling people there's going to be a coup. Boy, he's really mad at you. He said you're spreading outrageous lies! What have those generals been telling you?"

Murphy couldn't stop laughing, but now I was really scared.

"But I told you that was just my personal opinion," I insisted to Murphy. "I don't have any inside information."

"Well, you don't have to explain to me," Murphy replied. "But maybe you better keep your mouth shut."

I thought I better call Solomon and tell him not to repeat what I'd said. But Solomon didn't wait for me to speak. "Ambassador Martin's very upset with you," he reported as soon as he came on the phone.

I realized then that Solomon had tried to check up on what I'd told him. Somehow, it had all gotten back to the U.S. ambassador to Argentina, who just happened to be in Washington at that moment instead of Buenos Aires.

"Do you remember I said this was just my personal opinion? I don't know anything for sure," I pleaded. "I'm just guessing."

"I told the Ambassador that," Solomon said. "But he's pretty upset all the same. Apparently what you said is against the law."

I felt sick with worry. But I had to keep my lunch appointment. I hurried over to the Capitol, where Hartke greeted me with his usual friendly high spirits, and once we were seated in the Senate Dining Room, I blurted out to him everything that had happened to me since the night before. I had barely finished when Hartke hurriedly got up from the table and went over to a nearby table. I hadn't noticed before, but Vice President Hubert Humphrey was sitting in the Senate Dining Room. As Senator Hartke spoke into his ear, the vice president stopped eating and looked over at me, then he and Hartke had a worried tete-a-tete. Finally, the vice president got up, and he and Hartke walked back to where I was sitting.

I had actually met Hubert Humphrey twice before, although I scarcely expected the vice president to remember me. But he did, and he smiled as he looked me right in the eye.

"You're the fellow whose been saying that there's going to be a coup in Argentina?" the vice president asked.

I was absolutely terrified.

"I never said that, Mr. Vice President," I managed to say. I carefully explained how I had received a surprise call from Argentine Airlines regarding the closing of this loan, which had led me to speculate about the reasons for their urgency. "It's just my personal opinion," I emphasized.

Humphrey relaxed a little.

"Well, Ambassador Martin is here in Washington for a vacation and, you know, I'm in charge of Latin America for the president. The ambassador called me this morning and told me that the situation in Argentina was stable. Naturally if it wasn't, he wouldn't have come up here for a vacation. He said the generals assured him it would be fine for him to take his vacation now."

"Fine," I said to the vice president. "This was just my personal opinion. I wasn't trying to spread rumors. I don't know any more than the ambassador. It was only this sudden urgency about closing the airplane deal that had me concerned."

Satisfied, Humphrey returned to his table. Senator Hartke, who sat on the Senate Foreign Relations Committee, now explained the McCarran

*Executives from Aerolíneas Argentinas, the Boeing Corporation and the
U.S. Export-Import Bank formally commemorate the signing of an aircraft
purchase agreement. (The author is standing third from left.)*

Act to me, which prohibits Americans from making statements intended to destabilize foreign governments. But Hartke laughed and told me not to worry. He said he was sure that I wouldn't be put in jail for trying to provoke a coup in Argentina. I felt a little better.

After lunch, as I strolled back to the Washington Hilton, I stopped by the National Press Building on an impulse to pay a visit to the journalist Robert Novak, who was another acquaintance from New York. While waiting for him in the reception area, I idly stood by the Associated Press newswire and watched the stories being typed out automatically on the news machine, one letter at a time:

"DATELINE BUENOS AIRES–JUNE 27 1966: ALL TROOPS IN ARGENTINA ARE CONFINED TO QUARTERS AS OF FIVE PM THIS EVENING."

That was all it wrote. But it made me smile. And I finally relaxed. I assumed Vice President Humphrey was seeing the same news I was or that he soon would. I'd been right after all. Just then, Novak invited me into his office, and I told him I might have a big scoop for him, but I made him promise he wouldn't name me as his source. Novak was amused when I told him the whole story, but he wasn't interested in Argentine affairs, so he didn't think he'd want to write about it anyway.

Once I was back at the Hilton, I was handed a message that Carlos Scherpa and Brigadier Baltar had checked into the hotel. I called Scherpa to let him know that the closing was set for 2:00 pm the next day, and that this was the best everybody could do. Apparently that was perfectly acceptable, and Scherpa said he would inform the Brigadier. Scherpa also invited me to join him for dinner at eight, explaining that the Brigadier would be dining with the Argentine military attaché in Washington. I readily accepted, wondering how much Scherpa could tell me about what was happening in Argentina.

Within a few minutes, Brigadier Baltar called my room and thanked me for arranging the closing. Tomorrow was fine with him and he told me he'd see me there.

Baltar and Scherpa sounded so relaxed, my curiosity only grew. I called Argentina to speak with Mario Robiola, who was a very good lawyer, a very smart fellow and very well connected politically, especially since he had married into the Di Tella family. In those days, it was never easy to call anyone in Argentina, and once I got him on the phone, I got right to the point by asking him how things were going in Argentina. "Not very good" was all he would say. Even in the best of times, let alone the worst, Argentines do not think it wise to say too much on a telephone. So I hung up, no more enlightened than before.

During what I felt was the right moment over dinner, I shared with Scherpa the news I'd seen at Novak's office. The man instantly stopped eating and turned a deathly shade of white.

"We were told it would not happen until Thursday or Friday!" he barely whispered in his state of shock. "That we had three days!"

Then Scherpa clammed up. For the remainder of the meal, he wouldn't go anywhere near the subject. We didn't linger after dinner and when we parted, I was certain that Scherpa's next stop was Brigadier Baltar's room.

SHOULD I HAVE BECOME THE NEXT AMBASSADOR TO ARGENTINA?

Coup or no coup, I saw no reason not to get a good night's sleep. But at 6:00 am, my phone rang. It was Senator Hartke on the line.

"You must work for the CIA," the Senator said instead of good morning.[1] "I want you to be in your hotel lobby in an hour. I'm taking you to the White House. There's been a coup in Argentina and a General Onganía is going to be replacing President Illia."

Before I even got out of bed, I asked the hotel operator to connect me to Brigadier Baltar. I was told that the Brigadier had checked out at five. I then asked to be connected to Carlos Scherpa. I got the same answer.

At seven in the morning, I climbed into the back of a long limousine

---

1. Three years after this incident, Senator Hartke happened to be in London the same time I was and we arranged to have dinner. At the last moment, a well-connected business friend told me that the Israelis were about to attack Egypt, and he recommended that I immediately discontinue my travels in Europe and fly directly home. When I told Senator Hartke why I was cancelling our dinner, the senator replied that the information I'd been given was absolutely wrong. He revealed to me that the U.S. had specifically sought and received assurances from the Israelis that they would not attack Egypt. Within twenty-four hours, Israel had launched a surprise bombing run on Eygpt's airfields and the Six-Day War had begun. From then on, whenever Senator Hartke introduced me to anyone, he warned them they might learn a government secret they weren't supposed to know.

that already had Senator Hartke in it. As we sped through traffic, Hartke asked me to brief him on General Onganía. I told him that Onganía was head of the first army, and explained the meaning of that in the Argentine power structure. I explained that I had heard that Onganía had been asked to lead a coup against Illia once before, but had declined, believing the elected president should sit out his term. I had no idea what had now changed his mind and since I'd never met him, I couldn't be much more helpful to Hartke than that. Besides, the very short ride from the hotel to 1600 Pennsylvania Avenue didn't give us much time to talk.

We were quickly passed through security at the White House and then escorted to the president's private quarters. Vice President Humphrey was waiting for us and he gave me a very big smile. Almost immediately, Lyndon Johnson, dressed in a business suit, walked out of his private suite. He didn't wait for us to be introduced.

"I know all about you, Levine," the tall, Texan president drawled loudly at me. "You have great information. You're a friend of Eliot Janeway's. And you know Joe Califano. You pour the coffee."[2]

With that, LBJ headed back into his private suite, followed by Humphrey and Hartke. I looked around. I didn't see any coffee. I wondered if there might be some inside the president's suite, but I simply couldn't get up the nerve to go in and look. Inside that room, I could hear the President of the United States screaming at the top of his lungs.

"That stupid son of a bitch!" Lyndon Johnson was hollering—and those were the cleanest words I heard coming out of that room. The president went on ranting and raving in language so obscene that thirty years later, I am still too embarrassed to repeat it. "He's not going back anywhere!" I finally heard the president yell.

This was followed by muttering and murmuring from Humphrey and Hartke, and then much calmer tones from Johnson. I could no longer hear what was being said. After about ten minutes, Humphey

2. Eliot Janeway was a noted economic columnist in the 1960s, and it was he who introduced me to Senator Hartke and Robert Novak. I had known Joseph Califano from my days at Harvard law school and I later recommended him for a job in the Kennedy administration (which I had already turned down) as counsel to the secretary of the army, who at that time was Cyrus Vance, later Jimmy Carter's secretary of state. Califano parlayed that initial government post into a wide variety of Federal appointments, including a Cabinet position in the Carter administration.

and Hartke emerged from the president's room and walked over to where I had taken a seat.

"Mr. Levine," the vice president addressed me, "the president wants to appoint you ambassador to Argentina. We've checked up on you. You know an awful lot about it. We need you to make a decision by twelve noon tomorrow."

I simply sat there, open-mouthed. The vice president turned around and went back to be with the president. I can't remember if I said good-bye or not. Somehow, Senator Hartke guided me out the door.

"This is a great opportunity for you," I remember him saying to me.

"What do you think I should do?" I asked.

"It's up to you," he replied. "Just let us know by noon."

There was no chauffeured limousine waiting for me outside the White House. So I walked back to the hotel alone. Thinking.

Hartke was right. This was a great opportunity for me. I loved politics and I loved the notion of public service. And I certainly loved Argentina. But at thirty-four years old, is anybody really qualified to be a United States ambassador? True, by this time I had learned a lot about the country. It was a fair bet I knew more about Argentina than anyone already serving in government. But a lot of what I knew made me hesitate. Argentina was in turmoil. It now had a military government—the first one since I had begun working for Argentine Airlines. I wasn't sure I knew how to handle the military. I didn't know what an ambassador did during a military regime or how I would be received. Would the Argentines accept someone who wasn't from America's blue-blood elite? I knew I wasn't afraid of failure, but I wondered if my appointment to be the United States ambassador to Argentina would really be good for both countries. And what would my future be?

By the time I'd reached the hotel, I'd made up my mind. I wasn't going to do it. Looking back on my decision, I sometimes think I should have been more selfish. I know I would have loved being ambassador to Argentina. I didn't really understand at the time how Washington worked, or I might have just grabbed it, like so many other young men would. Probably I was wrong to say no. But I called up Hartke and said that was my answer.

"Are you sure?" Hartke asked.

"Yes, I'm sure," I said.

I could tell that Hartke was disappointed.

"These offers come only very rarely," the senator said to me.

Thirty years later, I had reason to vividly recall those disappointed words from Hartke. When Bill Clinton was elected president, I actively sought the job of U.S. ambassador to Argentina. After thirty-five years of experience with the country and serving as a director and the president of U.S.-Argentine Chamber of Commerce, I felt more than ready to take on the role of being my country's ambassador to Argentina. Despite having the support of both the majority and minority leaders of the Senate Foreign Relations Committee, I was called by the White House and told I would not be nominated to the post. Those opportunities only do come rarely.[3]

As for the purchase of the Boeing 707s, the closing of the loan was postponed but the deal went through six months later, by which time Brigadier Arnaldo Tesselhoff had become president of Argentine Airlines, and the situation in Argentina had changed dramatically.

3. From 1997 through the end of the century, the U.S. did not have an ambassador in Argentina. This was due, in no small part, to the Clinton administration's unfortunate tendency to reward large political contributors with ambassadorial nominations, which the U.S. Senate Foreign Relations Committee rightly disdained. Finally, in late 2000, a State Department professional, James Walsh, was successfully appointed our ambassador to Argentina.

FIVE

1964–1970
HOLDING THE LINE
AGAINST CIVIL WAR
IN ARGENTINA

Argentine authorities clash with demonstrations in the province of Córdoba in 1969.

W hat I didn't have time to fully explain to Senator Hartke during our early morning limousine ride to the White House was that General Juan Carlos Onganía was not your usual sort of Latin American military dictator. He was a unique product of Argentina's unique political situation, and of the Argentine military's peculiar history with Juan Perón.

Although Perón had been a military man himself, almost all of the military had come to despise Perón and everything Perón stood for by the time he was deposed and exiled in 1955. In the immediate years that followed, the military was unified—one hundred percent—against the Peronists. It took the position that every political, social, cultural and intellectual manifestation of Peronism should be outlawed, dismantled and eliminated from Argentina's landscape.

Frondizi saw that, politically, such a thing was impossible without inviting a full-scale civil war, so he made a deal with Perón which ultimately led to allowing Peronists once again to participate in elections. For this, the military threw Frondizi out.

But, during the brief presidential term of José María Guido that followed Frondizi's, the military became divided. A small but very smart and determined group in the military began to realize that it probably would be impossible to eliminate Peronism; there were simply too many Peronists. Yet they also still believed that Juan Perón himself was dangerous for the country. This group in the military, which became known as "the Azules", or "the Blues," believed that the best thing for Argentina was to maintain a system of electoral government but to develop a leader, either from the military or a select civilian group, who could represent and lead the Peronists, instead of Perón.

The military man who led this "constitutionalist" wing of the armed forces was General Onganía. He and the rest of the Blues advocated continued civilian rule and elections, which would necessitate giving the Peronists some kind of satisfactory role. Opposing Onganía and the Blues was a dictatorship-minded wing of military men called "the Colorados," or "the Reds," who insisted there should be absolutely no accommodation with anything even remotely resembling Peronism. Within the first six months of the Guido presidency, the Reds sent tanks into the streets of Buenos Aires in an attempt to topple the civilian government. Onganía's Blue forces drove them out and kept them out. Guido remained in power long enough for elections to be held in July of 1963, just as the Constitution demanded. But when President Illia assumed office, he forced Onganía out of the army, a very foolish error.

Unfortunately, as I have mentioned previously, the man who was elected president, Arturo Illia, was a decent man but an inexperienced politician; he won office with only a sliver of the popular vote. He had no feeling for the new economic realities of the post-war world. He couldn't control the Argentine economy and he couldn't control his own government. He had no understanding of how to build a power base. He even ignored his own supporters in the army!

But most of all, Illia couldn't satisfy the Peronists, whom he sometimes tried to placate with concessions but otherwise kept outlawed. The Peronist unions began staging strikes that paralyzed the country, but the military held back from removing Illia until they felt sure the situation had careened into chaos. That was June 28, 1966.

THE RETIRED GENERAL WHO
MIGHT HAVE SAVED ARGENTINA

There appeared to be a sigh of relief in Argentina when Illia was removed by the military in June of 1966. By that time, General Onganía was retired from the army, which made him an interesting choice for running a new government. Although the Argentine people wanted relief from

Illia's inexperience, they didn't really like having the military run the country. And the military very shrewdly realized that the United States didn't like it either. What the military wanted was to continue to receive aid from the United States as a reward for its efforts to stop communism. And yet increasingly, the U.S. frowned on military dictatorships.

Among Onganía's first acts as president was to outright dismiss the military junta that had put him in power and appoint a civilian cabinet. He positioned himself as an independent leader. Onganía was, in fact, a self-made man who was raised very far from the inner circles at the Jockey Club. He had no visible connections with the old families, the oligarchs, the unions, the banks or the intellectuals. Onganía was considered so absolutely honest, I heard him referred to as "The Pope of the Army." But I also heard that Onganía had lost some respect for democracy as he watched Illia rule so poorly. He began believing that at least some period of dictatorial rule was needed to set Argentina on the right track.

Onganía proclaimed "La Revolución Argentina," which was to take place in three stages: first, a single-minded focus on economic renewal along nationalist lines; second, a fair redistribution of the resultant domestic wealth; third, Onganía promised, he would return power to the people once new political parties had been born out of the presumably richer and more stable society. Onganía's mission was to develop, in himself or through other people, the leadership necessary for absorbing Peronism, thus bringing the Peronists back into the mainstream of Argentine politics. Only Perón himself was to be excluded.

All across Argentine society, the Onganian coup and "revolution" were welcomed as a fresh start, and many believed Onganía would find a solution to the nation's many ills. I myself thought that Onganía could find success. In the beginning, it appeared that he had defused the military's hard-liners and was paving the way for political rationality. Because of my work for Aerolíneas, I regularly talked with several high-ranking air force men, and learned that the military wanted Onganía to succeed. In the beginning, the unions supported Onganía, too. And the business community was soon impressed by the performance of the Onganía's civilian minister of economy, Adalbert Krieger-Vasena.

Krieger-Vasena was a talented man, who enjoyed great prestige not only in Argentina but in international business circles as well. He enacted a program to reduce inflation, fixing the exchange rate at 350 pesos to the dollar, a devaluation of forty percent. To his credit, that rate was maintained for all of Onganía's four-year rule, an achievement no other modern minister of economy ever came close to until Domingo Cavallo came in under Menem.

Under Krieger-Vasena, public spending was reduced and tax collection improved, greatly reducing the budget deficit. He won the confidence of the investment community by eliminating exchange controls, while at the same time renewing contracts with the multinational oil companies and signing new agreements with the International Monetary Fund. By the end of 1968, the economy was growing at such a strong pace, people were talking about the "Argentine miracle."

With so much optimism in the air, what went wrong?

NO PERONISM WITHOUT PERÓN

My own opinion is that Perón and the Peronists got very jealous. And they began to be afraid that Onganía might actually succeed at his plan at creating a Peronism without Perón. The truth was that any number of people could have run the country if the Peronists had helped. But they didn't want it. And Perón himself saw to it from Spain that no one would take his place. He never backed anybody.

During Onganía's regime, a small fraction of the Peronists in Argentina developed their own underground armies. Perón knew what these guerilla groups were doing in his name and he did nothing to stop them. Onganía's repeated attempts to win over the Peronists failed. They wanted no compromises. They wanted Perón.

In the Argentine province of Córdoba, university students and local workers began to stage strikes and violent demonstrations in 1969. In fierce rioting at the end of May, the protestors routed the police and government buildings were sacked and burned in an explosion of civic unrest that became known as "the Cordobazo." Onganía, who had opposed using

Juan Carlos Onganía, whose grand visions for Argentina were never realized.

military force against the Peronists during Illia's regime, now wanted to use the armed forces to wipe them out. General Alejandro Lanusse, who had always been part of Onganía's "Blue" faction, argued for concessions to the Peronists in order to obtain a more lasting peace. The army was sent in to restore civil order in the streets of Córdoba, but Onganía lost control of his government.

Onganía had pinned his hopes on creating a strong economy that would deprive Perón and the guerrillas of political support and make them both disappear. When Krieger-Vasena's austerity measures seemed to be producing the opposite political result, Onganía got rid of his economy minister, but the economy took a nosedive while, at the same time guerrilla gang activity increased. With the country verging on open civil war, Onganía wanted to wield a stronger, repressive hand, while most others in the military argued for a political settlement with the Peronists. And the military wanted to share the responsibilities of government with Onganía, who was ruling as a dictator. When Onganía refused to bend, there was another military coup.

Onganía was replaced on June 18, 1970, by a man I had met a few years earlier when I gave a luncheon at the Georgetown Club in Washington to celebrate the closing of the loan on the Boeing 707s purchased for Aerolíneas. General Roberto Levingston, who had been a military attaché in the U.S., was chosen to lead Argentina largely because the military faction that had taken over (led by General Lanusse) knew they could govern through him. But this backhanded effort to rule the country didn't really help to solve its problems. On the contrary, the economy worsened and terrorism was becoming rampant, tacitly encouraged by Perón from abroad in hopes that social chaos would produce a call to bring him back. I didn't predict it but I wasn't surprised when Levingston was gone in less than a year.

While I was greatly dismayed by the continuing instability and knew it was bad for Argentina's image abroad, I was glad to see that the next president, General Alejandro Augustín Lanusse, began with a willingness to tackle Argentina's fundamental political problems. He had learned that it was impossible for the military to destroy Peronism or to create a substitute "Peronism" that was not controlled by Perón. Lanusse surrounded himself with good people and began the incredibly difficult task of finding a legitimate, viable way to openly re-integrate the Peronists back into the political life of the country, which I had always believed was absolutely necessary for Argentina to move herself forward, politically and economically.

1972–1974: OPENING BANCO DE LA NACIÓN IN THE UNITED STATES

Right from the beginning, General Lanusse's presidency showed healthy signs of abandoning some of the parochial attitudes of previous Argentine governments. In fact, one of the more disturbing episodes I witnessed during the previous rule of Onganía was the appearance of Argentina's foreign minister, Nicanor Costa Méndez, before a Senate hearing in Washington, D.C., which ended up portraying Argentina poorly. At the beginning of Onganía's administration, in a wrong-headed move to control all of the nation's financial structures, the government abruptly had closed the small, privately owned currency exchange establishments known as "financieros." Some claimed this act was necessary because these exchanges were all "owned by Jews." This anti-Semitic untruth damaged the reputation of Argentina around the world, and the United States Senate immediately called hearings to review U.S. policy toward Argentina. I quietly attended the hearings as a spectator and felt Costa Méndez's testimony unfortunately did little to satisfy his questioners, nor did it reassure the U.S. government or U.S. investors that Argentina was ready to join the club of first world nations.[1]

I had long advocated that Argentines develop a more sophisticated understanding of the world financial community by opening a bank in New York. In 1958, I had written a memo to Dr. Juan Francisco de Larrechea, then the president of Banco Industrial, recommending that the bank open a branch in New York City. I argued that it would greatly enhance Argentina's knowledge of post-war international banking and

---

1. Many years after this event, I met Nicanor Costa Méndez at a forum at Harvard University, and during the lunch break, he refused to eat with any of the Americans present.

add immensely to Argentina's global stature. Dr. Larrechea wholeheart-edly agreed with me in 1958, but he simply could not persuade his coun-try to make the leap.

Now, under the new Lanusse government, Dr. Larrechea was appointed the first vice president of Banco de la Nación, and much to my delight he told me that he'd dusted off my memo of eleven years earlier and found all my points were still valid, and perhaps even more applica-ble to Banco de la Nación than Banco Industrial. He made a few perti-nent changes and sent the memo off to his new superiors with his strong recommendation that Banco de la Nación open a branch in the United States. The idea was welcomed by General Lanusse and approved. My law firm was retained to handle all the business arrangements in New York.

My efforts to help open this bank branch for Argentina proved a text-book study in how little Argentina understood the world twenty-five years ago, and why it so frequently shot itself in the foot just as it was beginning to move forward. People often blame the military for the eco-nomic problems Argentina endured during the 1970s, and those who don't blame the military blame whichever Argentine political party they don't like. But the truth of the matter is that Argentina's isolation, espe-cially its inability to come to terms with the United States, bred inexpe-rience and immaturity in its rulers, across the board. They simply did not understand how the world worked. Fortunately, the almost comical mis-takes made by the Argentine government on the way to opening a branch of Banco de la Nación did not have catastrophic consequences, as did other ignorant decisions made by later governments. But they did make my life interesting, if somewhat nerve-wracking, for several years.

In 1971, Banco de la Nación was among the first foreign banks to attempt to open a branch in New York City, and I had little doubt that the New York State Banking Department would ultimately approve our application for a license. Strongly in our favor was the fact that Argentina already offered "reciprocity" to American banks—which meant she already allowed American banks to open branches on her soil. Other Latin American countries, such as Brazil and Venezuela, did not offer "reciprocity," so Brazil and Venezuela had been forbidden to open banks in the U.S.[2] But in 1971, there were quite a few American-chartered banks doing business in Argentina (two of them New York-chartered banks), enough so that Argentina more than met the "reciprocity" requirement for opening a branch of Banco de la Nación in New York.

Nonetheless, my legal advice to my clients in Argentina was that they take nothing for granted and that we proceed in strict accordance with all the formal and informal customs of the New York State Banking Department when applying for our license. I instructed them that our first formal act would be to open what is known as a "representative office" (or "rep office"), whereby two representatives from Banco de La Nación in Argentina would come to New York City and establish themselves at a location with a business address. (In this case, we obtained space within the Argentine consulate.) The two representatives, Drs. José Franza and Juan Kenney shortly arrived in New York, along with a gentleman, very appropriately named Mr. Cash, who would oversee the day-to-day operations of the bank branch. I took them all to meet the head of the New York State Banking Department. There, the Argentine representatives were handed all the complicated forms required to get approval for opening a branch, which they were required to return in timely fashion. Naturally, the Argentines had no idea how to fill out these forms, so in essence, our law firm gave the bank's representatives a college education in U.S. banking law and American financial practice over the space of a few short months.

It was customary for a rep office to stay open for about eighteen months before actually opening a branch. In the summer of 1972, however, everyone in Argentina began rushing me to get the branch opened—and they didn't have to tell me why. General Lanusse, hoping to move Argentina toward democracy and gain greater legitimacy for his own administration, had scheduled elections for the following March of 1973. Even though Lanusse believed (incorrectly, it proved) that the military would be returned to power by the voters, he and his subordinates very much wanted to complete the opening of the bank branch in New

2. Under the Federal Banking Law of 1981, the Comptroller of the Currency is now permitted to open up foreign branches of banks with no demand for reciprocity.

York under his current administration.

So I secluded myself for a week in August at the seaside home of friends in Massachusetts to write the required "Certificate of Merit," which meant providing the New York State Banking Department with a complete history of Banco de la Nación's operations. Since no other Argentine bank had ever operated in the U.S., it was necessary for me to write a one hundred-page history of Argentina and its banking system.[3] In the meantime, back in New York, my exceptionally talented brother Jay worked furiously to complete all the other highly complex application forms.

We were able to ship all the legal papers to Argentina for signature by September 1972, and when they were promptly returned to us by the bank's board, I immediately went real estate shopping in New York City. In order to open a branch in New York, we needed to provide the Banking Department with a permanent business address.

299 PARK AVENUE: THE IDEAL LOCATION

From the very beginning, I had apprised Argentina of the need to select just the right location for the bank branch. After all, Banco de la Nación's branch in New York City would not be just another bank; it would serve as a kind of ambassador for the nation. The location of the bank would either enhance or detract from the international image of Argentina. The bank's directors knew very little about New York City and its snobbery about "location," so in a highly detailed memo to them, dated March 12, 1972, I explained the subtle differences between downtown, which (by virtue of Wall Street) was the traditional home of American finance, and midtown, which (by virtue of zoning laws designed to deter the proliferation of ground-floor airline offices) was fast becoming a prestige location for international banks. The choice of location was theirs.

Luckily, a recent stock market dive had drastically reduced real estate prices in New York, so Banco de la Nación was entering a shopper's par-

3. Flatteringly, Argentine banks subsequently opening branches in the United States appear to have used my Certificate of Merit as the model for their own, probably having obtained it under the Freedom of Information Act.

adise. I first took Drs. Franza and Kenney downtown to assess the twelve-story Societe Generale Bank at 64 Wall Street, one of the most beautiful bank buildings in New York City.[4] It had vaults, conference rooms, and was fully furnished. At a price tag of $2.5 million, it was a steal. (The vaults alone were worth well over a million dollars.) But since the Argentines seemed to be leaning toward an uptown location, I also took them to see an office building at Madison Avenue and 61st Street, also a bargain at $3 million. (Today, these buildings are worth at least $50 million each.)

My enthusiastic ally in this real estate hunt was Argentina's consul general, Ambassador Rafael Vázquez, one of the very best promoters of Argentine interests abroad that Argentina ever had. Uptown, he located a terrific pair of eleven-story buildings, highly visible on Fifth Avenue, each selling for less than $3 million. When he learned that a local bank would help finance the purchase with a thirty-year mortgage at 7 ¾ percent (with 10 percent down), the Ambassador could not contain himself. He took the very next flight down to Buenos Aires to beg his government to buy at least one of the Fifth Avenue buildings. He proposed to house in it not only the new branch of Banco de la Nación, but Aerolíneas Argentinas and the national office of tourism—and name all of it Argentina House! It was a wonderful idea, but unfortunately his government wasn't prepared to go that far. (I say 'unfortunately' because today those two buildings are worth $35 million a piece.)

In the end, the Lanusse government and the board of directors of the Banco de la Nación decided they would prefer to rent than buy, since it was sensitive to any appearance of impropriety that might accompany investing in foreign real estate, perhaps especially during an election year. Now that it was clear we were looking for a rental, a broker I had been working with brought to my attention a once-in-a-lifetime leasing opportunity: TWA had recently spent $2 million renovating one half of the lower floors of 299 Park Avenue, but since it was losing money badly in the ongoing financial recession, it was desperate to sublet the space. TWA was prepared to give us a twenty-one-year lease at $21 per square foot for the ground floor, and

---

4. Walsh & Levine was one of the first tenants in the building when it was built in 1961.

$9 per square foot for the offices upstairs. The deal included electricity and an option to buy the furniture, which was worth at least $1 million—and which I ultimately negotiated to buy for $60,000.

I knew from experience this was such a fabulous deal that I pleaded with the Argentine representatives to take an option on the spot, without waiting for approval from Buenos Aires. When they refused, I rashly wrote the broker my own personal check for $10,000, securing an option on the lease and the right to purchase the furniture for $60,000. It was foolhardy and it was risky, but I simply could not pass up that opportunity for the bank branch, which by now I wanted with all my heart and soul to succeed.

I wrote a five thousand word telex to the board of the Banco de la Nación in Buenos Aires, explaining my headstrong action and using all my powers of persuasion to sell them on 299 Park Avenue. Approval was not immediate. Instead, the board sent up a delegation to New York City to consider what to do. After looking at a number of other sites and arguing with each other in Spanish (while I chewed my nails), they finally resolved their internal disagreements and reimbursed me for the option.

That hurdle crossed, an even bigger one faced me: The other half of the ground floor at 299 Park Avenue was occupied by a branch of the Morgan Bank, which had inserted a clause in its lease prohibiting the building's owners from renting space in the same building to a rival bank. Furthermore, I knew from experience that the New York State Banking Department only rarely approved two banks operating at the same address. So I really had my work cut out for me.

Persuading Morgan to relax on the clause in its lease proved easier than I expected. I then put forward my best arguments to the New York State Banking Department, which kept me in suspense about its intentions until the day before our option-to-rent was about to expire. As it turned out, the Banking Department actually didn't care if there were two banks at one location if one of them was a foreign bank. So to my great joy, the first international branch of Banco de la Nación now had clearance to set up shop at 299 Park Avenue—right next door to the famous Morgan Bank! All we were waiting for was final approval from the Banking Department of our entire application.

It was right at this moment that Argentina almost pulled the rug right out from under—not just me—but its own state bank and the nation as well.

1973: THE PERONISTS RETURN—
AND ALMOST RUIN THE DEAL

Argentines went to the polls in March of 1973 and the elections did not turn out the way General Lanusse had hoped they would. His hand-picked favorite, General Ezequiel Martínez, did poorly in a contest won by Héctor José Cámpora, who was really just a stand-in for the still-exiled Juan Perón. The Peronist party cornered more than forty-nine percent of the vote. While I remained absolutely true to my principles of never taking sides in Argentine politics, I confess that privately I had mixed feelings, because I had known General Martínez since his days as an air force attaché in Washington and I felt he would make a marvelous president. Yet at the same time, I knew that a victory for the Peronists was a needed step forward for Argentina and that it was necessary for Perón himself to come back. No military alternative could be elected.

But my optimism about Peronist rule was sorely tested when, five days after taking office, on May 30, 1973, President Cámpora voided the licenses of five U.S. banks doing business in Argentina, claiming that since their licenses were issued by the previous military government without Congressional approval, they were not legal.[5] With one stroke of his pen, Cámpora completely undermined the existing "reciprocity" Argentina had with the U.S. in banking—and threw into total chaos our efforts to open a branch of Banco de la Nación in New York. Cámpora's actions demonstrated, without a doubt, that the Peronists had been banned from holding political office for so long that they knew absolutely nothing about how the modern world functioned. Their long banishment had deprived them of the day-to-day experience needed to govern intelligently.

I soon received notice from the Banking Department that it was holding

---

5. Included among the banks that Cámpora's decree would close were branches of the Morgan Bank, Chase Manhattan and Manufacturers Hanover Trust—in short, some of the most important banks in the United States.

up the license to open the bank branch. I immediately wrote a letter to the Department, requesting a meeting, and I contacted Governor Nelson Rockefeller to enlist his support. Although I knew Governor Rockefeller could not dictate to the Banking Department to give me a favorable ruling, I nonetheless felt that with his long experience in Latin America, it would be helpful if he said that it would be good for an Argentine bank to open here, and he did say that. I also wrote to Henry Kissinger, who was then secretary of state under Richard Nixon. He also agreed with me that, despite this sudden loss of "reciprocity," it would be good for both countries if Argentina were to open a branch of Banco de la Nación in the United States. Throughout all this, I also had the solid support of U.S. Ambassador Robert C. Hill, one of the best political diplomats the U.S. ever had.[6]

The Banking Department granted my request for a meeting. With Drs. Franza and Kenney in tow, I met with the highest officials in the Department. I spent thirty minutes explaining why the loss of reciprocity should not stand in the way of Banco de la Nación opening a New York City branch. If anything, I argued, there were more reasons than ever before to approve the branch. I explained to the Department's officials that this was a delicate moment in Argentina, and in the history of U.S.-Argentine relations. The long-banned Peronists had grown inexperienced in foreign affairs, and they harbored out-of-date but deep suspicions about the United States because of our bad behavior toward them during the 1940s. Our State Department at that time, headed by Cordell Hull, had allowed the U.S. ambassador to Argentina, Spruille Braden, to openly interfere in Argentina's elections in a crude attempt to prevent the people's choice, Juan Perón, from winning. Perón won despite the bad behavior of the U.S., but Argentines never forgot the insult. Now that the Peronists had been returned to power, and Perón himself was likely to come back, it was extremely important to allow the opening of the branch to go forward. It would demonstrate to the new government and all its newly appointed Peronist officials that the U.S. was not the enemy of freely-elected Peronism—which the people of Argentina had believed

6. Robert Hill was a genuine upper class "WASP" from New England and it was through conversations with him that I learned a great deal about how the cultural bias of the U.S. State Department under Cordell Hull did much to set U.S.-Argentine relations on the wrong track for years.

was the case for nearly thirty years.

I also said that, in my expert opinion, based on my long association with Argentine governments, any closed American banks would be fully compensated for their losses. But that in the unlikely event things turned out otherwise, having a branch of the Banco de la Nación in New York would give U.S. investors terrific leverage over Argentina—since the home branch of Banco de la Nación in Buenos Aires would be forced to keep money and other assets here. And New York in particular would be in a better position to recover any money lost by the closing of the two New York-chartered banks in Buenos Aires.

My arguments worked. We were approved by the Banking Department. Yet no sooner had I jumped that high hurdle, than another, even higher one was set in my path. The new Peronist government in Argentina quite naturally had appointed new directors to run Banco de la Nación in Argentina. Now that these men had assumed their positions behind their desks, they decided they didn't want to open a new branch of Banco de la Nación in New York, even though we had just gotten our license approved and signed a long-term lease for office space on Park Avenue. Instead, they thought it would be smarter to open a branch in Italy![7]

Upon hearing this from our two Argentine representatives, I sat down and wrote the longest telex that I had ever written in my life. I addressed it to Alfred Gómez Morales, the new minister of economy in Argentina, whom I knew to be a loyal Peronist but whom I had never met. I said I hoped he agreed with me that state banks, such as Banco de la Nación, do not serve political parties, but that they serve the state as a whole, and that the Argentine state needed a state bank in New York to supervise its foreign currency purchases and certificates of deposits, and to add to its prestige. I added that not only was such a bank in New York likely to make a lot of money for the Argentine state performing these functions, it would also serve as a base for promoting trade and increasing Argentina's knowledge of international trading and business practices, since New

---

7. I did not know at the time that the new Peronist cabinet was deeply and fiercely divided between Peronists allied with the leftist Monteneros and Peronists allied with Perón's almost literally "right-hand" man, José López-Rega, the minister of social welfare. Fortunately for me, the minister of economy proved to be a centrist.

York—not Rome—was the hub of these affairs.

I received a cable back from Minister Gómez Morales saying that he was flying to New York to see me the next day, accompanied by the new director of the bank, Edgardo Hillaire Chaneton. I met these gentlemen at the airport, as requested, and found them a taxi, but I took a different taxi back to the city. I wanted to avoid any appearance whatsoever of being personally close to the new Peronist regime, especially since the still highly-active guerillas in Argentina were so anti-U.S.[8] I did escort Gómez Morales and Chaneton on a tour of the proposed site of the bank branch, and they were deeply impressed by its Park Avenue location, especially once they realized we would be right next door to the Morgan Bank. Then we talked over the issues with Drs. Franza and Kenney, who pressed these gentlemen as hard as I did about the need for an official Argentine financial presence in New York.

Gómez Morales was a Peronist through and through, and he was a smart and courageous man. He finally turned to me and said: "Dr. Levine, I am an old man with a long memory. You are a young man. I hope you are right. I hope you are not Hull and Ambassador Hill is not Braden. But let's go ahead!" Gómez Morales returned to Buenos Aires and apparently we had supplied him with plenty of good arguments to use at home. President Cámpora decided it would be a good idea, after all, to establish a branch of Banco de la Nación in New York City.

So, just when I thought everyone in Argentina finally understood the importance of having a bank in New York and getting it open, I received a frantic phone from the bank's representatives saying that the government had ordered them to immediately transfer all the cash in the bank's reserve account back to Argentina. Doing so would have meant not open-

8. Despite my regrettable but unavoidable aloofness, Gómez Morales and Chaneton were very friendly toward me, to the point where a year later, while I was walking alone down a street in Buenos Aires, they spotted me from their limousine and stopped traffic trying to get my attention by shouting my name. But since during that time it was a tactic of the guerillas to kidnap American businessmen off the streets, after first confirming their identity by getting them to respond to their names being called out, I refused to so much as turn to look when I heard my name repeatedly shouted. Gómez Morales and Chaneton finally got out of their limousine and stood right in front of me. I gladly accepted their invitation to accompany them to a cocktail party. I soon regretted my decision when I discovered that the party was at the summer residence of the president, Isabelita Perón. I feared that being seen there would surely make me a marked man for the guerillas. I spent a very uncomfortable hour socializing with members of her administration, and although I was fascinated to meet such rising Peronist stars as Jorge Domínguez and Armando Blasco, I left as soon as I politely could.

ing the bank branch, because by law, every bank in New York is required to keep a set amount of cash in a reserve account. Drs. Franza and Kenney didn't know what to do. The order had come from the highest levels of government, because the new Peronist government was desperate for cash. Once they fully understood that Banco de la Nación was opening a branch in New York, their first thought was to borrow the money!

With Drs. Franza and Kenney afraid to lose their jobs if they didn't execute the order, I called the Argentine consul general in New York, Rafael Vázquez, and explained the situation.[9] He immediately got on the phone to Argentina, and we were able to keep the bank's reserve account in New York, enabling the branch to open.

But there was still more work to do before that could happen. My brother Jay and I had to show Hillaire Chaneton how a bank is run in New York City. It was hard but it was gratifying work, because once the bank opened, Peronists from every sector in Argentina visited the branch in New York and were very proud of it. They were proud that an Argentine bank was in the same building as a Morgan bank, right next to the famous Waldorf Astoria![10] And it gave the government a clearer window into how America really operated today, rather than the distorted view they obtained through the mists of the past. In fact, it may have been the very earliest education the Peronist Party had in how business got done in the United States.

And what did I get for all my pains? Well, the new vice president of the bank, Dr. Juan Carlos Paz, asked me to reduce my fees by half, claiming that was all the bank could afford. We had billed the bank for $80,000 in time and expenses for three years work, but now we were offered $40,000. Because I so much wanted to see the bank become a success, I foolishly agreed to the lesser amount. I didn't much mind the loss of the money but four years later I had reason to deeply regret my confusing love with business—but that is for a later chapter of this tale, when Banco de la Nación caused me a lot more trouble than this.

9. Rafael Vázquez later become Argentina's ambassador to the United States, and was among the very finest to serve in that post.

10. A later Argentine government thought it could save money by giving up the bank's street level location for an upstairs suite at 299 Park Avenue. The bank remains upstairs today, and I've always thought the move was penny wise but pound foolish, since Banco de la Nación is now far less visible a presence in New York.

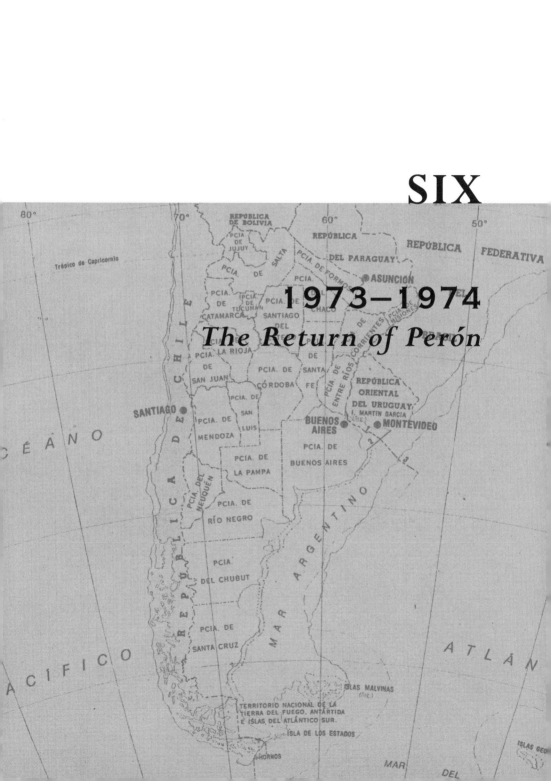

SIX

1973–1974
The Return of Perón

President Juan Domingo Perón returned in 1973 for a second, short-lived term.

The presidency of Héctor Cámpora only lasted forty-nine days. In reality, his election had merely set the stage for the re-election of Juan Domingo Perón, who by law was unable to run for election directly as a candidate. General Lanusse had realized, after the failed presidency of Roberto Levingston, that it was impossible to replace the leadership of the Peronists with anybody but Perón, military or civilian. The Peronists wouldn't let anyone else succeed. By paving the way for elections, Lanusse knew he was paving the way for the ultimate return of Perón from exile.

Perón did return to Argentina on June 20, 1973. Tens of thousands of joyful Peronists gathered at the Ezeiza airport to welcome him, where a horrifying gunfight broke out between guerrilla groups—which were Perón's own creation—and whose leaders had been released from prison by President Cámpora. Perón's plane had to be diverted to a distant military airport, the triumphant celebration now spoiled.

At the time, people thought this outbreak of violence would be the last of its kind in Argentina. For years, the nation had been plagued by terrorism, some of it sanctioned by Perón himself, some done in his name by rival gangs within his own party. They were vying for control of the Peronist apparatus and ideology, anticipating the day when Perón would return and their dreams of power would be realized. Now that Perón was actually inside the country again, it was presumed that he would order the guerrillas to stop the violence. People imagined it would only take a few words from the Great Leader, and the warring groups would lay down their arms and abide by the rule of law. "Today Perón is

Argentina," Perón simply told his people upon his return, asking them to join together as one. But those words, sadly, did not spell the end of political violence in Argentina.

To facilitate Peron's return to the presidential palace, Cámpora resigned the presidency and called for new elections. Raúl Lastiri, the president of the Congress, was sworn in as an interim president until new elections could be held on September 23, 1973. It was a foregone conclusion that Perón would win those elections.[1] I, like many other people, had a sense that history had come full circle. Although he was in his seventies and obviously ailing, Perón embodied the hope of Argentines across the board for renewal and rebirth. When Perón once again entered the Casa Rosada as president on October 17, 1973, I saw it as an extraordinary opportunity for both the United States and Argentina.

I thought the United States had a chance to rectify the mistakes it had made the previous time Perón was elected president. The first time around, our State Department had formed a totally wrong image of Perón. We spent years isolating and punishing Argentina for freely electing him, to the detriment of both countries. Now that Argentines had again freely elected him, I did not want to see the U.S. give the Argentines any further reasons to become anti-American, a posture that had crippled Argentina for more than twenty-five years.

I knew that Argentina needed better relations with the U.S. if she was to move forward economically, and the only leader who could help straighten things between the two countries was Perón himself. Only he had the authority to "forgive and forget." I felt that if we made it plain that we had changed our policy toward Perón and the Peronists, the attitudes of the Peronists toward the U.S. would change as well.

JUAN PERÓN: THE RICHARD NIXON OF ARGENTINA?

To me, the single most important symbol of a fresh start for both countries would be a meeting in the United States between President Juan Domingo Perón and President Richard Milhaus Nixon. In my view, Juan

---

1. Perón won by a landslide with nearly sixty-two percent of the vote.

Perón was a figure whose historical situation in 1973 was very much like that of Richard Nixon's in 1968, when he was elected president of the United States. Richard Nixon had made his political career during the 1950s by being a hard-line anti-communist. What that meant, paradoxically, is that he later become one of the very few political leaders who could take the risk of opening relations with communist China, which he did just a year before Peron's return. Similarly, Juan Perón famously campaigned against the United States in the 1950s, and his loyal followers never questioned his anti-American patriotism. Now only he could take the political risk of renewing relations with the United States, and thus lead the Peronists in a different direction.

I hope the reader will not mind a digression from the main narrative of this book to explain why I saw such strong parallels between situation of Perón and Richard Nixon in 1973. To a small but (I have been told) significant extent, I played a role in facilitating the U.S. rapprochement with China after Richard Nixon became president in 1968. I gladly played this role despite the fact I was, in those years, actively a Democrat, not a Republican. I simply believed that the time was ripe for a better relationship with China and that the moment should be seized.

During the 1968 presidential campaign, I had worked for Eugene McCarthy (the Democratic senator from Minnesota who ran a noble but failed effort to wrest his party's nomination away from Vice President Hubert Humphrey, the establishment favorite) because McCarthy strongly opposed the war in Vietnam. As the Democratic party fell into violent disarray early on in the campaign, it became plain to me that Richard Nixon, the Republican nominee, would win the general election. I further realized that this would create an extraordinary opportunity for America to change its relations with communist China.

At that time, our law firm represented the American branch of an international trading firm called Biddle Sawyer, whose British branch had been conducting business with communist China for about fifteen years. The way in which that had come about was very interesting: Like the U.S., the British had passed laws forbidding trade with China after its communist revolution, but by 1953, British traders were becoming ever more eager to do business with China. At that point, Biddle Sawyer decided to divide itself into two distinct entities—one in Britain and one in the U.S.—because the British side of the company wanted to move boldly without harming its interests in the States. In Britain, Biddle Sawyer then assembled forty-eight British companies into a trade delegation that it called "The Icebreaker Mission" and that "48 Group" went on an unofficial visit to mainland China to explore trade possibilities. The "Icebreaker Mission" was a total success and by the late 1960s, British traders, with their government's approval, were exporting millions of pounds worth of goods to China each year. As one of the leading companies in the "48 Group," Biddle Sawyer had built an outstanding reputation of trust with the Chinese government. In 1968, I began to think the American branch of Biddle Sawyer could have a similarly successful and profitable relationship with China, provided that the political obstacles in the U.S. could now be overcome.

The political obstacles, however, were still formidable. Ever since World War II, American politics had been deeply distorted by anti-communist paranoia. "Witch hunts" within our own State Department had deprived the government of expertise on communist China, and politicians who expressed interest in improving relations with China or Russia or Cuba were labeled "soft on communism" and hounded out of office. Honest political discussion of China and Russia fell victim to self-censorship and timidity in the media. Anti-communist fervor permeated every corner of American government, from schools to the post offices to the military, where people were expected to take "loyalty oaths" and the penalty for refusing was losing one's job.

In this atmosphere, an American businessman or politician who suggested opening up trade and relations with communist China took a tremendous risk. Yet, as the 1960s wore on, things gradually began to change. Americans grew increasingly suspicious of the anti-communist mindset that had led us into war in Vietnam; they were also eager for a reduction of the tensions that held the world hostage to the constant threat of nuclear war. Americans still wanted to remain "Number One" in the world and look strong to all potential enemies, but they weren't happy about leaving their children a world locked in an endless Cold War. And, of course, American business leaders saw a potentially huge consumer market in China, and were not at all happy to see other nations getting in ahead of them.

So, even though I had recently been working as a Democrat, I wanted to encourage better relations with China during the Nixon years. And I saw plenty of reasons to move as quickly as possible, because I thought a Republican could probably succeed where a Democrat could not, and opening up China to trade with the U.S. was too important to just let the moment slip by.

So on business trips to London in 1968 and 1969, I began to talk more frequently about China with members of Biddle Sawyer in Britain. I became more and more convinced that their "Icebreaker Mission" of 1953 could serve as a model for the U.S. in creating a similar opening to China.

In late July 1969, only six months after Richard Nixon's inauguration, I visited London and, almost on an impulse, I called and arranged to meet with two representatives of the Bank of China, owned and operated by the Chinese communist government. On the strength of the Biddle Sawyer name, I was received promptly and cordially, and greeted with a great many pleasantries. Over tea, the Chinese and I talked at length about U.S. politics and why, in my view, the U.S. government's attitude toward China was about to change, and why a man like Nixon was the one to do it. I told them candidly that I hoped that the American branch of Biddle Sawyer would come to enjoy the same success in China that Biddle Sawyer of Great Britain enjoyed.

The Chinese were also candid with me. They said they thought the U.S. trade embargo against China was absurd. "What has twenty years of American policy gained for your country except two wars?" I was asked, referring to the Korean and Vietnam wars. "There is nobody in the U.S. government that knows a thing about China," another stated. "And now when the climate in changing in your country and responsible politicians of both parties know that China is here to stay, who do you have to make constructive policy? Nobody!"

Nonetheless, they all agreed that Richard Nixon was a "practical politician" whom they felt would want to go down in history as a great president. It made them hopeful that the U.S. would soon change its policies toward the Chinese mainland, but they cautioned me that normal relations might not come quickly, because the Chinese might find it hard to forget past grievances.

At that point, the conversation ended nicely but abruptly. "There is no sense in talking any further, Mr. Levine," I was informed politely. "Your government is a fraud. It has recognzied Formosa [Taiwan], which we cannot—and we have another urgent appointment."

I suspected that this abrupt termination of our conversation was actually for "show." The Chinese felt an obligation to show strength to a U.S. businessman and to convey their party's position. But the mere fact that the conversation took place was extraordinary. Very few Americans ever had the opportunity to talk at any length with Chinese communist officials, and these men were giving me every indication that their government saw a great benefit for both countries in having better relations and doing more trade. I thought it was very encouraging.

Using my other social and business contacts in London, I tried to learn from those who frequently went to China whether the Chinese government in Peking would receive a trade mission from the United States.[2] Resoundingly, the answer was positive. I became so excited by the idea of the U.S. sending its own "Icebreaker Mission" to China that, instead of flying back to New York from London as I had planned, I booked passage on the S.S. *France* and spent the five-day crossing organizing my thoughts into a plan of action. I sat aboard the ship writing what became a twenty-one page memorandum detailing what I had learned in London, and I thought about who in government I should approach with my idea. To create such a trade mission could only be done with the complete backing of the White House.

I knew almost no one in the inner circles of the Republican Party. But

2. Two of the most helpful and interesting men in England with whom I frequently spoke about China were Roland Berger and P.A. Timberlake, who ran a trade group called Monitor Consultants and who edited the *China Trade and Economic Newsletter*. Both these men traveled to China on a regular basis and often met with officials from the Chinese government. It was ultimately through them that I came to understand, and relayed to Washington, that the Chinese government would look favorably upon an overture from the United States.

a good friend of mine, Larry Merthan, was now in business with Bob Gray, a very influential Republican. Together they operated the successful Washington public relations firm of Hill & Knowlton, and I knew that Bob Gray enjoyed a good relationship with President Nixon. I decided that would be one line of approach to the White House.

Another line of approach was through Robert Hill, who was then serving as U.S. ambassador to Spain (and whom Nixon would soon appoint ambassador to Argentina). Hill was a lifelong Republican whom I had met when he served on the board of directors of Northeast Airlines when I was its lawyer. We became good friends and, over the years, we had developed the habit of calling each other regularly on the phone just to talk about politics. I knew that Nixon had the highest regard for and trust in Robert Hill, so I felt I should discuss with him my trip to London and my conversations with the Chinese.

Ambassador Hill immediately embraced the idea of a U.S. trade mission to China, and although he gave me every indication that Nixon would welcome my ideas, he cautioned me that making it happen would be a very hard thing to do. Simultaneously, with the help of Larry Merthan, I communicated to Bob Gray my interest in forming an "Icebreaker Mission" to China. Gray was very enthusiastic. In addition, through my friend Lou Aragon of California, I met Murray Chotiner, who had recently been appointed general counsel in the Office of the Special Representative for Trade Negotiations in Washington, D.C. Although I had never met him, I knew that Chotiner had been a key political associate of Richard Nixon's for decades. I told Chotiner that if Nixon recognized China, it would ensure Nixon's re-election in 1972.

Chotiner was fascinated by the report I gave him of my London trip. In a series of conversations and meetings in late 1969, he asked me to elaborate on my proposal for an "Icebreaker" trade mission, which he promised to work on within the Administration. He told me he was impressed with the Chinese contacts I had in England, as he had checked them all out.

On August 8, 1969, I also sent a letter to Henry Kissinger, who was then serving as National Security Advisor. I scarcely knew Kissinger at all:

my only previous contact with him had been in 1955-56, when we were both teaching fellows (in different sections) at Harvard University.[3] But on September 15, I received a reply from him expressing his interest in my conversations with Chinese communist government officials in London.

"It is unusual for Chinese officials to show interest in any sort of relations with the United States," Kissinger wrote back to me. "Since it may be worthwhile for us to learn more about your conversation, I am taking the liberty in suggesting that Mr. Paul Kreisberg, Director of the Office of Asian Communist Affairs in the Department of State, get in touch with you. I would appreciate it if you would be as frank and as forthright with him as you would be with me."

But when Ambassador Hill and Murray Chotiner learned that I had shared with Kissinger details of my conversations with the Chinese and my idea about forming a trade mission to China, both of them got upset. They made it quite plain to me that if this became a "Kissinger" idea, it would stay a Kissinger idea, and everyone else would be shut out of the process. Nor did they like the idea of my dealing with people in the State Department, as Kissinger had recommended. Hill told me that Nixon himself wanted the State Department kept in the dark, on the grounds that "they'll either kill it or steal it." Both men advised me to have no further communication with Kissinger or the State Department, and I followed their advice.

On December 22, 1969, Richard Nixon announced an important change in U.S. policy toward China. Visa restrictions would be lifted and American citizens visiting China would be able to purchase up to $100 in Chinese goods for their personal use. In economic terms it was nothing, but in psychological terms it was a fundamental breakthrough. The U.S. was taking its first baby steps toward normalizing relations with the largest communist nation on earth.

Murray Chotiner had arranged for me to meet with President Nixon on December 23, the day after this announcement. I went down to

---

3. It wasn't until 1973 that I wrote to him regarding the opening of the New York City branch of Banco de la Nación.

The author during a 1972 visit to China accompanied by (left) Chien Hua Quo,
right, his interpreter and (right) Kuang Qwuo Liu of the China International Trade Service.

Washington, but while I was in Chotiner's office next door to the White House, the President called to say he would be unable to keep the appointment. But Chotiner handed me the phone and President Nixon personally thanked me for the work that I had been doing and told me things were moving along.

Shortly after that meeting, Murray Chotiner was transferred to the position of special counsel to the president, directly serving Nixon inside the White House. Although I had sent Chotiner another detailed memo about the "Icebreaker Mission" in late December as he requested, I never heard from him again once he was in his new job. I did learn from Ambassador Hill that the notion of a trade mission to China had become less appealing to the White House than a straightforward diplomatic approach to normalizing relations. In April 1971, the Chinese government pleasantly surprised the world by inviting U.S. Ping Pong players to participate in their championship tournaments. Soon, a whole array of diplomatic initiatives unfolded, culminating in Nixon's visit to China in February 1972. [4]

Although I was somewhat disappointed that I was unable to persuade the U.S. government to form an "Icebreaker" trade mission to China, I can see the logic of Nixon's preference for a diplomatic initiative. Making peace in Vietnam was the single greatest challenge facing his presidency, and that was not possible without direct contact with the Chinese leadership. Once Nixon had reason to believe that the Chinese would welcome direct contact, it made sense to pursue it as quickly as possible.

It also made sense to me that the Nixon White House did not keep me informed of its plans. This was a White House that became infamous for its penchant for secrecy and its paranoia, and surely its inhabitants found out and never forgot that my last political activity had been working for a Democratic candidate. Besides, I had already learned from my experiences with Argentina that credit for good political ideas are never given to the creators.

There is a coda to this story. More than twenty years later, in 1993, I was working in my Wall Street office when my secretary interrupted to

4. Madame Sun Yat Sen invited me to visit China, which I did on May 15, 1972.

say that H.R. Haldeman, Nixon's former White House chief of staff, was on the telephone. I had never met Haldeman, but I of course took the call. Haldeman said he was calling me from a hospital room in California, and all he wanted me to know was that it was through my contacts with the Chinese that Nixon's opening to China had been created. Haldeman explained that he wanted to tell me this personally "because those two egomaniacs will never give you so much as footnote." I assumed he was referring to Nixon and Kissinger. I was so surprised, I didn't know what to say. Haldeman asked me if I still had my Chinese contacts, and I told him I didn't. Most of them were dead. I'm sure I thanked him for the call, but that's all I remember of that strange conversation. One week later, I read in the *New York Times* that H.R. Haldeman had died of cancer in his home in Santa Barbara.

In his memoirs, Henry Kissinger merely credited "other private parties" with assisting in creating the rapprochement with China. But whether or not I was owed any credit, I had seen first-hand what an extraordinary difference it can make in the life of a country if a nation's president is willing to do an about face and reach out to a people that he formerly rejected. Only old enemies can truly make peace, and just as Richard Nixon was the only man who could credibly extend all of America's hand to the Chinese people, I felt Juan Perón was the only man in Argentina with the power to reach out and lead his people to a new relationship with the United States.

Perón reminded me of Nixon in other ways, too: both were poor boys and self-made men who had come up their own way in politics, without the approval of the upper classes. In addition, many of Perón's problems with the U.S. had their roots in the old-fashioned attitudes of the U.S. State Department, which was populated by upper class, East Coast, establishment-type people with whom Richard Nixon had long done battle. Both men, too, were capable of spectacular political comebacks: Richard Nixon had lost two bitterly contested elections and yet overcame the despair he felt at his defeats to run again for the highest office in the land and win it. Perón spent years in exile, a pariah in his own country. It must at times have seemed to him like an impossible dream that he would ever return. I felt that these two determined men would be able to reach across the decades of division and form a personal understanding. In doing so, I thought they could establish a permanent political opening by which mutual cooperation and trade between their two countries could flourish.

PERÓN SECRETLY PLANS TO VISIT NIXON

In 1973, I was the first person to broach the idea of Perón visiting the U.S. with Robert Hill, who had just been appointed American ambassador to Argentina. In addition to being my friend, Ambassador Hill was an old friend of Nixon's. Despite being a member of the East Coast establishment that had often proved such a thorn in the side of both Nixon and Perón, Hill had an unusually deep understanding of both men, and of Argentine and American politics. When I spoke with him in Washington after his Senate confirmation hearings about the possibility of Nixon and Perón meeting face to face, Hill instantly appreciated what I was saying. He asked me to put down my thoughts in a one-page memo and then send it to the U.S. embassy in Buenos Aires by cable, so it would be there ahead of his arrival.

"I want to make sure it is read by everybody," the ambassador told me humorously—which meant he already knew that both his bosses in the State Department and the Argentines would be intercepting all his cables and reading them behind his back. Instructing me to send the memo by cable was the best way to guarantee that it would be eagerly read by all the necessary parties.

I sent off the cable as instructed, but I didn't hear anything back from the Embassy. Not very long after, however, two distinguished Argentine air force generals paid me a visit in New York. They told me that Argentine Airlines had just decided to buy another Boeing 707, which would be leased to President Perón for his use as his private presidential plane. They needed my help in arranging financing for the purchase through the Ex-Im Bank, but they also needed my assistance for a more delicate matter as well.

Confidentially they told me that this new Boeing 707 had to be out-fitted with advanced medical equipment, and they hoped I would direct them to the best American suppliers. In going over their long wish list of medical equipment, it became obvious to me that this presidential plane would virtually be a flying hospital. I had heard that Perón was sick, but I didn't inquire into the nature of his illness, or ask many questions at all. Obviously the true nature of the president's health was being kept a state secret. But it appeared to me that the presidential plane was being equipped to enable Perón to safely fly long distances. I was very hopeful that one of those long flights might soon be to the United States.

I found all the information the Argentine air force generals needed, and helped make the complicated arrangements with Boeing to outfit the plane with the special equipment. Not long after, word came out that Perón's doctors had ordered the president to rest at home. Rumors began swirling in the Argentine press that Perón had suffered a heart attack, although the official story from the Casa Rosada was that the president had a bad case of bronchitis.

As it happened, other business took me to Buenos Aires in December 1973, and among the first things I did was stop by the American embassy to say hello. Ambassador Hill, who had just arrived in Buenos Aires and had yet to present his credentials to the Argentine government, immedi-ately escorted me into a private room.

"You're idea was terrific," he told me with evident excitement. "President Perón is going to visit the U.S., but he's got to be very careful how he does this. Right now, it appears that the plan is for him is to fly to New York and visit the United Nations for a session of the General Assembly. And then President Nixon could invite him down to Washington for dinner at the White House."

The date for the dinner was already set, Ambassador Hill told me. It would be December 7, 1974—almost exactly a year away. Only a hand-ful of people knew anything about it, however. The arrangements were being made so secretly that Perón's name had yet to appear on any cables or memos subsequent to mine. The words "the Argentine ambassador" were always used instead of "Perón" or "the president." In charge of the secret mission in the United States was Frank Ortiz (at that time the head of the Southern Cone division of the State Department, but who later became the U.S. ambassador to Argentina himself).

"How long are you going to be here?" Hill suddenly asked me. "I want you to meet President Perón the morning after next."

I had not planned to stay in Buenos Aires that long. Because of terrorism, it was not safe for any American businessman—even those considered longtime friends of Argentina—to stay in any one hotel for more than a day or two, and I disliked checking in and out of hotels. So I had arranged all my appointments back-to-back so I could leave Argentina almost immediately, even though I had just arrived.

Ambassador Hill told me I was welcome to stay at the American embassy, but I declined with thanks. If anybody was following me and saw me staying at the embassy, they might conclude I was not just an American businessman but somebody who was also working for the U.S. government—which could make me a target twice over.

In the end, I simply changed hotels and paid a return visit to the embassy two days later, whereupon Hill escorted me to the presidential palace for my meeting with President Perón.[5]

A FEW MOMENTS WITH THE PRESIDENT

President Perón stood up when I came into the room. While I had seen Juan Domingo Perón many times in photographs and he always looked imposing, I was still surprised by what a very tall and big man he actually was. Perón did not, however, look healthy. His wide face was very sallow and it had a heavy look. His overall appearance reminded me of the pictures I had seen of Franklin Roosevelt before his death, and I couldn't help but be concerned. Perón, however, was smiling a big smile.

Ambassador Hill spoke very little Spanish but he nonetheless introduced me to the president in Spanish. I heard myself described to Perón as the man who had shown Nixon the way to restore relations with

5. Since Hill had yet to present his credentials to the Argentine government, I asked him how he was able to take me to meet Perón. He simply told me it was "a good secret."

Ambassador Robert Hill, who introduced the author to President Juan Domingo Perón.

China. "It was his idea that you visit Washington," Hill told Perón, now switching to English, "so you can be the Nixon of Argentina."

Perón's smile got even bigger and we shook hands. He gestured for me to please sit down, which of course I did.

"Señor Presidente," I said to him in my very careful Spanish, "it is my opinion that Argentina needs a good relationship with the United States. Because whether you like it or whether you don't, the investment community in the United States is now the leader in world finance. Why shouldn't Argentina be associated with the leader in some form?"

President Perón nodded at me solemnly. His breathing was very labored.

"I am in accord," he told me. "The ambassador is arranging my visit. But I suggest that there should be no publicity yet. We will handle that. Are you enjoying yourself in Argentina? I know you are a good friend of my people."

I told the president I was enjoying my stay as always.

"How is the country?" he inquired politely.

I felt that Perón knew the true condition of his country as well as anyone, so I simply told him "Fine." (In fact, in many respects, the economic conditions of the country were better: wheat prices were rising and foreign reserves had tripled from $500 million to $1.6 billion.) I knew that I shouldn't take up any more of the president's time. So I stood up, shook hands with President Perón, and left. I was probably in the Casa Rosada for less than fifteen minutes.

For the next two months, I heard nothing about the Perón's proposed trip, although I did make sure that his plane was being readied for delivery to Argentina with all the specified medical equipment. Then I began to hear rumors that Perón was planning to visit the United Nations. There was talk of a meeting with Henry Kissinger. Even speculation about a meeting with President Nixon. I listened to all these rumors without revealing that I knew anything at all about the situation.

Complicating planning for the trip was the political crisis of Watergate, which had dragged on and on for months in the United States. The scandal had kept President Nixon and his White House under siege for months, and less and less was getting accomplished in terms of policy, domestic or foreign. However, throughout the Spring 1974 I did not give up hope that Perón still intended to come to the United States in December and would be received by President Nixon. In my mind, this was still a necessary step for both countries.

At the beginning of July 1974 I took a trip to Helsinki to visit my friend Karen Koon, the secretary to the U.S. ambassador to Finland. There I read in a newspaper that Juan Domingo Perón had died. One month later, Richard Milhaus Nixon resigned the United States presidency, having been impeached because of the Watergate scandal. The meeting between the two men that I had hoped for was never destined to take place.

WHAT MIGHT HAVE BEEN

I've never lost the feeling that if it had happened, Perón's planned trip to the U.S. would have been very good for the Argentine people. Subsequent history showed that, in the 1990s, a Peronist president was able to re-invent Peronism and steer Argentina away from its futile path of anti-Americanism. Had Perón himself visited the United States two decades earlier, I believe that the extremism of political life in Argentina might have been softened, and Perón would have shown that Peronism could be flexible and capable of adapting to modern circumstances, a task later accomplished by President Menem. But early in the 1970s, Perón might have reinvented the party and movement he created in the 1940s, and set Argentina on a different course in her relations with the world.

As it was, following Perón's death, Argentines went to battle with themselves over the unchangeable past. The legacy of Perón was a reversion to a personality cult. I tried to interest the government of Isabel Perón in making a visit to the United States, but I think she and her advisors were too frightened of the political consequences to try. They lacked experience and vision, and their fidelity to the outmoded ideology of Perón brought the country to near ruin. Lurching economic policies sent inflation sky-high, causing widespread panic and financial instability. The warring factions of the Peronist party now fought ruthlessly for supremacy.

Barely two months before his death, in a speech on May Day 1974, Juan Perón had openly encouraged his followers on the right to attack Peronist activists on the left. The right and the left factions of the Peronist party became warring armies. In addition, terrorist activity against the military and the business people of Argentina went on as it had before. The military again began organizing itself to fight and wipe out Peronism once and for all. Now violence permeated every sector of Argentine society. The ongoing civil war that everyone had expected the return of Perón would end was about to get unimaginably worse. Even as far away as New York I found myself uncomfortably close to the deteriorating situation.

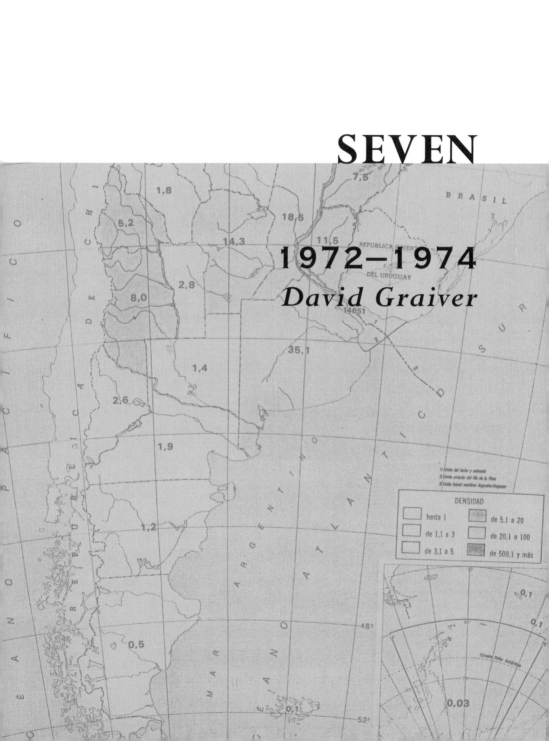

SEVEN

1972–1974
David Graiver

A newspaper photograph of David Graiver
published after his mysterious disappearance.

O n March 27, 1972, while I was in the midst of doing legal work for the opening of the branch office of Banco de la Nación, I was visited in my Wall Street offices by a very cordial young Argentine named David Graiver, who handed me six letters of introduction and a highly impressive resume. He told me that his father, Juan Graiver, a real estate magnate in Argentina, wanted to buy a small bank in New York City. When I asked David Graiver how much money his family was prepared spend on the purchase, he replied: "No more than $5 million." Graiver said he wanted my help in locating just the right bank to buy.

Five and a half years later, when a ten-seat Dessault Falcon jet presumed to be carrying David Graiver crashed outside Acapulco in Mexico, it set off an explosion of scandal, vituperation and recrimination in Argentina from which the nation has yet to completely recover. I sometimes look back on my first encounter with this confounding young man, and wonder why things didn't turn out otherwise.

Barely had Graiver walked into my office in 1972 when he paused and pointed to a painting that was hanging on my wall. "Is that a real Mary Cassatt?" he asked with genuine curiosity. I couldn't help but be impressed. The painting, which I was a keeping for a client, was believed to have been painted by Mary Cassatt, although its authenticity could not be determined for certain.[1] I immediately formed the impression that David Graiver was

1. My client, Reed Erickson, had bought the painting, along with two others, while on a European trip. He had them shipped to my office for safekeeping. The alleged Cassatt showed an older woman looking in a mirror in her bath, and supposedly was a self-portrait done in the last years of the artist's life. I once took the painting on a plane to Washington, D.C., to have Adelyn D. Breeskin of the National Gallery, a renowned expert on Cassatt's work, examine them. She said it was impossible to say "yes or no" as to whether the portrait was an authentic Cassatt. Reed Erickson never retrieved the paintings from my office. When he died, his relatives came by to claim the paintings, and I don't know where they are today.

a very sophisticated young man who had received an excellent education.

In the papers David Graiver presented to me I read that Juan Graiver had brought his family to Argentina from Poland in the 1930s, and quickly had set about establishing himself as a financier. (Eventually, I met David's father, whom I liked.) Over the decades, the Graiver family business had expanded into real estate and construction, in the private and public sectors of Argentina, and it developed projects in Brazil as well. The Graivers claimed they owned *estancias* in Paraguay with a total of 122,000 acres, upon which grazed 15,000 head of cattle, 3,000 sheep and 135 horses. I also reviewed the official financial statement's David gave me and saw his family had listed $5 million in liquid assets and not a penny more—exactly the amount David said he wanted to spend on a bank.

In 1969, David's father had bought Banco Comercial del Plata in Argentina, a private bank which by 1972 had $15 million in foreign credit lines. The family also bought Banco de Hurlingham in Buenos Aires, and it was about to purchase Compañía Metropolitana de Seguros, one of the ten largest insurance companies in Argentina.

And money was not the only measure of the Graivers. According to the papers David Graiver gave me, his family had created two philanthropic foundations, the Fundación del Hombre (of which Pablo Casals was the honorary president) and Gaceta de la Historia, dedicated to the preservation of Argentine history. According to his own resume, David had served as an advisor to the Argentine government and was the president of the Chamber of Commerce and Industry in La Plata.

I LOOK FOR A BANK FOR GRAIVER TO BUY

The credentials David Graiver presented to me were certainly enough for me to initially consider him and his father the kind of substantial citizens whom the United States looks upon favorably when they say they'd like to purchase an American bank. I let David Graiver know, however, that he would be wise to wait at least one year before purchasing a bank in New York City. The New York stock market had just suffered a crash, which traditionally meant that real estate prices would soon take a nosedive and a greater selection of banks would be up for sale. "1972," I told David Graiver, "is not the year to look for a bank."

Graiver listened to me very attentively and agreed to follow my advice. He asked me to telex him if I saw anything that changed my mind, which I agreed to do.

But with most of my attention devoted to opening Banco de la Nación's branch office, I scarcely thought about that meeting with David Graiver during the ensuing year, and to the extent that I did, it was to affirm to myself that my advice to him had been sound. In August of 1973, Graiver returned to New York to thank me for my advice, saying that he was aware that the prices of American banks had dropped, and in the meantime he had strengthened his assets. The family business was growing in Argentina, and he thought this was the right time to buy a bank in New York.

I agreed. I told David Graiver I would immediately set about looking for a bank his family could buy, but before leaving my office he mentioned that he was now a vice minister in the government of Héctor Cámpora, and asked me if I would provide him with a monthly report, by telex, of the economic and political situation in America. I told him I would try to find the time, and from September 1973 to April 1974, I did supply Graiver with a monthly telex, for which he paid me a small fee.

But the very first order of business was to have Graiver open a bank account in New York, which he did. Next, I called a friend of mine upstate in Buffalo, a man by the name of Steve Berg who often knew which banks were for sale, or could readily find out which were coming onto the market. Berg told me he would do some research.

Lastly, I wrote to eight highly respectable people in the United States and in Argentina whom I believed were in a position to know of the Graiver family, asking them whether the Graivers were serious, responsible business people. All eight responded in the affirmative, without reservation. David Graiver was admired as a very smart young man and a successful first-generation Argentine; his father was considered excellent. I learned that the family was politically associated with José Gelbard, the Peronist who next became Argentina's minister of economy.

I thought that in many ways they sounded typical of Argentina's successful immigrant families.

Steve Berg soon got back to me and told me that there were three banks that I ought to consider. I read the reports on each and talked informally with their owners. All of them told me they weren't really interested in selling, but I could sense that they very much were.

The three banks differed considerably in price. One, the Chelsea National, could probably be bought for $4 million, well within the $5 million price range Graiver could afford. Another, the Century National Bank, was an extremely well run bank, and it might go for less than $8 million. That was more than Graiver had said he was willing to spend the year before, but he'd since told me that his assets had grown. The third bank, the American Bank and Trust Company, was likely to go on the market for $15 million, although I had my doubts it was worth that much.

When I telexed Graiver with all this information, he said there was absolutely no way he could afford to buy American Bank and Trust Company. He simply didn't have $15 million to spend. So we agreed that I would concentrate on obtaining either the Chelsea or the Century bank for his family, and I told Graiver that I would write him frequent letters to keep him informed.

Graiver surprised me by asking me not to write to him anymore. Unlike almost every Argentine with whom I'd ever done business, Graiver preferred to talk on the telephone. He said he wanted to keep his family's interest in buying an American bank a secret, and preferred not having things set down on paper. But I knew there was a lot of instability in Argentina at that moment—everyone was waiting for Cámpora to be replaced by Perón—so I felt I understood his caution.

I BECOME SUSPICIOUS OF DAVID GRAIVER

Buying a bank in New York City is not quite like making any other kind of purchase. The sellers often like to develop a rapport with potential buyers, and learning the true financial condition of a bank is a delicate affair. I did find out that The Chelsea Bank was not in good condition, so I put my energy into acquiring Century, which was owned by two Italian Americans named Lawrence Marchini and Vincent Albano, who was the leader of the Republican party in New York county.

They drove a hard bargain, and so did we, but overall the chemistry was good. Negotiating the details extended over a period of months, and Graiver sent as his surrogate a man named Dr. Jorge Rubinstein. Almost from the beginning I didn't like this arrangement. Buying a bank is too important an affair to be left to a surrogate, especially one not intimately familiar with the American banking system. It also didn't help that Rubinstein, who spoke perfect English, never seemed to pass up an opportunity to indicate that he thought our family law firm, Walsh & Levine, was not high enough on the social register for him. I quietly checked up on Rubinstein's background in Argentina. Politically he was very well-connected: he was actually the brother-in-law of Juan Perón's new minister of economy, José Gelbard. But people did not speak warmly of him and no one could explain to me precisely what his relationship to Graiver was. Nonetheless, I cooperated with Rubinstein one hundred percent.

My brother Jay, the most skilled lawyer I know, handled most of the negotiations, and we arrived at a deal to buy the Century that I thought was very much in Graiver's interests. We were determined that the bank be delivered in tip-top condition, so Jay insisted to the sellers that any problematic loans had to be covered by a reserve account by the time of purchase, or else the purchase price of $7 million be reduced accordingly. The sellers proved balky on this point because there were only a few such loans on their books, but we were both particularly concerned about a $100,000 loan that had been made to a former mayoral candidate in New York City, which I sincerely doubted would or could be collected.

So in November of 1974, when Graiver flew up from Argentina for a meeting to help close the deal, I was extremely annoyed when, right in front of the sellers, he simply dismissed our insistence on protecting him against the bad loans with a wave of his hand and "Forget it." Graiver joked that it was a good thing he had finally arrived, because if everything was left up to lawyers and accountants, nothing would ever get done. My objection having been overruled, a binding contract was signed and everyone claimed to be quite happy, but walking back to Graiver's hotel, I let him know that I was infuriated. I told him that his behavior in front of the sellers had been stupid, flippant and dangerous, because a client should never undercut his own lawyers in the midst of their efforts to save him money. I added that what had disturbed me most was to watch him treat $100,000 so casually. I told him bluntly that Americans might come to regard him as simply the spoiled son of a rich Argentine and they would take advantage of him. And I warned him that, as a young banker starting out with limited assets, he would soon land in real trouble running an American bank unless he was more careful with his money.

Graiver simply looked at me. "I have lots of money," he told me unpleasantly. "And I mean lots." He then turned to one of his Argentine associates and very cockily said: "I'll bet Levine doesn't believe me."

I was completely taken aback by Graiver's statement and his attitude. Up until that moment, I had been coming to the opinion that David Graiver was immature and sometimes annoyingly arrogant, but now I wondered if there was something more seriously wrong with him. His cavalier attitude about legal advice and the suggestion that he hadn't always been level with me about his assets didn't bode well for our future relationship as lawyer and client. But there was still so much work to do on the purchase of the bank I simply plowed ahead. The deal had to be approved by the Banking Department, the Comptroller of the Currency and the Federal Reserve Board. This required investigations and reviews by the FBI, the CIA, the State Department and the U.S. embassy in Argentina. Juan Graiver submitted to an interview and Ambassador Alejandro Orfila in Washington wrote the usual pro forma letter verifying that the Graivers enjoyed a good reputation in Argentina.[2] Everything

2. After the death of David Graiver and the exposure of his financial dealings, former Ambassador Alejandro Orfila was unfairly castigated for having written this letter, which simply stated facts as they were known at the time, and which was Orfila's duty to write. United States Ambassador Robert Hill also was unfairly criticized for writing a letter vouching for Graiver's good reputation, which at the time of the Century Bank deal he certainly had. Both Orfila and Hill were among the best foreign service professionals that I have ever known.

proceeded without a glitch and all we were waiting for was approval from the Banking Department.

But suddenly, on January 10, 1975, I received a call from Buenos Aires requesting that I and my brother Jay meet with Jorge Rubinstein at the Regency Hotel the following morning. Over a pot of tea, Rubinstein informed us that Graiver no longer wanted the Century Bank because he intended to purchase another, bigger New York bank that he liked better. Rubinstein wanted to know the consequences of breaking our contract with the sellers of Century Bank.

I was dumbfounded.

"What bank are you going to buy?" I asked.

"It is none of your business," Rubinstein replied.

So I told Rubinstein the consequences of breaking the contract: "You will not only be sued for $7 million and lose, you will be the laughing-stock of the New York banking world. And the New York State Banking Department will rate you as 'lousy.'"

Rubinstein told me that he planned to offer the sellers of Century $1 million to tear up the contract.

"Good luck," I told him, "but it won't happen." My brother Jay couldn't help but roll his eyes. "You guys are nuts," he told them bluntly. Century's public stockholders had approved the sale on the expectation of soon receiving $7 million for the purchase of the stock. They would hardly let the buyer's off the hook at this stage for a paltry $1 million. Graiver had signed a binding contract.

I immediately went back to my office and dictated a twelve-page letter to Graiver in Argentina. I figured since he was still paying for my advice (even though he'd yet to pay my bills), he would hear it directly from me. I wrote that if he did what Rubinstein claimed he was going to do, Graiver could look forward to losing an expensive lawsuit that would make it impossible for him to do business in the United States. His reputation would be reduced to zero; he would never be approved to buy any other bank. Privately, I had already deduced that the bank he wanted to buy was American Bank & Trust, and I was deeply troubled that he had previously told me that he couldn't afford it, and now mysteriously could. I expect my clients to be honest with me, and I saw that David Graiver was being dishonest.

But as much as anything, what caused me to lose confidence in Graiver and his sidekick Rubinstein was their stubborn belief that political connections mattered more than working hard, being smart or being honest. The sellers of American Bank & Trust Company were a blue-ribbon group of men who were very active in our national Democratic party of the United States. Some had even served as Cabinet secretaries to Democratic presidents, and while they were a fine group of men, they were not particularly talented bankers. I had heard on the street that AB&T was not in solid condition. Yet as far as I could see, all that Graiver and Rubinstein cared about was its social pedigree, and for this they were trying to worm out of a signed contract!

But while simple logic allowed me to deduce that Graiver was interested in buying American Bank & Trust, I did not guess—and would not in my wildest dreams have guessed—that Graiver had already given the owners of AB&T a $12 million deposit to purchase their bank stock. Yet that is precisely what I later read he'd done. Had I known that, it certainly wouldn't have altered my advice that he honor his contract with the sellers of Century, but I would have resigned as his attorney. And I might have understood slightly better the baffling events that unfolded over the next two years.

As it turned out, on the evening of the same day I met with Rubinstein and wrote to Graiver, I attended a reception at the Argentine Consulate in New York to honor the Argentine minster of economy, José Gelbard. Naturally his brother-in-law, Jorge Rubinstein, was there as well. Over cocktails, I casually asked how his afternoon meeting with Marchini and Albano had gone. Rubinstein, in an altogether civil tone, told me that the meeting had not gone well. The sellers of the Century Bank had threatened to sue. He was genuinely surprised.

I felt that this man was almost hopelessly stupid. I said to him: "Jorge, I don't know your relationship with Graiver, but I'm assuming you are his lawyer. If you are, listen to me and honor this contract, because if you don't, you will not only lose $7 million, you will never do a deal in the

United States again. You don't know anything about our legal system, but it's good and honest."

I DISTANCE MYSELF FROM THE GRAIVERS

I left the party and heard nothing for a few days, and then I got a sur-prising call from the Century Bank lawyer, a very pleasant man named James Garrity. Somewhat angrily, he told me that his clients were head-ed to Buenos Aires to resolve the situation with Graiver himself—and that he hadn't been asked to go along. I told him that neither Jay or I had been asked to go, and that we knew nothing about this. I even called Marchini and Albano and advised them to be careful, and suggested that they consult with their lawyer.

Down in Buenos Aires, the sellers amended the contract to induce Graiver to go through with it. Instead of purchasing all of the bank's stock for cash, Graiver would be permitted to buy just the public stock for cash, and hand the owners a promissory note for the purchase of the remaining privately held stock. Although the sellers' own lawyer had told them that doing this might complicate matters, Graiver walked out of the meeting believing that there would be no problems with anyone. As it turned out, Graiver had to hire, at his own consid-erable expense, a lawyer specializing in Securities and Exchange Commission work to get the deal to go through. And I was left won-dering why Graiver, after telling me that he had "lots of money," now had trouble paying cash for all the bank stock. And if he didn't have "lots of money," then why had Rubinstein told me Graiver preferred to purchase a bigger bank?

But I saw little reason to solve these puzzles because now my main objective was to be finished with the Century deal and be rid of David Graiver as a client, since I was not at all happy with the way he way behav-ing (and at that time, I didn't know the half of it). So when Century's stockholders approved the final, amended deal, my office redid the papers for the Banking Department. When the approval came through on April 29, 1975, I packed up all my Graiver files and delivered them—

along with my bill—to Graiver's doorstep, which now was a swank office in the heart of Manhattan.

Obviously Graiver was determined to build an empire in New York City, and I was well aware that he and Rubinstein had begun hiring fancy and politically connected law firms to handle other transactions. Ordinarily I admire Argentines with high ambitions, but by this time, I'd become so wary of David Graiver's operations that my only further interest in his business was that my bill be paid—which it was not, month after month. I told the Argentines who had recommended David Graiver to me what was happening. They were genuinely saddened and surprised that things had taken such a turn.

I wasn't totally surprised when American Bank & Trust Company sent out a letter announcing that it was about to be purchased by Graiver. My intuition that Graiver wanted that bank had been right. But I was surprised that things had progressed that far. It was rumored that the selling price of AB&T was $26 million—more than twice the amount the Graiver family had listed as their total assets in their application to buy Century Bank! It also didn't seem possible to me that Graiver would be approved to buy a second bank, since he hadn't formed a holding company to do so, as usually required by law. But since he was no longer my client, it wasn't my problem. My only response to the news as a lawyer was to write Graiver a nice but tough letter saying that if he could afford to buy another bank, surely he could afford to pay my bill. In case he missed my point, I enclosed a draft of a summons and complaint, signaling my intention to sue. He wrote back promising to pay the bill in three installments, which he did.

Just when I thought I'd heard the last of David Graiver, I received a telephone call in February 1976, from the Argentine consul general in New York, Rafael Vázquez. David Graiver was pestering him to help persuade the superintendent of banks in New York, a very fine man named John Heimann, to approve his purchase of AB&T. Gravier was urging the consul general to host a dinner or reception for him at the consulate, and publicly endorse him as an important Argentine citizen. He also wanted Vázquez to write a letter directly to Superintendent

Heimann pleading his case. The consul general asked me for my opinion.

I told him that, in my opinion, there was no reason for the consul general to give a dinner in honor of David Graiver. Whether the bank purchase would be approved was strictly a matter of finance and law, not connections. In my experience, Graiver did not understand that the American banking system is far less political than the Argentine system, and his belief that a dinner at the consulate would get his bank purchase approved was born of faulty logic. What the Banking Department needed to know was whether the Graivers could afford to own two banks at once, and, if so, exactly where they were getting the money to purchase the second bank. Only the Graiver family could provide that information.

To turn down a request for a dinner from a member of so prominent and politically well-connected family as the Graivers required some courage on the part of Vázquez. But he thanked me for my advice and, in the end, did everything formally required of a consul general, whose job is to assist his countrymen abroad. Although he did not hold a dinner, Vázquez wrote a letter to the Banking Department stating that the Graiver family operated legitimate and successful businesses in Argentina, and the family enjoyed a good reputation there—which, as far as anyone at that time knew, was most certainly true.

MY LAST CONVERSATION WITH DAVID GRAIVER

I later had an occasion to again become concerned about David Graiver when one of the managers of Banco de La Nación in New York City mentioned to me at a dinner party that the bank had just concluded an agreement to make overnight weekly loans to the "Graiver group" on the same terms as other New York banks. I sensed that the officers of the bank were proud to see a fellow Argentine buying up banks in the United States, but I told the bank's officers that I no longer represented Graiver at my request, and that my experiences with him had taught me to be careful. I told them that they should only make loans if ordered to do so by their head office in Buenos Aires, and I suggested that since I was the lawyer for Banco de la Nación, they ought to send over the paperwork on any agreements with Graiver so I could review them. Finally, I reminded them that with regard to any loans, the managers should always make sure the loans are secured. The bank's officers appeared to listen, but they did not subsequently send me any paperwork regarding the Graiver loans for my review, despite repeated requests.

Then, much to my surprise, in May of 1976, I received a phone call from David Graiver himself. His first words were: "Larry, are you still mad at me?" I told him that I was disappointed in him, because I once felt he would do good for Argentina in America. Graiver then said he was going to send his chauffeur to pick me up and bring me to his Upper East Side apartment, an apartment he described as among the most beautiful in New York. I told him not to. I said if he thought there was some reason we should meet, he could make an appointment to meet in my office.

After I hung up, I wondered what had made David Graiver seek me out again, since when we parted, he and Jorge Rubinstein had tried to make it plain they didn't respect me. Two months earlier, there had been a military coup in Argentina, and I heard that the country was no longer being run by people friendly to the Graiver family. For a man as concerned with political connections as David Graiver, no doubt this seemed a very worrisome situation, and perhaps he wanted to talk politics. The general financial condition of Argentina no doubt troubled Graiver as well: In the final throes of Isabelita Perón's regime, spiraling inflation made everyone dizzy. Any Argentine operating an international business had all he could do to keep his head above water, and in the past, I had sometimes given Graiver good investment advice, although I doubted that he listened. But it had been so long since I'd had anything to do with Graiver's business, I really had no idea what he might now want from me. And I wasn't sure I wanted to know. By that time, I had begun hearing rumors that David Graiver might be getting his money from groups who were accused of kidnapping people for ransom. I never saw proof of this, and I certainly never heard such things said about other members of his family or their business associates, but it was a very troubling accusation.

So it was with considerable reluctance that I admitted David Graiver into my office at 60 Wall Street on May 18, 1976. After taking a moment to admire my view of the New York harbor, Graiver sat down and said: "Larry, my father says you are the only person in the United States who ever helped us and, therefore, I have to talk frankly to you. I apologize for not listening to you before. You were right. I never should have tried to buy American Bank & Trust. I paid $26 million for a bankrupt bank."

I suppose I should have known he would only talk to me if he'd gotten himself into deep financial trouble. I asked Graiver if he had hired accountants to assess the bank's condition before he bought it.

"I didn't," he replied sadly. Then he named two New York lawyers involved in the sale of AB&T whom, much to my surprise, Graiver described as "the most prominent Jews in the world." He explained that "these people, I thought, represented the best. I found out they didn't."

I was dumbstruck. The lawyers named by Graiver were hardly the "most prominent Jews in the world," even if one were to believe that such mythical people exist. And even if "the most prominent Jews in the world" existed, it would have no bearing whatsoever on buying a bank! I understood right then that Graiver had thrown all caution to the wind in buying AB&T because the group of businessmen who owned it were not only Jewish, as was Graiver, they were active in American politics. In buying this bank, Graiver fantasized that he was buying the political influence he would need to build an American empire! Yet what he had bought, illegally, was a load of bad debts—all of which he could have avoided if he had only listened to the things I told him.

Graiver then showed me a piece of paper which bore his signature. It appeared to be a one-page contract to buy American Bank & Trust, although I couldn't be sure it was authentic.

"Did you make your contract subject to approval by all the appropriate banking authorities, like we did with the Century contract?" I asked him.

"No, I didn't," Graiver answered.

I remember putting my hands to my head. How could anyone be so stupid as to sign a multimillion-dollar promise to buy a bank "as is" and "come hell or high water"?

There was silence until Graiver finally said: "Larry, I have great plans.

I want to buy, after this, the Long Island Trust Company. I have talked to a bank broker and he said we can do it. I want you to be a director of the bank, but first, I must get this contract approved by the New York Superintendent of Banks. But that bastard, John Heimann, hasn't done it! Will you be my lawyer again and take charge of this matter?"

I reminded Graiver that the last time I had taken him on as a client, he had disregarded my advice, jeopardized my reputation, insulted me and did not pay my bill until dunned. "And now you want me to come back?" I asked.

I further pointed out that John Heinmann was not a "bastard," but a man who was both smart and honest. He could not be led around by the nose. "When you bought the Century Bank you gave him a balance sheet which said your father was worth $12 million. Less than year later, you want his approval to buy a $26 million bank. The Banking Department has a right to know where that new money came from. And you made me look foolish in front of the Banking Department.

"Heimann is a fine person doing his job," I told Graiver, "which is to protect the American banking system from people who think they can buy anything. You have conducted yourself terribly in this country. You behaved like a rich spoiled kid, not a professional. You have given yourself, your family, your country and even me a bad name, and unless you change, you will get into even deeper trouble."

I finished up by telling Graiver that he couldn't buy me either.

"I don't want to be your lawyer again. I don't want to be the director of any bank you own. It would make me look like a whore, which I am not. I know you have other lawyers. They are good lawyers. You should be speaking frankly to them. You have no loyalty or character, and no credibility with me."

Graiver didn't get angry. He merely stood up, thanked me for my time, and took one last look at my harbor view. Then he turned to me.

"I have two choices, Larry. One is that I can open that window and jump. The other is I can work this out. I'm not a jumper."

"This isn't all that serious, David," I assured him. "Talk to your lawyers. Either supply the information the Banking Department needs or write AB&T and get your money back. There will probably be a lawsuit, which I'd bet can be settled out of court. You may have to give up a couple of million dollars, but you were prepared to do that in the Century deal, so you shouldn't mind doing it here." I had no idea at that time how much trouble he was in.

Graiver shook my hand and left. He called me the following Wednesday and asked me again to please be his lawyer, and once more I refused.

GRAIVER NEARLY BANKRUPTS BANCO DE LA NACIÓN

Then out of the blue, I received a phone call concerning Graiver from one of the most respected and senior bank examiners in New York State Banking Department, a man named Bernie Gassman. It was Wednesday, the 25th of May, and he called me just as I was halfway out my door to catch a plane to San Francisco.[3]

"Mr. Levine, is Banco de la Nación financing David Graiver's purchase of the American Bank and Trust?"

I was almost too startled to answer.

"Mr. Gassman, anything is possible, but I seriously doubt it. I doubt the government of Argentina would allow its state bank to do such a thing. Why do you ask?"

Mr. Gassman told me that his department had just completed its yearly examination of the New York branch of Banco de la Nación and found $30 million in loans to a bank in Belgium owned by the Graivers.

"So you can put two and two together," he concluded.

But it didn't add up to me. Banco de la Nación, according to the information I had, had a lending limit of $12 million in New York. It would be madness to go over it. Yet Bernie Gassman rarely made mistakes. What truly disturbed me was that while I was no longer the lawyer for David Graiver, I still was the lawyer for Banco de la Nación. I had asked the bank's officers months before to please send me the paperwork on any loans to the Graiver group so that I could review it. It was an embarrassment to have Bernie Gassman calling me with these suspicions. I couldn't

3. At the time, I was co-owner of the San Francisco Merchandise Mart.

believe the bank would do something so foolish as he was suggesting it had, but I had to admit I didn't know what they were doing.

"Mr. Gassman, I don't own Banco de la Nación and they don't use me as their mother confessor," I told him. "I'm not on any loan committees and I don't know their loan portfolio. But I will try to find out what's going on. I honestly don't believe the state bank of Argentina is trying to assist the Graivers in buying a bank, because the new junta government is allied with the old-line Argentine banking families, and the Graivers are 'new money' with strong ties to the government that got overthrown. But I will find out what I can." It occurred to me that perhaps the prior board of Peronist directors had approved the transactions.

I thanked Gassman for calling and raced to the airport. There was just enough time before my flight to call Banco de la Nación. I asked one of the bank's officers if Banco de la Nación was financing Graiver's purchase of AB&T.

"Of course not!" came the reply.

I then asked if the bank had $30 million in loans to a Graiver bank in Belgium. There was a long pause on the line, after which I was reminded that Banco de la Nación had an agreement with the Graivers to provide short-term loans in the same way that other New York banks did. I was told, however, that it would be unlikely that anywhere near that amount had been lent, especially not to some mysterious Belgian bank.

I insisted on finding out and being told the whole truth. I believed that one of the reasons that Banco de la Nación had been a success in New York was that, right from the beginning, the bank had benefited from my good reputation in New York and Argentina, which aided its getting a license to operate in New York. I was not now going to have my credibility in both countries ruined by the very bank I had brought into existence.

The bank assured me it understood and asked for a little time to check things out. I left to catch my plane, and within a few days, I received a call from the bank while I was San Francisco, confirming that Banco de la Nación had loaned $30 million in short-term, overnight, seven-day money to a Graiver bank in Belgium—all of it guaranteed by AB&T. I was told the loans had been made by low level employees of the bank who felt they were merely acting in accordance with the bank's agreement with the Graivers, which followed the lead of other major New York banks in lending money to the "Graiver group." I was asked for my advice.

"Start cutting the loans tonight," I advised. The entire capital base of Banco de la Nación in New York was less than $30 million. If the Graivers defaulted, the bank would go under. I also once again requested that the original paperwork on the agreement and the loans be sent to me, adding that I asked for this paperwork months before and had never received it.

I was thanked for my advice and promised I would be sent the paperwork. (In fact, I never was.) I was not at all happy. It seemed to me that the present administration in Banco de la Nación's head office in Buenos Aires was probably unaware of these large loans, which perhaps were initiated during the previous Peronist regime. Accordingly, I drafted a telex to Narciso Ocampo, the new president of the bank in Argentina, and while I didn't make accusations, I alerted him to the risky loans and expressed my concern about them—and then I tore up the telex. In my years of representing the bank, I had never gone over the head of a local manager. In addition, I had heard through the Argentine rumor mill that Ocampo didn't like me. Not only might he dismiss my cable, thinking it was none of my business, he might also think I was trying to ingratiate myself to him. I had also heard that Banco de la Nación in Buenos Aires had outstanding loans to the domestic Graiver empire, and I feared my long telex might have too many unforeseen consequences.

So instead I wrote a short note to Ocampo suggesting that he send someone to the U.S. to talk with me about ongoing problems at Banco de la Nación in New York. And I let Bernie Gassman know that the loans were being called in.

On August 7, 1976, the *New York Times* reported that David Graiver was missing, presumed dead in a plane crash.[4] And immediately I was contacted by Banco de la Nación and was rather frantically informed that there was

4. By sheer coincidence, it turned out that I knew one of the owners of the plane that crashed. He, along with others unknown to me, had bought the plane for private business use, but chartered it occasionally to outside parties to help defray the costs of owning it. A further coincidence is that American Bank & Trust, through a loan that predated Graiver's involvement in the bank, financed the plane.

still $2 million in outstanding debt, due by the end of the week. I congratulated the bank on recovering the other $28 million so quickly, but obviously the remaining $2 million was a problem for the New York branch—one which it now appeared I was expected to solve. But I reminded the bank that I had yet to see a single piece of paper regarding those loans, so I had no idea at this point what was legally possible and where Banco de la Nación stood. Once again I was promised the paperwork.

I then received a strange and urgent phone call from one of the officers of American Bank & Trust, an old acquaintance of mine named Spiro Donas. AB&T's Board of Directors had discovered something "shocking," he told me. It involved David Graiver, and they needed the help of someone with contacts in Argentina. That's all Donas could say on the phone. Would I meet with them?

I replied to Donas that I certainly would not if the meeting was being arranged without the knowledge of AB&T's regular lawyers from the firm of Reavis & McGrath. A few phone calls were then made, and a meeting was arranged that included the Reavis lawyers, the Board of Directors of AB&T, Donas and myself.

THE COLLAPSE OF AMERICAN BANK & TRUST

The "shocking" thing revealed at the meeting was shocking: While the directors of AB&T were waiting for David Graiver to be fully approved to buy their bank, they had been allowing Graiver to run the loan committee! Now there was $7 million in unsecured debt on the books—loans made by David Graiver, some of them to non-existent entities.

I couldn't believe that this distinguished and experienced Board of Directors had been so foolish as to allow an unknown, inexperienced Argentine kid control their loan portfolio. But they all shrugged their shoulders at me and said that they had thought their savior had come when David offered to buy their bank, and they were just biding time until he paid up and took over.

Then the chairman of the bank said to me: "We need someone to go to Argentina and get security for these loans. We'll take cash, bank stock or mortgages." They wanted—and needed—fast action. Without that security in hand within a week, the New York State Banking Department would surely liquidate their bank.

Even though I felt absolutely no responsibility for what had happened, and even though I felt that I was being asked to join what looked like an impossible mission, I felt an obligation to help out if I could. The liquidation of a bank always hurts innocent people, and if money could be found in Argentina to secure these loans, then no liquidation of AB&T need occur. The board of AB&T thought I was the obvious choice to go to Argentina and speak to the Graivers about securing those loans. Perhaps I could persuade David Graiver's father, whom David said respected me, not to let this bank go under. Even though I felt certain no one else in the Graiver family had participated in anything illegal, I thought Juan Graiver had to take an interest in what David had done. I believed that the Graivers probably did have some assets in Argentina that could be used to collateralize these loans. Maybe I could help the Graivers understand the severity of the situation. A spectacular bank failure in America, with possible accusations of fraud and criminality, could ruin them in Argentina. I doubted that the new junta government would show much patience or mercy for the Graivers, who had been so closely allied with the personnel and policies that the military had so angrily overthrown.

Nonetheless, my first professional loyalty was to Banco de la Nación, which was also at risk of losing money because of David Graiver's behavior. It was my obligation to get those loans secured first. When I consulted with the bank, however, I was encouraged to go to Argentina to save AB&T, on the grounds that its solvency would guarantee the payback of the $2 million owed Banco de la Nación. I knew it wasn't quite that simple, so before agreeing to fly to Argentina on AB&T's behalf, I secured a guarantee for the complete repayment of the $2 million Banco de la Nación was owed.

With that out of the way, I set some further conditions for my taking on this task for AB&T. I insisted that the bank's board of directors pass a resolution hiring our firm, Walsh & Levine. And I insisted that I be given the authority to hire an Argentine team of experts—a lawyer, an economist and an accountant—who could value the Graivers' assets if I could get them to open their books to me. AB&T's directors gave me everything I asked for.[5]

So in New York, the president of AB&T and I boarded a flight for Buenos Aires—feeling ill with dread. Terrorism and "the dirty war" were in full swing, and we were warned to keep a low profile. Rumors were now swirling everywhere that David Graiver had deposited millions in ransom money that Argentine guerrilla groups had gleaned from numerous kidnaps. And now some people were saying that Graiver had stolen from these groups as well, double-crossing them to expand his business empire. I could not and did not believe this, but any number of people in Argentina might have felt I was their enemy.

By pure chance, Jorge Rubinstein turned up at the airport in New York and boarded our same flight. Even though he was the man I was flying all the way to Argentina to see, I kept as far away from him as I could on the long flight down. I felt in my heart that whatever had occurred in David Graiver's complicated dealings, Rubinstein probably knew something about it. I didn't want to be seen anywhere near him in public.

Within six hours after my arrival in Buenos Aires, I was sitting opposite Jorge Rubinstein in a lawyer's office, my team of Argentine experts by my side. I felt exhausted, but I made the speech I had come to deliver:

"Jorge, I am spending only three days in Buenos Aires and then I am returning to New York. So I cannot afford to waste time. Substantial additional capital—$8 million in mortgages, or in bank stocks, or in cash—is needed to secure loans made by David Graiver through American Bank & Trust. Without that capital, the Superintendent of the New York State Banking Department will probably begin proceedings to close and liquidate AB&T, and many people could be hurt.

"I am returning to New York on Saturday evening. On Monday morning I will report to the Board of American Bank & Trust as to whether I think you and the Graiver family will post that additional security. We have to act fast. If the security is posted, I think the bank can be saved. If

5. I hired Ricardo Zinn, the financial director of the SASETRU Group, as my economic advisor; my old friend Héctor Grinberg as the team's legal advisor, and Dr. Silvio Becher, who had been the financial vice president of Aerolíneas Argentinas, to do the accounting.

it isn't, then I predict that in one week, the bank will be closed and liquidated. And you and the Graivers will be sued.

"And I also predict that should all or any of this happen, the government here in Argentina might come after all the Graivers' institutions and take over all your properties. I'm no expert on your country's politics, but I believe there could be a political explosion against all of you. Those loans appear to have been fraudulent." The president of AB&T confirmed what I said.

Jorge Rubinstein simply sat there and said nothing to us.

"Mr. Rubinstein," I continued, "I gather that you now are head of the Graiver family business, or Juan Graiver's advisor, so the decision is yours. I realize that you were not put in your job, as Churchill once said, to preside over dismantling the empire. But if you don't get the situation in New York straightened out, I predict you will lose everything that Juan Graiver ever built. My team of experts is here to assess your assets. What is needed is $8 million in cash or good mortgages on real estate here, and it is needed fast. I know that you alone can't pledge bank stocks, but you must be able to produce this other material quickly, or at least let me know by the time I board my plane for New York what you have to offer as security."

The best I could get out of Rubinstein was an agreement to meet with me Friday morning, when he said he would produce a list of the Graiver assets for my team to review. I returned to my hotel and tried telephoning Narciso Ocampo at the Banco de la Nación, because I felt Ocampo probably could be of some assistance in this matter. But Ocampo never returned my telephone call (nor did he respond to a letter I had delivered to his office).

THE DOWNFALL OF THE GRAIVERS

On Friday morning, Rubinstein produced a list of mortgages and properties owned by the Graivers, and it became perfectly obvious to me and my team that they had no cash. According to what we were shown, all of the Graiver assets were frozen. I also got the very strong feeling that Rubinstein was only pretending to be willing to put up additional security for AB&T.

"Jorge, I am not kidding," I told him. "I didn't travel down here with the president of AB&T for my health. American banking authorities don't like to close banks, but they are going to be forced to close AB&T because of what it appears that David did. He apparently made unsecured loans to non-existent entities. You have to let me know now if you can post the security."

"I don't think the New York authorities will move so fast," Jorge replied nonchalantly. "After all, the owners of the bank are some of the most prominent people in New York."

I guess I knew right then that Rubinstein would be of no help. He simply couldn't free himself of the illusion that all that really mattered in America was who you knew, not whether or not you were on the level. I certainly didn't feel that Rubinstein was leveling with me. And I suspected that if the Graiver family had the kind of money that was needed, David Graiver would not have been making those loans in the first place. It now appeared to me that David Graiver, in trying to amass his empire, probably had made enormous commitments to buy things in dollars, while the Graiver family income was almost all in pesos. In the last months, the peso had skyrocketed from 1,000 to 24,000 to the U.S. dollar. I wondered if David began making those loans to himself, in U.S. dollars, in a desperate attempt to cover his existing commitments. I couldn't believe that any member of his family knew anything about it.

The president of AB&T and my team of advisors stayed behind to continue to work with Rubinstein, looking for assets that could be used as collateral. I left Argentina on Saturday night, and on Sunday night the team called me to say that Jorge Rubinstein had promised nothing. On Monday morning, I reported the news to the Board of AB&T. By the end of the week, the Superintendent of Banks had moved in and taken over American Bank & Trust Company.

What the banking examiners found was far worse than I ever imagined. Not only did it appear that Graiver had made loans to dummy companies, he apparently also had sent a representative from AB&T to Mexico to attract big depositors with a promise of high interest rates, but their money was actually sent straight overseas and deposited into the Belgian bank. The chief targets were Jewish émigrés to Mexico, who were reassured by the notion that they could safely deposit their money in AB&T because it was a bank owned by fellow Jews. All of them lost their money when the government of Belgium moved in to liquidate the Graivers' bank there as well. (Again, I felt sure that David's family knew nothing of these activities.)

In the United States, the New York City branch of Banco de la Nación at least had the guarantee that I had secured for it repayment of the $2 million that the bank was owed. And what was my reward for not only getting them that guarantee, but also for advising Banco de la Nación to rapidly call in the other $28 million lent to Graiver which they surely otherwise would have lost?

THE BANK HIRED A NEW LAWYER

The news that my law firm was being dismissed was conveyed to me by the bank's first vice president, Jorge Pratt Gay. Narciso Ocampo, the bank's president, had never met me, but supposedly he suddenly decided down in Buenos Aires that I was not "prestigious" enough to represent Argentina's state bank in New York —even though this bank branch never would have seen the light of day had not I been there to help its birth, nor would it have survived had not Bernie Gassman called about the suspect Graiver loans, which caused me to alert the bank.

I was told by third parties that Ocampo concluded that Walsh & Levine was not "prestigious" enough after learning how little we charged the bank to do its legal work. Three years earlier, under an impoverished Peronist government, I had foolishly allowed the bank to reduce our fees because I so much wanted to see the bank succeed, for Argentina's sake. I agreed to take a lesser amount because I was told that was all the bank and the nation could afford. Apparently Ocampo was now using this to fire me, reasoning that since other New York law firms would charge him two and three times more than what we did, surely we must be second or third rate! Of course I was angry.

A year later, when a criminal investigation was opened to examine what role, if any, Banco de la Nación played in the collapse of American Bank & Trust, the bank's managers quickly came back to my law firm and asked us to help them. I wrote a letter to Ocampo refusing. "If we can't handle the good stuff because we're not 'prestigious,'" I asked him, "why should we handle the garbage?" When other representatives of the bank and the government privately approached me and asked me to reconsider, I finally relented, and my law firm took on the work of helping Banco de la Nación perserve its good name. We succeeded. When indictments were brought in the American Bank & Trust affair, no one at Banco de la Nación was indicted.[6]

In the meantime, factions within Argentina slowly and inexorably had mounted a vendetta against the Graivers. The Graiver family assets were seized and the Graivers themselves, along with José Gelbard, were scapegoated by anti-Semites within the junta and within the press. Members of the Graiver family and their employees were arrested and sent to prison.[7] Jorge Rubinstein died in police custody and his body was dumped on a street corner for his wife to find. David Graiver had told me that he owned the Argentine newspaper *La Opinión*,[8] and its editor, Jacobo Timerman, was taken into custody. Timerman's story of how he was tortured became an international cause celebré, which, along with many other terrible stories, helped blacken Argentina's reputation around the world.

For some time after David Graiver's flight crashed outside Acapulco, the military junta in Argentina refused to confirm that David Graiver had been killed. Various people, for their own political purposes, wanted to keep alive a rumor that perhaps David Graiver had faked own his death in an elaborate scheme to disappear with a lot of money. But I knew

6. A great deal of the hard work for the bank was done by my brother Jay, Ray Fersko and Paul Ambos, who all helped Banco de la Nación tell its side of the story. It was especially difficult because the bank had become rather lax in its paperwork. We never received a thank you from anyone.

7. It wasn't until August 25, 1982, that the Argentine courts finally released many of these people.

8. In his book, *Prisoner Without a Name, Cell Without a Number*, Timerman said that he was the owner of *La Opinión*. Graiver never showed me any documents proving his claim although others have also stated Graiver owned at least part of the newspaper.

almost immediately following the crash that Graiver had died on board that plane. The U.S. ambassador to Argentina, Robert Hill, had previously served as U.S. ambassador to Mexico, and through his connections he learned within days (and Hill told me in my office) that Graiver's dental records matched the teeth found in a charred corpse recovered from the plane's wreckage.

Why David Graiver died the way he did is still a mystery to me. It might have been an accident. It might even have been suicide, although I very much doubt it, since David Graiver told me he wasn't the type to kill himself. Personally, I think it was sabotage, although I can't say that I know who was behind it. By the time he died, David Graiver had made a lot of enemies.

EIGHT

1976–1980
The Videla Proceso

Rafael Trozzo, the founder of Banco de Intercambio Regional.

One of the great tragedies in Argentine history is that Juan Perón returned to Argentina too sick to take over as a strong political leader. I believe he was trying hard to turn the country in a positive direction and that he had personally changed as well. But it is also true that Perón was unable to control the negative forces which he himself had helped create, particularly the guerrilla organizations which acted as his armies. When Perón suddenly died in July of 1974 and his wife, Isabelita, took over, she lacked the prestige and the know-how to rule. Within two years, the peso was valueless, the guerrillas were killing union leaders, the government had begun waging its secret war against the guerrillas, and Mrs. Perón was having a nervous breakdown. Argentina once again was in the violent throes of a civil war, only now Perón was dead, never to return.

A military junta replaced the government of Isabelita Perón. Its members came from the faction of the military that supported elections, and they promised future elections. The junta's arrival was widely supported, even by the Peronist unions, even though the junta appointed a civilian economic team that quickly showed itself determined to put an end to Peronist economic policy. They wanted three things: to increase foreign investment, an end to state-owned industries, and low tariffs to increase imports.

I agreed with those goals as a necessary step for Argentina. And I had been hoping that Perón would be the man to peacefully begin the process. But I became concerned about the attitudes of the junta's economic team not very long after it assumed power because of a disturbing story I heard from Robert Hill, the departing United States ambassador to Argentina. Ambassador Hill, who served so heroically in Buenos Aires from 1974 to 1977, had dinner with me in New York just after completing his tour of duty.[1] He told me that prior to returning to the U.S. he had paid courtesy calls to various members of the new Argentine government, making his formal goodbye. One of the men he visited was José Martínez de Hoz, who had been appointed Argentina's minister of economy. In a break with the past, the military junta had taken the unusual step of giving this new economy minister almost unlimited powers and sole discretion in running Argentina's economy.

José Martínez de Hoz came from one of Argentina's great agricultural families, and although I did not know him, everything I knew about him persuaded me that he was an intelligent, practical and decent man who knew his country well. As minister of economy, I expected that he would work for the smoothest possible transition from the state-run Peronist industrial economy that was still in place to the newer models of free enterprise that I knew he and his economic team believed in so strongly.

But Hill reported to me that, after being invited to sit down by Martínez de Hoz in friendly fashion, Hill seized the occasion to wish the economy minister the best of luck and prosperity. Martínez de Hoz thanked him and then Hill expressed another wish: In the coming months, he hoped that Martínez de Hoz and his economic team would find ways to successfully amalgamate the Peronists, who still represented so much of Argentina's economic wealth.

At this point, Hill reported to me, Martínez de Hoz turned white. He stood up stiffly with his hands clenched behind his back and stated flatly: "Mr. Ambassador, when I am finished, the word 'Peronist' will no longer exist!" Silence fell and the visit obviously was over. Martínez de Hoz did not extend his hand to the U.S. ambassador when Hill stood up to leave.

Hill concluded our conversation in New York that evening with two

---

1. During the worst years of guerilla terror in Argentina, Ambassador Hill and his wife slept with a loaded gun at their bedside and had been instructed how to commit suicide if captured. They were guarded every step they took. One evening, when the Hills attempted to dine out in Buenos Aires, other diners recognized the Ambassador and, fearing an ambush, began exiting in droves, leaving behind food on their plates. The Hills quickly departed before ordering their own meal so as not to ruin the restaurant's business. The high stress of his service in Argentina cost Ambassador Hill his health and he died not very long after he returned to his home in New Hampshire, where he had hoped to enjoy a well-deserved retirement.

predictions: "This government will be deadly," he said. "And if Martínez de Hoz thinks he's will finish off the Peronists economically, he never will." Robert Hill was right on both counts. It is now thought that the government of the military junta had a dual mission. On the military side, the army's task was to eliminate the collective bargaining power of the unions and all socialist tendencies in the country. The economic team took on the role of dismantling the Peronist legacy of subsidizing the industrial sector.

Still, I have to admit that most of my own initial impressions of Martínez de Hoz were favorable: I thought he was a smart, shrewd man who behaved in a way that gave people confidence in Argentina's economic future. He was eager to make a good beginning, so much so that he even hired a U.S. public relations firm to build up confidence in him abroad. Since Martínez de Hoz came from one of Argentina's oldest agricultural families, he assembled a high-powered group around him that considered itself Argentina's "elite."[2] David Rockefeller, the scion of America's banking elite, was largely responsible for introducing "Joe" to the American financial community, and Martínez de Hoz got a warm reception.

In anticipation of Martínez de Hoz coming here, I organized the U.S.-Argentine Chamber of Commerce to take out a large ad in the *New York Times* welcoming him and his new economic team. Copies of the ad were widely distributed by the Ministry of Economy, and I think that helped set the tone of the trip. I soon found out through the grapevine, however, that Martínez de Hoz and some leading members of his "elite" economic team were telling people that they did not like me personally (and I was surprised when I wasn't invited to several Argentine functions). It appeared that my long time practice of working with Argentines of every political stripe had earned me the label of "Peronist sympathizer" in the eyes of the Martínez de Hoz group. They were simply too ideologically rigid to understand the ways of an American lawyer with a varied practice. It also appeared that some of them disliked me without ever having met me, preferring to cultivate Americans with blue-blood names.

2. They included Franciso Soldati, Christian Zimmerman, Jorge Lanusse and Jorge Pratt Gay, all of whom were recruited from Argentina's oldest banks and investment firms.

But I remained committed to promoting Argentina's best interests, and did nothing to undermine the new economic team, or the image of Argentina abroad, and I continued my attempts to assist them.[3] But now that Argentina's state bank had said my services were no longer required (after all the work we had done for them in difficult times), I felt free to represent private Argentine banks, and let it be known through the Argentine grapevine that I was available.[4]

RAFAEL TROZZO AND HIS BANK'S GROWTH IN THE U.S.

The first Argentine banker to contact me about possibly opening a bank branch in the United States was a delightful, thoroughly honest gentleman named Pérez Companc, whose family owned Banco Río de la Plata.[5] Despite his family's enormous wealth, Mr. Companc was a thrifty man who rode the subways instead of taking taxis when he visited New York and stayed in two-star hotels. I spent several enjoyable hours with Mr. Companc discussing American banking law, the current economic situation and the policies of Martínez de Hoz. But ultimately it was Mr. Companc's judgment that the time just wasn't right for him to undertake opening a bank branch in America.

Not long after my encounter with Mr. Companc, I met Dr. José Rafael Trozzo, the head of the Banco de Intercambio Regional. He was very eager to open a bank branch in the United States, and he had been sent my way by a first-rate group of civilian and military Argentines who were the directors of his bank in Argentina.[6] When I consider taking on a major client, I arrange a casual, relaxed meeting to get a good sense of who they really are, but when I first met with Trozzo in his modest New York hotel room, he was initially extremely reticent and reserved. Having a drink together might have eased the awkwardness, but among the very first things I learned about José Rafael Trozzo was that he never drank. Period.

3. In 1976, Argentina turned around a billion dollar deficit into a $650 million surplus, but wages dropped by about fifty percent, which was planned by the Ministry of the Economy.
4. Although I had represented David Graiver in the purchase of Century Bank, I did not represent the bank itself in its day-to-day operations.
5. I came to knew Mr. Companc through Manuel Basaldúa, formerly Juan Perón's personal pilot and, subsequently, the general manager in the United States of Aerolíneas Argentinas from 1973 to 1976.
6. Among them was Brigadier Arnoldo Tesselhoff, a former president of Aerolíneas Argentinas.

The author attending a luncheon in honor of
U.S. Ambassador Raúl Castro in Washington, D.C.

Although it took a little while for the conversation to warm up, especially since Trozzo spoke no English, when it finally did Trozzo revealed himself to be a fascinating, self-made man.

Trozzo had started out in life as a poor boy in Mendoza. Somehow he had managed to attend law school, and then had gotten himself into a position to open a small bank in Argentina. By working hard he had become a successful banker, to the point where now, he told me, Banco de Intercambio Regional was Argentina's largest private bank, with branches all over the country. From his own experience he had concluded that Argentina was a marvelous nation, with all the elements necessary for success, but that the chief cause of its economic distress was that people did not work hard enough.

He was also deeply concerned, however, with the conflict between the old-line Argentine agricultural families and the up-and-coming Argentine industrial class. The conflict was severe, he said, because the old-line families still controlled the country politically but no longer had wealth, while the new industrial class could create prosperity, but was now politically shut out. But Trozzo had confidence in the make up of the new military government, whose members, he thought, really understood the country.

Trozzo told me his vision for the financial future of Argentina: It rested on policies encouraging private saving in Argentina and the development of industry. He wanted to use his own banks as a means of realizing this vision, but worried that others would get jealous and try to stop him.

I was aware that to some extent, Trozzo was giving a performance. He had become a successful man because he possessed the talents of a showman and a salesman. Trozzo must have talked for an hour before he finally asked me for my personal opinion of the situation in Argentina. Ordinarily I would not have answered such a question on a first meeting, but Trozzo came so well recommended, and obviously was so intelligent, I felt it would be all right to share my private views.

I told Trozzo that Argentina was like a giant that had been tucked away sleeping for seventy years, and only now was emerging and awakening. I pointed out that while the U.S. had been fighting with itself internally over "Who lost China?" ever since World War II (and its China policy had suffered accordingly), Argentina had been fighting with itself internally over "Who lost Argentina?" and United States had become a whipping boy in that fight to Argentina's own financial detriment. Argentine needed the financial expertise that only the U.S. could provide, but politically that had been made impossible, and there was blame on all sides.

I said that while I believed it had been necessary for the nation for Perón to return, unfortunately he had been too sick to do what was needed, and his wife had been too inexperienced. Now, I said, it was the time for Argentina to wake up and expand commercially, but they needed branches of their banks in the United States, England and Germany to do it. I believed these bank branches could serve as economic intelligence centers for the nation although, as things stood, it would take years to develop a generation of competent Argentine bankers. Nonetheless, I was convinced it was necessary to do it, and I told Trozzo that I had written all of this in a memo to Dr. Narciso Ocampo, the new president of the Argentina's state bank. I had hoped to persuade Ocampo to appoint an advisory Board of Directors to the New York branch of Banco de la Nación. I told him that a board comprised of Americans could help educate Argentines to the workings of the world's financial markets and improve trade, and this was crucial to Argentina's economic development. But I never received a reply from Ocampo.

Trozzo startled me by saying he had read a copy of my memo. He said my idea was so excellent that Ocampo might very well "steal" the idea for a bank he privately owned, Banco Ganadero, instead of trying to make it happen with the state bank that he ran. Trozzo then told me that all my memos written from 1971 to 1976 regarding Banco de la Nación had been read by Martínez de Hoz's economic team, which I doubted, but Trozzo went on to say that the team had been very impressed by the idea of using banks in America as a source of commercial intelligence.

It was Trozzo's belief that state banks would find it hard to change and do what I was proposing. But since the private banking system was now being deregulated by the Martínez de Hoz team, banks like Trozzo's—

Banco de Intercambio Regional—were in a perfect position to seize the opportunity. Trozzo wanted to begin as soon as he could, and he wanted me to be his lawyer.

I was both surprised and happy, but before I made a commitment, I needed to check up on Trozzo. I wrote more than half a dozen letters to my professional acquaintances in Argentina asking about Trozzo and—amazingly—all the replies I received were identical. Trozzo is a smart man, I was repeatedly told, but egomaniacal. Apparently there was a hatred for Trozzo in Argentina from the old-line bankers, many of whom now controlled the Central Bank and the Ministry of Economy. (But if that was so, I wondered, why had Trozzo been issued the licenses that enabled him to open banks in the U.S.?) You should take him as a client, came the unanimous advice, but don't count on it lasting long.

I was startled, but not surprised—although I'm aware that sounds strange. The man I had met was obviously dynamic and determined to keep moving up in the world, but he shunned fancy clothes and expensive hotel suites. Trozzo adhered to the strict faction of Catholicism known as Opus Dei, which includes liturgical worship and monastic practice. He went to Mass every day, was devoted to his wife and he neither smoked nor drank. I believed him when he said his life was work, and I could readily see why he was so disliked by the traditionalists of Argentina, who reveled in the luxuries of the Jockey Club.

So, despite the warnings and even my own misgivings that it all might be over soon, I decided to work with him.

INTERCEPTING THE ROCKEFELLERS, CALLING OFF A COUP

On his own, Trozzo had established a "rep office" in New York, so I took over the legal work for the branch application and worked on organizing an Advisory Board of Directors. In my memo to Ocampo, I had mentioned that former Ambassador Robert Hill would be the ideal man to be the chairman of an Argentine bank's board of directors in the U.S., and I now suggested to Trozzo that he could do no better than to ask Robert Hill to lead his board. I knew for a fact that Hill had been very disappointed when he retired from the foreign service that no Argentine bank had asked him to serve as a director. (I was amazed he was not asked by Banco de la Nación.) It wasn't that Hill needed the money or the prestige. He simply loved Argentina and wanted to remain connected with it and to help it. When Trozzo asked him to organize a Board of Directors for a new U.S. branch of Banco de Intercambio Regional, Hill was immediately interested.

Hill, too, took the trouble to check on Trozzo's background with all his Argentine friends, and found nothing discouraging. One former Argentine ambassador to the U.S. was already sitting on the board of Trozzo's principal bank, and he encouraged Hill to take the job. Hill, of course, met with Trozzo himself and came to his own conclusions. "I've met people like this before," Hill said to me. "He's not a bad fellow, but he's very ambitious. Argentina needs ambitious entrepreneurs. We don't come from the same social background but, hell, I find nothing dishonest about him. Why shouldn't I try to help him and his bank?"

Hill took on the formation of the BIR advisory board with zest.[7] Trozzo, who had deep respect for Hill, gave him carte blanche in organizing his board. He also allowed Hill to educate him to the ways of banking in the United States and to help him cultivate support here. Hill arranged for Trozzo to visit the United States every month and meet with various bankers to help bring Banco de Intercambio Regional into the American banking community.

Trozzo would use these occasions to provide American bankers with an explanation of what was currently happening in the Argentina economy. I never heard him say one bad word about the Videla government's economic team. In fact, I vividly recall a speech given by Trozzo to an elite group of financiers at the Metropolitan Club in Washington, D.C. He said he supported President Videla and the process of reorganization, and he specifically approved of the overall plans of Martínez de Hoz. Although he was well aware that the Martínez de Hoz group did not like him personally, in the U.S. Trozzo said publicly that it was

7. None of us could have foreseen that within a year Hill would be dead from illnesses developed because of the strain of serving in Argentina during its worst years of guerrilla terror, when the ambassador and his family were prime targets for violence.

essential for José Martínez de Hoz to be successful because the opportunities for reform of industry would not come around again soon. Trozzo was not without criticisms of the Martínez de Hoz economic plan, and he predicted modifications would be necessary. But seldom have I heard such a convincing speech in support of the Videla government and Martínez de Hoz. It was hard to understand why such support was not returned.

I did learn, however, that Trozzo's judgment was not perfect. In 1979, after the BIR had opened up its office on 57th Street and was in operation, Trozzo called my office to say he was flying to New York and asked if I would meet him the next morning at the Waldorf Astoria. When I arrived for the appointment, Trozzo introduced me to three Argentine military officers—one each from the air force, army and navy—who had flown up with him from Buenos Aires. A limousine was waiting for all of us downstairs, and Trozzo asked if I would please accompany the group to an important meeting with David Rockefeller. I readily obliged.

Once we were all in the limousine, the military officers and Trozzo fell to talking among themselves. My Spanish is good but it's not good enough to follow four people all at once. So I asked in Spanish if one of them would please explain to me what this meeting was about. Trozzo told me that since the Videla government in Argentina had been accused of anti-Semitism, Trozzo and these military officers thought it would be a good idea to host a forum with Jewish participants in Argentina to demonstrate that Argentina is not an anti-Semitic nation. So the purpose of the meeting we were about to attend was to invite David Rockefeller to Argentina for this forum—because, Trozzo pointed out to me, everyone knew David Rockefeller was the most prominent Jewish banker in America.

I wasn't all that sure of my Spanish. Had I heard something wrong? I said to Trozzo: "No puedo entender". He repeated the exact same thing.

I thought I better ask specifically just to double check.

"You are going to invite David Rockefeller to speak in Argentina because he's the most prominent American *Jewish* banker?" I asked.

Trozzo said, "Sí." And the three military officers said, "Sí."

I said: "Mr. Trozzo, the forum is a wonderful idea, but David Rockefeller is not Jewish. If anything, he's one of the most prominent Protestants in the United States. He supports a Christian church on Park Avenue and is head of several Protestant organizations. He has very good relations with the Jewish community, but he is not Jewish."

There was complete silence as all four men stared at me. They obviously didn't believe me. By that time, we were almost at David Rockefeller's office building, just minutes away from the meeting, so I quickly said to them all: "My suggestion to you is that you invite David Rockefeller to Argentina to speak. He'd be very honored because the Rockefellers have been hurt in Argentina. Argentines have often been very anti-Rockefeller; they burned down his family businesses there. I think David Rockefeller will regard it as a great honor to be invited to speak in Argentina by three representatives of the government. Just leave out the Jewish business."

All four of them began jabbering among themselves. They finally asked me to go inside with them to the meeting, but I suggested they would be more impressive doing it alone. So I sat outside David Rockefeller's office, hoping for the best. And when the group came out they all looked very happy. David Rockefeller had accepted.

When we all got back in the limousine, the generals asked me to please now come with them to the Argentine consulate's office in midtown Manhattan. They didn't tell me why, but I could see it in their faces. They still didn't believe me that David Rockefeller wasn't Jewish.

I waited in the car while the Argentines went into the consulate's office. Trozzo paused before leaving the car to say to me: "You better be right, or you and I are in a lot of trouble."

The consul general did indeed confirm to the group that David Rockefeller is not Jewish, and when the Argentines returned, each of the military men shook hands with me and thanked me. They also asked me whom else they should invite. I suggested that they would do well to invite Arthur Burns. Burns, who is Jewish, was at that time the head of the Federal Reserve. (I never bothered to find out if they followed through on my suggestion and whether or not Burns went to Argentina.)

I also became aware during the time that Trozzo, no doubt unwisely, had gotten himself involved in the internal political machinations of the Videla government. We now know that there were three groups inside the junta. One was the group headed by Videla and Viola, which advocated economic recovery in order to gain a stability in which the political parties could run again. A second group in the junta was led by Generals Carlos Guillermo Suárez Masón and Luciano Benjamín Menéndez, which supported continued military dictatorship, permanent elimination of the Peronist Party and the unions. The third faction was led by Admiral Eduardo Emilio Massera, which advocated President Lanusse's line of the early 1970s: "Peronism without Perón."

One day, I received a visit in my Wall Street law offices from Robert Hill. He told me that he had gotten wind of a rumor that Trozzo was backing Admiral Emilio Massera in his maneuvers to replace Videla as president. Neither Hill nor I at that time knew the inside story of what was happening in Argentina within the junta. We only knew that Videla and Viola were on top, although they constantly had to placate the extreme right wing elements in the military to retain control. At the same time, Videla and Viola had given Martínez de Hoz total control of the economy, and Admiral Massera and General Ramón Genaro Díaz Bessone disagreed with the minister of economy's policies toward industry.

Hill was convinced that any attempt by Massera to unseat Videla was doomed, so Hill asked me to please phone Trozzo and give him this simple message: "Cut it out." I placed the phone call to Trozzo with Hill sitting right next to me and, since I thought all international phone calls to Argentina were tapped, I repeated the Spanish equivalent of Hill's words, but that was all I said. Trozzo only replied that he would take the advice, and nothing more was discussed.

So it may be that Trozzo did much to contribute to the hostility José Martínez de Hoz and his group felt toward him. But if they were driven by personal and political animosity toward Trozzo, it blinded them to the fact that they were ruining the economy and destroying international

*The author with Argentine Ambassador Jorge Aja Espil (right) and
Alberto Moore, aide to U.S. Ambassador Raul H. Castro.*

confidence in Argentina in their attack on BIR. There were other ways to rein in Admiral Massera than to destroy the banking system.

WAS TROZZO TELLING ME THE TRUTH?

It was at a different Metropolitan Club—in New York, not Washington—that I met with Trozzo on December 18, 1979, after Banco de Intercambio Regional had successfully established its branch office in New York and had applied to open another branch in Washington. It was by now evident that the economic plans of José Martínez de Hoz had not developed the sound basis for overall Argentine prosperity as promised. He had kept the value of the peso artificially high and lowered the tariffs on manufactured goods, which caused foreign imports to become much cheaper to buy in Argentina. That caused Argentina's foreign reserves to swell to $24 billion, enriching the Central Bank and pleasing the military junta and agricultural entities in Argentina, but the plentiful imports made it almost impossible for Argentina's domestic manufacturers to make money. Bankers like Trozzo had built up their businesses by making large loans to industry, and now these loans weren't getting repaid. Trozzo claimed his once successful banking enterprise was being threatened with extinction by this change in government policy. He told me industry as a whole was desperate.

"In 1976, the government freed the system," I can recall Trozzo saying to me. "I was prepared for it. I took people's deposits and loaned them to industry because I believed in Argentine industry, and I believed in its ability to produce and repay the loans. But now we are headed for a depression, and it is the fault of Martínez de Hoz and his group. They are deliberately working to destroy the industrial base of Argentina, for their own political reasons. Don't they see that you can't change a domestic policy of helping Argentine industry overnight. It has to be done gradually."

I knew that the economic situation in Argentina was very difficult for bankers like Trozzo. In 1977, Martínez de Hoz gave substantial tax breaks to foreign investors, which caused a flight of dollars and a sharp rise in domestic interest rates. It was hard for Argentine industrialists to borrow and expand their businesses and to make them competitive with low-tariffed goods from Europe. Imports grew three times faster than exports in 1977, and Argentines voraciously consumed these cheap imported goods because it helped distract them from other doings by their government that they preferred not to think about: news censorship, disappearances, the constant threat of war with Chile.

Still, I told Trozzo that I found it hard to believe that Martínez de Hoz was actively pursuing policies to undermine industry. I believed Martínez de Hoz to be a smart and shrewd man. Surely he understood, despite his family's connections to the Argentine agricultural oligarchy, that it was essential for Argentine industry to thrive, especially if he was to be successful as the country's minister of economy.

"Dr. Levine," Trozzo replied, "you don't know my country. This group thinks Perón and Perón alone killed Argentina. But in fact, Perón came to power because this group's fathers did what their sons are now doing. The fathers wanted only rich old families from England and Spain to run the country. No Italians. No Jews. Perón allowed those people in. The oligarchs were displaced by Perón and now their sons have come back. But today is not 1945. In the past thirty years, a new generation of immigrants has grown up and we have been working hard. We may not have inherited our wealth, but we have acquired wealth. This economic team hates us and wants to destroy us. They want to kill us forever so they can keep the power and wealth of the country for themselves and their friends. They want to destroy the new Argentine money so that we can never have political power."

Trozzo argued to me that the "false" value of the peso and what he viewed as the other anti-industrial policies of the Martínez de Hoz team had thoroughly undermined the position of his Banco de Intercambio Regional, which by that time was the largest private bank in Argentina. In the midst of his tenure, Martínez de Hoz lifted the rule requiring private Argentine banks keep a cash reserve of twenty percent against the money they borrowed from foreign banks. The banks quite naturally began loaning out their reserves, and made riskier loans in the process. It was Trozzo's and BIR's specific business strategy, he told me, to offer depositors very high interest rates, and use those deposits to make even more loans to industry, and to other small banks that also loaned to industrial enterprises. Trozzo said he believed that by helping to develop Argentina's industrial base, he would make a profit, pure and simple, but he would also help develop his country.

Day by day, as profits flagged, industry was losing its ability to repay those loans to BIR and to other banks. And the large network of smaller banks dependent on BIR would collapse if BIR collapsed. In fact, a good part of the entire private Argentine banking system could go under in a flash if what Trozzo was saying was true.

It was hard for me to believe, and I did not. I wanted to think better of the Argentine government. I wondered if he was exaggerating the antipathy some members of the government felt toward him because of his poor background and his political leanings. Trozzo was a proud man who wanted credit and acceptance for his hard-won, self-made success. I wondered if the failure of the "elite" to embrace him as one of their own caused him to imagine plots that were not there.

It was undeniably true, however, that the current economic situation in Argentina had weakened BIR structurally. Trozzo now asked me to please fly to Argentina on his behalf and appeal directly to Martínez de Hoz not to close his bank.

That was a tall order for a lawyer, and not my role. I told Trozzo that this was not a good idea. I pointed out that first of all, I sincerely doubt-ed that his bank would be put out of business. The economic repercus-sions would be too great. But I said that even if Martínez de Hoz and his economic team were determined to put BIR out of business, which I doubted, an appeal from me would do more harm than good. The eco-nomic team did not like me. I was not an expert on the bank's loan port-folio and had no real influence. So I was unlikely to persuade anyone to follow my advice. Furthermore, word of my visit might be leaked to the press to make Trozzo look desperate and weak. Rumors alone could destroy his bank.

Trozzo wanted to know if he should appeal to David Rockefeller, who had been the patron and escort of Martínez de Hoz in the United States but whom Trozzo did not know. Again, I said no. Such a move would only increase suspicions and enmity against Trozzo in Argentina—in the unlikely event David Rockefeller agreed to see him.

I did promise to help him, however. I said I would contact Eliot Janeway, the American business writer, to try to interest him in doing a story on Trozzo and BIR, pointing out the dire domestic and international consequences if BIR were to fail. I felt that if the junta and the economic team read constructive criticism of their actions from a well-regarded international writer, it might check their moves. I also counseled Trozzo to seek a foreign bank partner to shore up BIR's financial position if that was needed. Trozzo, as it turned out, had also been thinking along these lines and felt acquiring a partner was no solution.

He told me that the European manager of BIR had offered to help bring in a French bank as a partner. But Trozzo was convinced that such a move would never be approved by the government, which he said would not allow the largest private bank in Argentina to be half-owned by foreigners. He had considered taking on an Argentine partner, but the only plausible candidates were not members of the establishment, and Trozzo felt that joining with another "new money" Argentine would only make him more vulnerable to liquidation.

Trozzo concluded by telling me that his only remaining option for keeping alive the bank that he'd created and built into a success was to accept an offer recently made to him by a "friend" of Martínez de Hoz. In Trozzo's eyes, the only reason this offer had been made was because the "elites" wanted his bank for themselves. They'd made him an offer, and if he didn't sell, they had the political power to liquidate his bank and ruin Trozzo.

I left my dinner with Trozzo at midnight, and when I went home, I couldn't sleep. Was he mad? Was he telling me the truth? Should I get involved?

The next day, I only did what I'd promised Trozzo I would do: I called Eliot Janeway and interested him in taking a trip to Argentina. Janeway even went so far as to spend his time there talking with Martínez de Hoz, whose ideas about economics Janeway found "off the wall." He visited various branches of BIR and reported back to me that no one seemed in a panic.

Although Janeway didn't write a story about his trip, it nonetheless bought Trozzo some sense of relief. According to Trozzo, Janeway's appearance in Argentina asking questions about BIR put a different frame around Trozzo's image in the eyes of the Martínez de Hoz team, who began to worry that he might have powerful friends in the U.S. Trozzo believed they had been slowed in their efforts to hurt BIR, although his optimism did not last long.

HOPING TO AVERT CATASTROPHE IN
THE ARGENTINE BANKING SYSTEM

Within a month, Trozzo was back in the United States, this time in Miami, for a few days rest. He asked me to fly down from New York to meet him, which I did.

Our meeting was sad. When I looked at Trozzo, I felt I was looking at a great wounded animal. Nonetheless, he still had plenty of energy, and an unusual charm. We drew up two chairs to the window of his hotel room, overlooking Miami. We conversed in Spanish.

"You see this beautiful city," he said to me. "If you worked ten percent as hard here as I've worked in Argentina, you would be accepted into the establishment. You could join a golf or luncheon club. You'd be respected. But in my country, where I work very hard, have built up the largest private bank, have established a foundation and have done much good, the economic team wants me out of business, and now it looks like they can win. I haven't lost yet, but I think I will."

I asked him why he believed that a handful of people, who didn't even speak for the entire government, could or would destroy the largest private bank in Argentina. It made no sense to me. Trozzo insisted that it as a personal vendetta by "the sons of the old" who did not want a newcomer to be so big.

"The junta gave all the economic power to one man," Trozzo answered me, launching into another of his political tirades. "He controls the coun-

try. What Martínez de Hoz wants is multinationals, foreign corporations—and he wants to destroy the new domestic Argentine business
class. And the military are mesmerized by him and don't know economics well enough to understand what is happening to the industrial side.
It's the first time this has ever happened in our country. I can't do anything about it."

He finally told me straight out the reason for our meeting: "I have to
find a foreign partner they will be afraid of, or I have to sell out to them.
What do you think I should do?"

I didn't know what to say. I felt that if his situation was as he
described, there was in fact very little he could do. If the economic team
hated him as he said and if he wanted to hang on to his bank, Trozzo
would have to kowtow to them. I did suggest that Trozzo keep a lower
public profile; perhaps that would give them pause. Perhaps he could find
some way to work with them and slowly win them to his side. I told him
to have hope: I still could not believe that his bank would be put out of
business. It would simply be too injurious to the nation as a whole.

When I left, I had the odd sensation that I was saying goodbye for
good. When I arrived back in New York, I received a phone call from
another Argentine banker who was not a friend of Trozzo's but was a
member of the group holding political power. He was a first-class person,
however, and a man with a heart. He told me that, in his opinion,
Martínez de Hoz was a little obsessed with power and he was not listening to anyone. BIR was likely to be eliminated if Martínez de Hoz wanted it that way, according to my friend.

Once I heard this, I immediately sat down and wrote, non-stop, a
telex which I sent without hesitation to Guillermo Walter Klein, the
well-respected number two man in Argentina's Ministry of Economy. It
was one of the longest telexes I have ever written and I sent it on an open
wire because I wanted it read throughout the Argentine government, and
I hoped someone would leak it to the press.

In that telex I said: "The government is on a self-destructive course
because there appears to be a self-destructive desire to knock not only

Trozzo out of business but to cause chaos in your system." I pointed out that unless the economic team worked hard to quiet rumors that BIR was in trouble and reassure investors that it was safe, Martínez de Hoz would find not only his entire economic plan but also the Argentine economy in ruins. I wanted to help Martínez de Hoz by plainly alerting him to the dangers at hand.

"If the Argentines don't handle this one carefully," I wrote, "so BIR is saved if it is in trouble, or if a convenient merger is not worked out which gives the appearance that (a) all is calm and (b) you know how to handle a matter like this prudently, the entire Argentine banking community is finished here for a long time. No U.S. agency will believe anything said with regard to Argentina and you will find a retrenchment of private lines of credit." I added that I didn't know who was right and wrong, but that didn't matter. All that mattered was that some way be found to keep BIR from collapsing for Argentina's sake.

I spent much of the rest of the telex relating how the U.S. banking system had faced similar crises and how those crises were handled. In the United States we have the concept of "too big to fail"—meaning that the government recognizes that the failure of one very large bank could cause a panic in the entire system, and it steps into stabilize a bank in trouble. During a real estate crisis in the early 1970s, several large banks in the U.S. almost went under when the value of the land they had mortgaged suddenly lost a huge percentage of its worth. The federal government opened its money window every morning and it loaned those banks—for one day only—enough money to stay solvent on the books. At the end of the day, the banks paid the money back in full, only to borrow it again the next morning. The government allowed the banks to revalue their government bonds at cost rather than at market value if the market had fallen under cost. In that fashion, those banks were kept open, which kept the public from panicking while real solutions could be worked out. Quietly, in the background, the government worked to find new financial partners and investors for the troubled banks, or worthy, creditable buyers for those few cases where banks needed to be sold.

I closed by pointing out that Martínez de Hoz enjoyed a good reputation in the U.S. and that recently many positive things had been said about Argentina. "As things seem to be turning around," I wrote, "do not ruin it by starting another banking scandal."

As I suspected it would be, my telex was leaked to the press, and accusations flew that I was trying to meddle in the internal affairs of Argentina. I was irked by the criticism, but glad that the public controversy seemed to deter the government from closing BIR. Trozzo called me to tell me that things were better and that he was selling part of the bank to a group the government accepted. He said that I had been an enormous help to him and to Argentina. He even said he planned to take language lessons in the United States so that he could speak English with me. Trozzo sounded very happy, and I considered the drama to be over.

As a lawyer, my main concern is to deliver intelligence and quality in my work to my clients. But it is hard not to feel personally involved with a client who does not speak your language and therefore gives you his trust. I respected Trozzo in a way that I did not respect David Graiver. Trozzo became a success through hard work and he listened to other people. I knew his faults—impetuousness and ego—but I never felt he was dishonest, even though I could see he was terribly ambitious. I wanted Banco de Intercambio Regional to succeed because I thought it would be good for Argentina to have more bases for foreign economic intelligence and to cultivate a generation of trained international bankers.

Still, as an American lawyer, I knew there was a limit to how much I could or should get involved with BIR's problems in Argentina. In fact, for some months, the U.S. ambassador to Argentina, Raúl Castro, had been inviting me to visit him in Buenos Aires, but I kept saying 'no,' even though Castro was a personal friend. I simply did not want tongues wagging that I was in Argentina trying to lobby for BIR. However, Castro was about to end his tour of duty in Argentina, and now that Trozzo sounded so optimistic about his situation, I decided to accept Castro's final plea to be my host, and I made plans to fly to Argentina in March of 1980.

Just to make sure that no one would misinterpret my motives for the trip, I took a moment before leaving to write a letter to Walter Klein. I wanted to make sure that the government's economic team understood that I would not be in Argentina on behalf of Trozzo—or anyone else. The day before I left, I received a letter from the secretary of Banco de Intercambio Regional elaborating on what Trozzo had told me on the phone: The bank was being purchased by Piñeiro Pacheco, and Pacheco had already indicated that he wished me to continue to be BIR's lawyer in New York. A letter signed by Wenceslao Bunge, the director of BIR, was also sent to all the bank's depositors and shareholders confirming the deal.

I did not know Pacheco, although I once met him briefly in the company of Robert Hill. I knew him to be a successful businessman and several of my acquaintances, both here and abroad, spoke well of him. I had little reason to doubt he would be an acceptable buyer in the eyes of the government, but negative gossip immediately reached me from Argentina about the reported sale. People were saying they did not understand where Pacheco was getting the money to buy BIR, but I mostly wrote off the gossip to jealousy. I headed off to Argentina on a Saturday night feeling relieved that the crises surrounding BIR had subsided. I thought a solution had been found that was good for the stability of Argentina, and which spoke well of the economic team of Martínez de Hoz.

THE TRAUMATIC END OF
BANCO DE INTERCAMBIO REGIONAL

Ambassador Castro had told me he would be sending a car to the airport in Buenos Aires to be there for my arrival at 7:00 am. When I was not met by anyone in the terminal, I asked the information desk to please page "the American Embassy driver meeting Mr. Levine." No sooner was my name blared out over the public address system than an Argentine lawyer whom I knew quite well appeared at my side, surprised to see me but ready to embrace me.

"You must be here for the bankruptcy of Banco de Intercambio Regional," my friend said to me.

"There's no bankruptcy," I assured him. "Piñeiro Pacheco has just bought the bank."

My lawyer friend shook his head.

"That was a phony purchase," he informed me. "The Central Bank will liquidate BIR Friday night."

I almost died on the spot.

I met my driver and we soon arrived at the embassy, where Ambassador Castro simply could not believe what I told him was true. He didn't know Trozzo personally, but he could not fathom that the economic team would take such risks with the Argentine economy. I was suddenly relieved, feeling that my lawyer friend at the airport probably wasn't sufficiently well-informed. Ambassador Castro agreed with my prediction that if BIR were closed, the entire Argentine banking system would go into a tailspin.

The Argentine ambassador to the U.S., Aja Espil, just happened to be in Buenos Aires that weekend, and he invited me to a small dinner party on Sunday night. I considered Espil an old friend, and I agreed to go to what I believed was a purely social gathering. So when one of Espil's guests at the table, the noted Argentine journalist Claudio Escribano, asked me a few questions about BIR, I felt comfortable discussing the matter. I told Escribano how I had delayed my trip to avoid any possible accusation that I was in Argentina to assist Trozzo, which even if I wanted to do, I could not do. I discussed with everyone at the table of my letter to Walter Klein, explaining how the closure of BIR could create chaos, and how such matters are handled in the U.S. I discussed the letter I'd received from Bunge confirming the purchase of BIR.

I enjoyed the dinner but was appalled the next day to read in *La Nación* that I was in Argentina lobbying for Banco de Intercambio Regional. My dinnertime comments were written up into the news story as if I had arrived in Buenos Aires with an agenda. The distress I felt at breakfast reading the newspaper only got worse when, at lunch, several friends from the Severgnini law firm told me that it was their considered opinion that BIR would in fact be liquidated shortly. And after lunch I spoke with Félix Uno, a former president of the U.S.-Argentine Chamber of Commerce who happened to be in Argentina just then, and he concurred in that opinion.

By pure chance, I later ran into Ambassador Espil walking up the Calle Florida. I told him of the rumors I was hearing about BIR, and the ambassador divulged to me that he had just come from a meeting with Martínez de Hoz. He could not reveal, the ambassador said, anything of his conversation with the minister. But he did not contradict my information, and the look it his eye told me it was true.

I went back to the American embassy, where I was staying as the Ambassador's guest,[8] and told Raúl Castro all that I'd heard that morning. He still could not make sense of any effort to liquidate BIR—and then he came up with an interesting idea. In two days, Ambassador Castro was set to host a very large reception at the embassy, where everyone from the Argentine establishment was likely to be present. He now decided to also invite Pacheco so we could observe how the establishment treated him. The establishment would be quite cordial to him, Castro predicted to me, if the bank sale was likely to be approved. But if we saw Pacheco shunned at the party, then we would know BIR was doomed.[9]

The ambassador had also been kind enough to arrange a lunch in my honor for Tuesday afternoon, and with my help, he made up a guest list that did not include a single person from the Ministry of Economy, the Central Bank or any other quarter in Argentina which might lead people to believe that I was in Argentina to help Trozzo. Instead, twenty or so personal friends came to the embassy Tuesday afternoon, where not a word about BIR was spoken. I might have enjoyed that lunch more had I not received a phone call that morning from my New York office which indicated that things were even more dire for BIR and the Argentine bank system than I had known.

My office told me that the New York State Banking Department had called to let me know that it had received a visit from Guillermo Reynal

8. This trip marked the first time I had ever accepted an invitation to stay at the American embassy in more than twenty years of representing Argentine interests and many invitations from ambassdors to do so. My close personal feeling for Raúl Castro, and the fact that he was soon to leave Buenos Aires, prompted the change of heart. It was also true that, by 1980, it was no longer dangerous for an American businessman to be seen coming and going from the embassy.
9. I also knew, through Ricardo Zinn, that Banco d'Italia and SASETRU, one of Argentina's largest agricultural businesses, was interested in buying BIR. But the Central Bank denied permission for the purchase. When BIR was closed, Banco d'Italia and SASETRU got caught in the ensuing financial chaos, and both later were forced into bankruptcy despite being two of the most prosperous agricultural export firms in Argentine history.

of the Central Bank of Argentina. Mr. Reynal had gone there to ask what would happen to the branch of BIR in New York if the Argentine Government liquidated BIR in Argentina! In response to Mr. Reynal's query, the New York State Banking Department had recommended that a serious effort be made to sell or merge the branch in New York, so that Argentina did not become the first nation in the world to have a bank with a branch open in the U.S. after the government had put its owner out of business at home. The Department tried to explain to Reynal how Argentina would suffer a loss of image, and I was told by people at the meeting that Reynal gave the banking department the distinct impression that he appreciated the advice. Nonetheless, the very fact such a meeting occurred only increased my anxiety that Argentina's government was about to jump off a financial cliff.

I spent the next day and a half doing other business and socializing in Buenos Aires without any reference to BIR. But on Wednesday evening, as arranged, almost the entire Argentine government arrived at the American embassy for the reception, and I kept my eyes glued to Piñeiro Pacheco. He walked around the reception, alone, smoking a cigarette. Everyone ignored him. At one point, the economic team of Martínez de Hoz had shifted to one corner of the room to talk and laugh among themselves. Piñeiro Pacheco was in the opposite corner of the room, by himself. Martínez de Hoz and his friends ignored me as well.

Once Ambassador Castro had said goodbye to the last of his guests at the door, he turned to me and said: "Larry, you see how they ignored Pacheco. They are going to liquidate that bank."

Now that I was certain BIR would be closed, I decided I did not want to be in Buenos Aires when it happened, simply because I did not want to be hounded by the press. Besides, once the government took over the bank to liquidate it, I would no longer be its lawyer, and there was no point to my being around. The earliest flight reservations I could make were for Saturday night, and even that was not soon enough. Castro woke me Saturday morning with his arms full of that day's newspapers, whose headlines announced that Banco de Intercambio Regional had been shut down by the Central Bank on Friday afternoon. I left Argentina Saturday evening with feelings of disgust and sadness. I had so much wanted Martínez de Hoz and his team to succeed in improving Argentina's economy.

The immediate fallout of the closure was, as I knew it would be, a spate of annoying press stories that tried to blame everyone but the Ministry of Economy for the bank's closure. Former ambassador Robert Hill and I were made out to be Trozzo's creators in the United States; Trozzo was made out to be a crook who dressed sloppily and lacked the social graces. I finally did agree to interviews and, in each one of them, I pointed out that I and Robert Hill (who came from the same kind of wealthy background as Martínez de Hoz) both had found Trozzo to be honest, and therefore had no problem introducing him to the American banking community. And I emphasized that the American banking industry was built by men like Trozzo: the sons of immigrants who did not wear silk ties and had not gone to Harvard University, but who had made their fortune through relentless hard work. I acknowledged that Trozzo was ambitious, but so were the men in the Ministry of Economy and the Central Bank. And I reminded everyone that if people now wanted to declare that BIR was a bad bank run by a bad man, people should be asking the government to explain why the Central Bank had given Trozzo the licenses to operate banks in the first place and to expand their business abroad.

The longer-term effects of the liquidation of BIR were dreadful. Bank after bank collapsed like dominoes, until nearly the entire banking system had collapsed and the Argentine economy had collapsed with it. The panic I had predicted when no one would listen now occurred. After a March 1980 currency devaluation, approximately $2 billion dollars left Argentina between April and June in 1980. Banks and business began to fail to such an extent that in October the government intervened and allowed banks that had remained open to give short-term loans to companies that were insolvent. In February 1981, there was another currency devaluation and $2 billion more fled the country. By March of 1981, the foreign debt had increased from $8.5 billion in 1980 to $25 billion— a full forty-two percent of Argentina's gross domestic product. At that point, Roberto Eduardo Viola took over as president and José Martínez de Hoz resigned as minister of the economy.

Many people ultimately concluded that the Martínez de Hoz team was driven by political hatred of Trozzo, not by any clear-headed thinking about how best to maintain and strengthen the Argentine economy.[10] If that was the case, it was certainly a shame. You don't close a bank and inflict pain on investors and depositors merely because you don't like the banker or share his politics. In the case of closing BIR, the pain inflicted was far-reaching and enormous. It took years for Argentina to recapture the confidence of the international banking community and set her economy on a promising path.

When José Martínez de Hoz was named minister of economy, I expected and hoped he would do an excellent job. With his marvelous background and education, and with his bright young associates full of new ideas, I felt he could send a message to the world that Argentina, after years of staggering under the unworkable economic policies of Perón, was now prepared to reward incentive in private industry and allow capitalism to work. Like the inability of Perón to seize the moment and set Argentina on a new course, the failure of Martínez de Hoz to set the right course for Argentina was a tragedy, too.

The Argentine government's persistent inability to merge or blend the interests of agriculture and industry, and thereby spare the country repeated economic crises, was the direct result of its persistent inability to develop a political system of checks and balances. In the United States, it took a bloody civil war to pave the way for integrating the interests of agriculture and industry, but once the nation was united and at peace, the American system of regular free elections and representative government helps guarantee that both agricultural and industrial interests always have very powerful voices in government. No politican hoping to be president can afford to defy the farmers or the manufacturers or the workers. Instead, he must work with all sectors in the nation, and with their elected representatives, too. And no American president ever becomes the sole arbiter of the coun-

10. I had a chance to discuss these matters with Martínez de Hoz himself when he visited Harvard University in the spring of 1988. Over a cordial lunch, I stressed to him what a tragedy it had been for Argentina when Banco de Intercambio Regional was closed. Martínez de Hoz denied that any personal or political feelings about Trozzo had played any role in the closure. He claimed that BIR had been overextended with too many outstanding loans, which made it necessary to close it. That was the law in Argentina, he told me. He said he was powerless to stop the liquidation of BIR.

try's direction and the law, as the dictators of Argentina so often did.

In retrospect, it is easy to see that the nation might well have been spared the consequences of the inadequacies of Martínez de Hoz's policies if Argentina had developed a true democracy and appropriate checks and balances. But at the time, people tended to believe just the opposite. The stated plan of the military junta for the five years from 1976 to 1981 was to put Argentina on the map as a first-rate power and people were enthusiastic. Operating without the interference of political parties, and by not allowing political opposition within the country, the theory was that the armed forces needed unlimited power to restore law and order after years of terrorism, while the economic team needed unlimited power to restore the country to prosperity after years of Peronism.

As it turned out, the unchecked plan of the economic team, while it briefly revived the economy, ultimately caused the ruination of the newer industries and the banks that supported them, dragging everything under. At the same time, the unchecked armed forces sought the elimination of the guerilla movements that had led to so much death and terror, but in the process, sectors of the military were created that tortured and murdered, and that brought the Argentine military to ruin as well.

NINE

1983

Looking Out for

Argentina's Interests

in the U.S.

*Argentina's struggle with Great Britain to regain the
Falklands Islands explodes into open warfare.*

B efore the period of the military junta came to its close in December 1983, I found myself involved with the Argentine government in two other limited but quite unexpected ways. The first concerned a long running, multimillion dollar lawsuit brought against Argentina in the United States, where my law offices successfully defended the Argentine government. The second came during the Malvinas War, which I and everyone else I knew regarded as a terrible blunder, but which helped hasten the birth of democracy in Argentina.

It seemed that no sooner than Jorge Pratt Gay at the Banco de la Nación told me, in 1977, that they no longer wished to retain me as its lawyer than the vice president of the Banco Industrial, Luis María Gottheil, was standing in my office in New York, asking me to represent a different government bank.

"Your law firm understands our country and you do good work," Gottheil told me, which I already believed but was still nice to hear. "As I'm sure you already know," he continued, "in 1962, the New York City sheriff's office seized $1.2 million of our bank's money as part of a strange lawsuit, and we are hoping you can help us get it back."

I had heard of the case—*Mirabella v. Banco Industrial de la República Argentina*—and indeed it was a strange one. It had begun nearly twenty years before, in 1948. Juan Perón had ordered Banco Industrial, which was the state bank created to assist industry, to cancel letters of credit that had been issued to a pair of Italian businessmen because the aluminum and hydro-electric plants that the pair had promised to build in Argentina never broke ground. An initial shipment of plant parts to

Argentina from Italy apparently contained nothing but crates filled with rocks. Infuriated, Perón jailed one of the Italians' business agents in Argentina and revoked the letters of credit, claiming they'd been obtained fraudulently. In retaliation, the Italian businessmen sued, claiming that the letters of credit issued by Banco Industrial were irrevocable.

For nearly a dozen years, the Italians tried to get the suit resolved in their favor in Italian and Argentine courts. When that failed, the Italian businessmen found a way to try their luck in the American courts. In 1962, they named as their "representative" an Italian Alitalia Airlines worker who happened to live in New York City, and this "representative" promptly filed suit on their behalf against Banco Industrial in Manhattan's Supreme Court. Because of the particulars in the way the suit was brought, the New York City sheriff's office now had the legal authority to freeze $1.2 million in an account held by the bank in New York, which it did. The money had remained frozen for fourteen years, collecting interest but inaccessible to Argentina.

It was a legally dubious lawsuit that probably never should have been in the American court system in the first place, since not a single U.S. citizen was involved in the issues in any way. Besides, bringing the case to the U.S. did not bring the Italians and Argentines any closer to resolving the issues, to a large extent because the national pride of Argentine had become involved. The almost funny thing was that lawyers for every elected civilian government in Argentina since 1948 had successfully negotiated a settlement to the suit out of court, only to see the elected Congress in Buenos Aires refuse to give its approval at the last minute, afraid of the political repercussions of making Argentina appear weak. The military governments had done no better. Their lawyers also negotiated settlements, but there was always at least one general or admiral in a junta who exercised his veto and rejected the deal. So year after year, government after government, the case went back to square one.

By the time Luis Gottheil was standing in my office in 1977, *Mirabella v. Banco Industrial de la República Argentina* was the single longest-running active case on the New York state court docket, and I wouldn't be surprised to learn it was one of longest-lasting legal cases in the world. It was certainly one of Argentina's longest-running headaches. The head of Banco Industrial's legal department, Antonio Frogone, had been commuting to New York for more than a decade to supervise the bank's legal defense. And now the bank president himself found it necessary to come to New York to move things forward. He told me that the Videla government wanted a new approach: It wanted the case to go to trial. The Argentines had always believed they were in the right on this matter, and now they were determined to prove it in court.

THE CASE NOBODY THOUGHT ANYBODY WOULD EVER WIN

Argentina had no further use for the American lawyers who had been handling the *Mirabella* case since 1962. I had no idea whether or not they'd done a good job, but obviously the Argentines wanted new representation for the litigation. "I'd like you to write up a report of what you charge per hour and how you would litigate the case," Gottheil requested of me. He promised to send to New York two of his bank's lawyers, who could provide my office with the complete history of the *Mirabella* case. I accepted the assignment on the spot, never once dreaming how long my office would end up being involved in this crazy case. I have to admit that, after being treated so badly by the new officers of Banco de la Nación, I was very pleased that other bank officers in Argentina, and the government itself, retained a high opinion of our firm's abilities and knowledge of Argentine affairs.

Gottheil went back to Buenos Aires and very shortly, two lawyers from the Banco Industrial arrived as promised. I gave them space in our office to write a memo on the history of the case, which our law firm, under the very able guidance of my brother, Jay, checked out against the court records. In truth, despite all the negotiations between the parties, and the repeated attempts to settle, very little legal action had been undertaken within the United States to put the case to rest.

My brother Jay and I were confident the case was winnable. What would prove crucial to our winning this case in court, however, was obtaining the full cooperation and coordination of the legal staffs of the

Argentine military: the army, the navy and the air force. For twenty-five years, each branch of the military had its own lawyers working on the case, in addition to the involvement of many successive Argentine attorneys general. Important original documents were scattered throughout several branches of the government, and we needed authority to assemble them. That authority could only come from the government. We contacted Gottheil, who assured us that the necessary decree would be issued, giving us all the authority we needed.

Complicating matters further, all of the potential witnesses were living in Argentina, so we told Gottheil candidly that day-to-day expenses to prepare for trial would surely run very high, even though we would keep our own fees modest. We pointed out that if we won, which we believed we could, all those expenses could be recovered from the plaintiffs, but that reimbursement might be a long time in coming. Once again, Gottheil assured us we would be given all the funds and cooperation we needed to go forward.

So for the next several years, our office was filled with Argentine military lawyers (who, by the way, were excellent), their interpreters and a whole host of aging witnesses who had been tracked down and flown up from Argentina to New York for depositions and examinations. The case was so difficult to prepare that it wasn't until 1984 that we were finally ready to appear before a jury. The actual trial itself lasted 30 days—and we won! Not only were the plaintiffs forced to relinquish the bank's $1.2 million—now worth close to $5 million with the accrued interest—they were told they would have to pay Banco Industrial's considerable legal costs as well.

When we calculated the exact cost of the damages, it came to several hundred thousand dollars, and the other side instantly objected. So we went back into negotiations with the plaintiffs' lawyers—and those negotiations also lasted years. Finally, the Argentine government dropped its claim for damages in return for the release of $1.2 million in the attached bank account (plus interest) and a judgment in our favor dismissing the suit once and for all. So on February 21, 1989, *Mirabella v. Banco Industrial de la República Argentina* finally disappeared from the docket of the Manhattan

Supreme Court and entered into the record books as the longest case ever to be tried in the New York courts—a record that remains unbroken today and likely will stand for many, many years to come.

Our victory made headlines in every major newspaper in Argentina. Argentines often felt that they never won anything and that they were treated unfairly by the world (perhaps especially by the U.S.), so they savored the vindication of their position by the American courts. The fees we charged Banco Industrial were paid up promptly and with gratitude, and I, and certainly the presiding judge, and probably all the rest of the New York legal community, were very glad we'd never hear of the *Mirabella* case again.

ASSESSING "THE DIRTY WAR" FROM AFAR

During the mid-1970s, reports began coming out of Argentina that the military, in its fight against terrorism, was torturing people who had been arrested and that people had "disappeared." The administration of Jimmy Carter had made human rights a focus of its overall foreign policy, and accordingly it took a very hard line against the military government of Argentina.

This is not a book about human rights, but it is impossible to relate a coherent story about Argentina (and its relations with the U.S.) without mentioning "the dirty war." People often ask me how I felt personally during that period, and I can only answer honestly that my feelings were very mixed and they changed over time. In the early 1970s, it did not seem to me possible that the terrorism which had plagued Argentine society for years could be ended without military action. And I felt by the time that the Videla junta took power, following the incompetent rule of Isabelita Perón, that Argentina was barely a country, her governmental structures and financial order had so deteriorated. By that time, many of the guerrilla groups were no longer fighting for a better country: They were gangsters, pure and simple, who kidnapped and terrorized for personal gain.

Accordingly, I felt, as many Argentines did, that the military was the only sector that could reorganize the government and restore order. Even union leaders welcomed the return of the military, especially since the wing of the army which ascended to power was generally considered to be the moderate wing. None of us expected the junta of General Videla would commit the crimes that they did: They violated every known law of human rights.

Unlike previous and subsequent Argentine presidents, I saw very little of General Videla. Apart from meeting him briefly at a reception at the American embassy, where he struck me as a very solemn and austere managerial type, and not at all a politician, General Videla remained quite a mystery to me. I heard from many sources in and out of the Argentine government that he did not have full control of his government, and that he was especially unable to control the most extreme right-wing members of his own army, who threatened coups if the junta failed to demonstrate it was zealously anti-communist.

For many years, because of my work with Aerolíneas Argentinas, my main contact with the Argentine military was with its air force officers. By and large I found them relaxed and friendly men with a modern outlook, who were less tradition-minded than their counterparts in the army and navy. I attributed this to the fact that they were from the newest branch of the armed forces, and many of their highest officers had taken their training in the U.S. My contact with the air force men shaped my overall view of the Argentine military, and made it more favorable than it might have been had I worked with a wider variety of military personnel.

Still, I must admit that it has been impossible to reconcile the reports I have read in recent years about military men who committed human rights abuses with my casual experiences of these men both here and in Argentina. Admiral Emilio Massera, for example, was ultimately convicted of having commited some of the worst crimes of that era, and yet all I ever knew of Massera from his behavior toward me what that he could be a delightful person who liked to laugh. A handsome man, he had the personality of a political candidate: When he walked into a room, he'd "work" it, shaking hands and making friends. Every year I received a Christmas card from Admiral Massera. I don't think I am alone in wondering how it

*The military junta that came to power in 1976: (left to right) Adm.
Eduardo Emilio Massera, Gen. Jorge Rafael Videla, Brig. Gen. Orlando Ramón Agosti.*

is that any human being can do to another human being the things that members of the Argentine military were documented to have done.

I have always believed it was for the Argentine people themselves to sort out the tragedies of their past and I think that is a very complicated process. Recently, in New York, I was visited by a man whom I have known since the early 1970s. He told me he had an association with the Montonero terrorists and said, quite candidly, that he believes now that had not the military taken over in 1976, he would not be alive today. I make no excuses for what the Argentine military did. It was terrible and immoral. They led Argentina into irrationality and people—even good people—degenerated. They also led Argentina to a humiliating defeat in war.

MISADVENTURE IN THE MALVINAS

In April of 1981, at the urging of myself and Dr. Wenceslao Bunge (a former director of the Piñeiro Pacheco Foundation), a forum was held at Harvard University's Center for International Studies entitled: "Argentina, the Road Ahead." It seemed to me to be just the right moment to focus international attention on Argentina. General Videla had just completed his five-year term of office, one of the longest periods of uninterrupted time that any Argentine president had served. In March of 1981, he had peacefully turned over the reins of power to General Roberto Viola, and even though these were military dictatorships, this orderly, institutionalized transfer of the presidency was considered at that time a sign that Argentina had matured politically.

General Viola came into office with the hope that during his term the Peronist and Radical parties would gradually rebuild their organizations and generate enough political leaders to make it possible for the country to return to civilian government. Although Viola stated "it was impossible" to set a date for the return of democracy, he appointed fifteen civilians to the governorships of Argentina's twenty-two provinces and invited more civilians than military men to join his Cabinet. He immediately allowed the unions to hold elections and generally won the public over to the idea of a gradual return to democracy, sector by sector. General Viola was regarded by many to be a talented politician who could reach out to the disaffected Peronists and guide Argentina back to more normal internal politics after five years of uninterrupted military rule.

All of these hopeful signs were thoroughly analyzed and discussed at the forum at Harvard, which was such a great success that I subsequently helped Ambassador Aja Espil make arrangements for President Viola to be invited to the United States. The front page of the *New York Times* carried a photograph of Viola being warmly received by President Ronald Reagan, who had only recently become president of the United States and was very eager to obtain Argentina's cooperation in fighting communism in Latin America. It might have been a snapshot of the beginning of a new era of international acceptance and stability for Argentina, but instead, it marked the beginning of a very fast slide into disaster for the Argentine government, caused solely by the Argentine military's failure to understand their country and the world.

GALTIERI LOOKS TO MAKE FRIENDS IN THE U.S.

For President Ronald Reagan, few things were as important as defeating global communism. In addition to his anti-Soviet policies and his advocacy of freedom for Eastern Europe, he was determined to eliminate communism in the Western Hemisphere. As part of a strategy for doing that, Reagan and his advisers thought it was necessary to isolate Fidel Castro in Cuba, and he wanted Argentina to help lead that effort. Most of the Argentine military was eager to help.

One of the few exceptions appeared to be General Viola and the group he had assembled around him. For one thing, Viola worried that joining forces with America to isolate Castro would upset the delicate political balance he was trying to create at home, where many admired the Cubans for defying the U.S. Viola certainly shared Ronald Reagan's distaste for communism, but since Cuba and Argentina had many business interests in common (Argentina definitely needed Cuba as a market for its exports), Viola was unwilling to go along totally with Reagan's agenda. This created an opportunity for General Leopoldo Galtieri, a very ambitious army general, to work at diminishing Viola's stature abroad for his own personal benefit. Galtieri had been a military attaché in Washington and was a close friend of President Reagan's Special Envoy, General Vernon Walters, as well as the U.S. ambassador to the United Nations, Jean Kirkpatrick. On a trip to Washington with his wife in October 1981, General Galtieri not so subtly hinted that there were other leaders in Argentina who were ready to work hand-in-glove with the White House, if Viola was not.

I could see what was going on and knew that without strong U.S. support (which wasn't quite there), Viola would not last long. When Viola had come to the United States to meet Reagan, I saw him at a luncheon hosted by the U.S.-Argentine Chamber of Commerce. (By that time, I had become a director of the Chamber.) I was quite disappointed in Viola's presentation. The Argentine economy was in much worse shape than Viola seemed to understand, even though, upon taking office, he had needed to spend close to $2 billion to shore up Argentina's remaining banks (a consequence of José Martínez de Hoz's economic policies and the closing of BIR). When the president of the Chamber, Ogden White, asked Viola if the peso would be devalued, Viola instantly responded, "No." No sooner had Viola returned to Argentina than the peso was devalued.

Privately I knew that in Buenos Aires Viola was trying to persuade the others members of the junta to have the government intervene in the economy in other ways in order to jump-start industry. But no one had much confidence in Viola's vision. Galtieri made himself a leading opponent of Viola's economic policies, although I don't think he had any better ideas for improving the economic picture. In addition, Galtieri made it plain he did not like the fact that Viola had freed Isabelita Perón as a conciliatory gesture to the Peronists; he used it to stir up trouble for Viola on this score, too. There was still a considerable faction in the military that did not want Peronism to return in any form. Friends in Argentina began predicting to me privately that Viola wouldn't finish his term but would be replaced by the end of the year.

In November of that same year, I vacationed in Arizona, where I paid a visit to Raúl Castro, the former ambassador to Argentina during the Carter administration. When I told him that I'd been watching Galtieri court favor in Washington and that very soon he might replace Viola as president, Castro surprised me by saying that if I was right, he would bet on Galtieri lasting less than six months in office. He doubted Galtieri could go that long without making "a catastrophic mistake." As was so often the case on matters concerning Argentina, Castro turned out to be right.

THE FALKLANDS: SINKING THE ARGENTINE SHIP OF STATE

Viola was gone by the end of 1981, while he was recovering from a mild heart attack. General Galtieri replaced him, and I suspected things would not go well. But the first inkling I had that Argentina was preparing for a military action was when, not long after the change in government, an air force general whom I knew from Argentine Airlines called to ask if I could direct him to major suppliers of cotton flannel underwear in New York. As it so happened, I was long acquainted with a family that had made its fortune manufacturing underwear, so I gave this officer the telephone number. It wasn't until I hung up that I asked myself: Why the hell is the Argentine military looking to buy flannel underwear?

Over the next few months, my friends in Argentina began telling me stories I simply could not and did not want to believe. The military was preparing for war. Supposedly Galtieri, who had enjoyed the assistance of the navy in his "palace coup" against Viola but had met with the opposition from the air force, was now listening to the new head of the navy, Admiral Jorge Anaya, who was drawing up plans to reclaim the Falkland Islands by force. (I heard that the air force was very much opposed this.) Still, when on April 2, 1982, Argentina attacked the Falklands, evicted the British governor and hoisted the Argentine flag over "Islas Malvinas," I was aghast. In a flash, Argentina had isolated herself from world opinion and her newly acquired reputation for maturity and good judgment was in ruins. I couldn't believe the folly of it.

I later heard that General Galtieri initially had no plan to fight the British to keep the island. His strategy—modeled on Israeli military tactics—was a quick surprise strike intended to force the British to the negotiating table, whereupon the Argentines would withdraw to neutral territory until the issues were resolved. But the capture of the islands was wildly popular with the Argentine people, so much so that Galtieri became afraid to withdraw. Instead he deluded himself into believing that the world would rally around the junta in its effort to liberate historically Argentine territory from colonial dominance, just like the Argentine public rallied around the junta.

But the United Nations condemned the invasion. Even the Organization of American States did not support it. Russia opposed Argentina; so did Ronald Reagan. General Galtieri had merely assumed his dinner party friends in Washington would support his rash actions. As Ambassador Castro had foretold, it was a catastrophic mistake.[1]

Argentina always had suffered from an extreme lack of knowledge of world affairs, but I thought that if there was any country that Argentina understood well, it had to be England. The United Kingdom had been the largest foreign investor in Argentina for more than a century. Yet when I flew to London on April 11, it became obvious to me just how badly the Argentines had miscalculated.

For the first few days of the war, everything seemed to be going in Argentina's favor, but British resolve simply couldn't have been higher. After meeting with a member of the British cabinet whom I knew, as well as a former intelligence agent who was now in the private sector, I drew the conclusion that Britons were united in a way that they had not been united since World War II. Every newspaper I picked up told me the same thing. England viewed the Argentine attack on the Falklands as no different from the Japanese attack on Pearl Harbor. Britons saw themselves as obliged to defend rule of law against brute aggression. They felt that the security of Gilbraltar and Hong Kong and other remnants of their colonial empire would be compromised if Britain failed to retake the Falklands and defeat the Argentines. They had absolutely no intention of giving in. They were sending troops to the south Atlantic, preparing for

---

1. It was not only a great political blunder; it was a great military blunder as well. The British were preparing to retire their only remaining aircraft carrier in the region within six months. Had Argentina simply waited before attacking, it would have been impossible for the British to mount the kind of swift response that they did.

war, full steam ahead.

To me it was all a tragedy, and a dangerous one at that. Argentina was a beautiful nation with very good people, but their leaders did not understand the world. They didn't even understand their own people. By trying to retake a group of useless islands, General Galtieri and his junta bet they could distract Argentines from the long lasting economic mess that was created when Martínez de Hoz liquidated BIR, among other banks. They were wrong. The junta members had merely assumed that England would do nothing because keeping the Falklands wouldn't be worth it to them. Again, they were wrong. The junta members assumed the U.S. would do nothing out of gratitude for Argentina's help in fighting communists in Latin America. In this too they were wrong. They thought the members of the U.N. would support Argentina on a "colonial" issue, that the Common Market would not react and that the OAS would stand with Argentina out of solidarity. They were wrong, wrong, wrong.[2]

Although the Argentines were euphoric at what appeared to be an instant victory in the "Malvinas," it didn't take long for the situation to turn frightening. With all international foreign aid and trade cut off, there was economic chaos. All the wonderful plans to integrate Argentina into the world economy were now down the drain, and every Argentine businessman knew it. Yet no one seemed prepared to be do the sensible thing. The Argentines simply dug in, believing the British would give up.

THE U.S. PUTS THE WRONG FOOT FORWARD

On April 22, 1982, both the Argentines and the British established a security zone around the islands. Round the clock negotiations took place in Washington, but within twenty-four hours, the U.S. announced that they had failed. President Reagan imposed a limited embargo on aid to Argentina: no Export-Import Bank credits, no loans from the Agricultural Commodity Credit Corporation, no arms sales. With the Common Market freeze now in place, I did not see how Argentina could

2. I am told that, prior to launching the attack, the junta asked its foreign minister, Nicanor Costa Méndez, to predict the world's reaction. Costa Méndez assured the military that Britain would do nothing and that the United States would support Argentina's claim to the islands.

repay her debts. Obviously bankers in Argentina and around the world saw this as well.

While it was obvious to many, even inside Argentina, that Argentina had made a terrific blunder, not everyone was altogether pleased with the way the U.S. State Department was handling the situation. Secretary of State Alexander Haig had injected himself into the crisis as a mediator, despite the fact that President Reagan's first choice was Vice President George Bush, who understood Latin America far better. Unable to obtain a quick solution, General Haig threw a temper tantrum, telling the press that he considered the Argentine junta "a bunch of thugs" and letting it be known that he personally favored the British. At that point, he lost all credibility with the Argentines as a mediator, and even though Haig was aware of this, he refused to step aside and let others in the U.S. government try to find a solution. On Friday, April 30, 1982, the U.S. began sending military supplies to Britain to aid it in defending the Falklands from the Argentines.

On the evening of April 30, I spoke with Victor Fidae, an Argentine who worked in Washington on behalf of politically conservative legislators in Argentina. He asked me if I would accompany him to Argentina on Sunday, possibly with Senator Jesse Helms, a Republican member of the Senate Foreign Relations Committee and also a political conservative. Fidae believed that now that Haig had shown his bias he was worthless as a mediator, but the Argentines with whom he had spoken with in Argentina all felt that an independent third party from the U.S. should be involved in setting up negotiations. Fidae also believed that the time for an independent approach was ripe, since he had detected, in a speech delivered by Margaret Thatcher the day before to the House of Commons, flexibility in the British position: For the first time in the Falklands crisis, the prime minister had stated publicly that "sovereignty was negotiable." Up until that point, the British had insisted that the Argentines must withdraw unconditionally from the Falklands before England would discuss anything.

It was flattering to receive Fidae's phone call, but I doubted that I or Senator Helms could accomplish much as third party negotiators. And I wasn't at all convinced the time was ripe: I expected at any moment for the British to attack the two airports on the Falklands to prevent the Argentine Air Force, which was quite strong, from using them as bases. I felt as soon as the British attacked, the Argentines would simply have to fight back. I thought the moment for a negotiated settlement had passed.

Nonetheless, I did make phone calls to several well-placed people in Britain to determine if there was any flexibility in the British position. Every single one of them told me categorically that Britain would not budge on her insistence that the Argentines withdraw from the Falklands unconditionally. I also phoned Raúl Castro, the former U.S. ambassador to Argentina during the Carter administration, who was now living in Arizona, where he had once been governor. He agreed with Fidae that a third party initiative was very much needed. But he believed that the Pope or the Papal Delegate would be needed for the task, and strongly recommended that I not accept Fidae's invitation to accompany him to Argentina on Sunday.

On Saturday morning, I awoke to the news that British planes had bombed the Port Stanley airport, and attacks against Argentine air bases continued through the day. Víctor Fidae abandoned his plans to travel to Argentina, but later in the week, he and I met with James Lucier, an advisor to Senator Jesse Helms. We felt sufficiently concerned about the deteriorating situation to put together a memo addressed to Judge William Clarke, Ronald Reagan's national security adviser, tactfully pointing out that future U.S. relations with Argentina might depend on explaining personally to the Argentine government that the highest levels of U.S. government recognized the problems created by the Haig's personality and his apparent bias in siding with England while trying to act as a mediator.

It seemed that others in Washington were also thinking that a new U.S. messenger might move things forward: The president sent General Vernon Walters, a personal friend of General Galtieri's, on a secret mission to Argentina. General Walters asked Argentina to comply with U.N. Resolution 502, which called for Argentina to withdraw from the islands to her own internationally recognized borders and gave her a deadline for doing so. It was the internationally approved solution, but the Argentine military voted against it. By that time, England and Argentina were already engaged in an all-out shooting match on the high seas.

BLOOD IN THE WATERS

The entire experience of watching the Falklands War unfold was a surreal one. I sometimes thought that what the world was witnessing was the Spanish Civil War all over again, where the big powers used Spain as a proving ground for all their fancy new armaments. Both England and Argentina were pounding each other with the most advanced technology they had in their arsenals, and each dealt devastating blows to the other side. On May 4, Margaret Thatcher took to the floor of the British Commons to gloat over that day's sinking of the General Belgrano, the pride of the Argentine Navy. Two days later, the Argentines sunk Britain's prize destroyer, the Sheffield, using sophisticated French Exocet missiles fired from thirty miles away.[3] More than four hundred men died in the combined events.

It was a horrifying display of high-tech stubbornness, with lives senselessly lost on both sides. I was extremely eager to see it end, but I was having a hard time seeing an end in sight. England was poised to mount an invasion to retake the islands, and the Argentines were spending every penny they could find in their national treasury to put up a fight.[4] One evening, I received a phone call from Aerolíneas informing that its cargo terminal in Miami had just blown up and burned to the ground. It was never said out loud, but it certainly occurred to me that the Argentine

3. One of the great ironies of this incident is that the Sheffield apparently began its life as an Argentine ship. I was told by an Argentine military attaché that the British vessel had actually been commissioned by the Argentines from a British shipbuilder some years before. But while the ship was under construction, a fire occurred in the shipbuilding yard, which totally destroyed a half-built British ship. The Argentines' ship was left intact. Unwilling to wait for another vessel to be built from scratch, the British government negotiated with the Argentine naval attaché, Admiral Jorge Anaya, to purchase the Argentines' half-completed warship. The British christened the finished destroyer the Sheffield when it was launched at sea.

4. Many years later I was told by a member of the British military that the Argentine Air Force actually hit every British warship (except the QE2) with a bomb, but they hit each ship with the wrong kind of bomb. The Argentine Air Force didn't have many bombs designed to destroy ships at sea, so they dropped conventional land bombs, which have delayed fuses. When the bombs hit the ships, they dropped clean through the aluminum hulls before exploding in the water nearer the ocean floor. The British ships were damaged, but not irreparably, and because of that, the Argentine Air Force sunk far fewer ships than they otherwise might have if they had possessed the right bombs. I was told that the British military felt sufficiently threatened during the war to draft a withdrawal order, which they never issued. It will be interesting to read the official records and military history when the British finally release them.

military might have been storing missiles or missile parts there. The explosion was treated as an accident, but privately I wondered whether British intelligence had something to do with that "accident" happening.

Neither Britain nor Argentina was prepared to give political ground. With the Falklands crisis in full swing, Margaret Thatcher's Conservative Party won Britain's off-year elections by the largest majority it had ever enjoyed. I knew that Argentina's generals felt backed into a corner. To concede anything now, in the face of an invasion, would be all but impossible for them.

On Friday, May 14, I placed a full-page advertisement in the *Christian Science Monitor*, widely considered to be one of America's most serious national newspapers, calling on everyone to stop and reflect on the truth. The truth was that Argentina and England were two old friends who needed each other, and both sides had blundered into this war. In print, I reprimanded the English for failing to appreciate the depth of feeling that Argentines had regarding the sovereignty of the Malvinas. There had been a long history of overtures by the Argentines to resolve the issue peacefully, which should have been taken more seriously by the British government. Its failure to do so was a moral as well as a political failure. I also reprimanded Argentina's leaders for resorting to force in their frustration. They had badly hurt Argentina by pursuing a violent course. I even reprimanded the U.S. government for not working harder to lay the right groundwork for negotiating a settlement after the damage done by Alexander Haig.

I was not alone in calling for renewed efforts to negotiate a settlement. Several similar articles appeared in newspapers, and even Margaret Thatcher and General Galtieri felt it necessary that weekend to affirm publicly their willingness to negotiate, although both insisted they were prepared to fight and lose more lives in order to prevail. The secretary general of the United Nations, Javier Pérez de Cuellar, personally became involved in the search for a solution, and he worked non-stop at it for a week. Within twenty-four hours of his giving up, the British landed troops on the island. It only took a week of fighting before the Argentines were forced to surrender. The Argentines had won nothing and ended up losing more than they started out with. Their international reputation was in shambles. They had squandered the lives of many young Argentine soldiers.

I knew from the beginning that this war would be the end of Galtieri, but even I was surprised by what happened next. On June 15, Galtieri called for mass demonstrations at the Casa Rosada in support of his government, but when the masses came, they came to jeer. When Galtieri blamed the defeat in the Falklands on the United States, which he called "the enemy of Argentina and its people," the crowd broke out in raucous rebellion. The people had been lied to one too many times.

On June 16, ten Army generals met all night and voted to prevent Galtieri from making any more speeches, and they stopped him from recalling the U.S. ambassador. Galtieri resigned on the 17th and was replaced on June 22 by another army general, General Reynaldo Benito Bignone. Everyone knew that arrangement was only temporary and that the public would sit still for nothing less than elections. The power of the military had been irrevocably broken in Argentina.

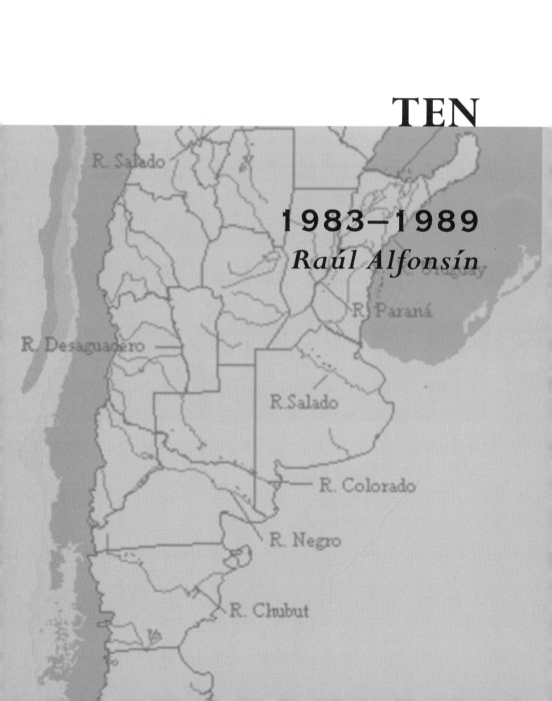

TEN

1983–1989
Raúl Alfonsín

President Raúl Alfonsín addresses the nation.

Not many who saw them are likely to forget the faces of those tens of thousands of Argentines who, on December 11, 1983, took to the streets of Buenos Aries for the inaugural of their new, democratically-elected government. With joyous expressions they celebrated, almost to the point of delerium, believing that they had finally ended the torments that had begun nearly fifty years earlier, when the overthrow of constitutional government led to a succession of civic calamaties that dragged their country into a general economic, political and social decline. Now the citizens of Argentina hoped they'd put all of that behind them.

Raúl Alfonsín, the new president at the center of this explosion of civic rejoicing, was a stocky, amiable country lawyer who came up through the ranks of the Radical Party as a hardworking politician. More than anything else, he campaigned and won on a promise of reinstating the rule of law. With the Peronist Party in total disarray and the public wary of any more Peronist rule, the Radical Party and Alfonsín were swept into office with a strong vote of confidence. Alfonsín was to enjoy one of the longest honeymoons ever to be accorded an incoming president in the Western Hemisphere. For his first few years in office, he faced little organized domestic political opposition, and he possessed the overwhelming good will of the West, the Third World and even some of the Communist bloc states as well. It was a fabulous opportunity.

During his first three years in office, Alfonsín did what no other leader in Argentina had been able to do in recent history: he simultaneously imposed his political will on the military, the entrenched agricultural oligarchs, industrialists, the labor unions and even the Catholic church, and he did so entirely within the constitution of Argentina. Although there were many compromises along the way and everyone had to settle for less than they hoped for, Alfonsín's memorable accomplishments included the bringing to trial of those military leaders accused of gross human rights abuses; a deft settlement of the dispute with Chile over the Beagle Channel (with crucial help from the Catholic church and the U.S. ambassador); maintaining Argentina's access to international credit markets despite a $50 billion foreign debt, and the implementation of a sweeping austerity plan that at least temporarily put a brake on galloping inflation.

But even Alfonsín's accomplishments and the triumph of democracy could not alter the fact that Argentina was in very serious trouble economically. Changing global patterns of trade had cost Argentina many of her most lucrative markets in Europe, the traditional mainstay of her economic health. Paying interest on her massive foreign debt deprived Argentina of the capital she needed to develop new industries. Worsening matters still was the fact that the Alfonsín government failed to send sufficiently strong signals to investors abroad that it was truly business and capital friendly, and it likewise failed to create a climate of business confidence at home. Although the Peronists and the labor unions were nowhere near as strong politically as they once had been, Alfonsín still found it necessary to make economic concessions to them that hurt private enterprise, and it made Argentina a prohibitively expensive place to do business. In previous years, more than $20 billion in capital had fled the country; Alfonsín's rule did not encourage that capital to come home and fuel growth.

Part of the reason for this was Alfonsín's choices in staffing his administration. His minister of economy, Bernardo Grinspun, was a decent and honest man, but the international business community didn't believe he had the experience and skill required to move Argentina steadily forward economically.[1] It was an unfair assessment, and investors abroad were made even more uneasy with Alfonsín's choice of a foreign minister, Dante Caputo.

---

1. Mr. Grinspun had indirectly been a client of mine many years earlier when he was an officer of the Dargent Corporation; I handled the company's legal affairs in New York.

I didn't know Caputo when he ascended to the post and was hoping he would do a good job; from all reports I heard, he was considered a very decent man. It was my belief that Dante Caputo had a dream of one day heading the United Nations, and it appeared that his agenda for Argentina was to make it the leader of the Third World. No doubt he hoped to turn the Third World into consumers of Argentine goods (and maybe even supporters of his campaign to get the top U.N. job). I thought it was a good idea if it could work. But perhaps Caputo also imagined that nations of the Third World had a resentment and suspicion of the U.S., and would therefore rather trade with Argentina, and follow its leadership, than be friends with America. If so, that was a very unrealistic view. The leaders of the Third World saw no profit in aligning themselves with a nation struggling just as hard as they were to set their economies on stable footing. They had no real reason to fall in line behind Argentina, and President Alfonsín was very poorly served by any advice that recommended he distance himself from the business community in the United States as a way of making himself a hero in the eyes of the Third World.

But to a large extent, Alfonsín himself was responsible for his poor image in the international business community. Many business people who met Alfonsín thought they detected in him a certain personal distaste for the United States. Others felt Alfonsín was too beholden to the outmoded economic policies of his Radical Party, which had never really come to grips with the innovative leadership of Arturo Frondizi twenty years earlier. The Radicals had not held power since the presidency of Illia in 1966, and Alfonsín was of a generation that didn't really understand the new high-tech world of global finance. As much as Alfonsín was admired for his commitment to sustaining democracy in Argentina, potential investors in Argentina worried that Alfonsín was not the man to lead Argentina into the world of free trade and private enterprise. I knew that a poor economic performance was a cheap price to pay for the establishment of democracy, but still I felt that Argentina could have had it all if Alfonsín exerted more leadership in the economic arena. I set out to help, if I could.

ALFONSÍN, MISSING IN ACTION

In March of 1985, I was elected president of the U.S.-Argentine Chamber of Commerce. For more than one hundred years, the historic mission of the Chamber has been to encourage better business relations between the two countries and bolster each other's economic growth. If ever there was a time when the Chamber could be of service to Argentina, I felt that time was at hand. I thought it was a marvelous moment to become president of the Chamber.

But unfortunately, like Argentina itself, the Chamber was bankrupt financially and its prestige was diminished. The Chamber's membership rolls were in disarray and the Chamber lacked a strong direction. With the help of a very able woman named Joan Faber and a fine Board of Directors, I set myself the task of getting the Chamber in shape to meet the challenges of the moment. In the end, I felt proud to have helped restore a very venerable organization to its rightful place of influence in the political life of both countries.[2]

In previous years, the Chamber's Argentine members had organized what are known as *encuentros* (or "encounters"): week-long seminars that brought together members of the U.S. and Argentine business sector with officials from the U.S. and Argentine governments. These *encuentros* had been quite successful in the past, and some of the Chamber's Argentine members now suggested to me that Alfonsín and his government would especially benefit from our quickly organizing another, since it would provide a forum for a reassuring dialogue between the American business community and the Alfonsín administration at a time when it was sorely needed. They believed this was a great opportunity to help get the country moving.

So in addition to re-organizing the Chamber, I listened to their good advice and began to organize an *encuentro*, hoping to make it happen as soon as possible. I knew it would help restore the Chamber and bring it good publicity, and I agreed that it would also give the Alfonsín govern-

2. Over the course of three years, I personally invested approximately $100,000 in the Chamber, to buy everything from paper clips to publicity for the organization's events. By updating and expanding the membership rolls, I was finally able to get the Chamber self-supporting by 1988.

U.S. Ambassador Frank V. Ortiz

ment an opportunity to present itself as actively pro-business. It might also help an aging Radical Party to forge better relations with the U.S.

Staging an *encuentro* is an immensely complicated affair, politically and logistically. It is also expensive, and I did my best to make sure that everything was done in first-class fashion. The Chamber's directors and I determined that the right time for the event was the following year, in June of 1986. I went to Washington in 1985 and spoke with those members of the State Department and the National Security Council who primarily dealt with Argentina, to tell them of the Chamber's plans. They agreed that an *encuentro* could help boost Argentina's standing in the world and they made a commitment to send people to the event.[3] I next convened a meeting of representatives from the U.S. corporations that were doing in business in Argentina, and they, too, were enthusiastic and eager to participate.

Working with both the Argentine ambassador to the United States, Lucio García del Solar, and the U.S. ambassador to Argentina, Frank V. Ortiz, Jr., the Chamber extended an invitation to President Alfonsín to open the Encuentro with a speech. To our delight, he immediately accepted. I knew Alfonsín's appearance would be a key element to the success of the event, and I set to work making sure that his appearance and his speech would be covered by the international press. Without the approval of Argentine Ambassador del Solar, I never would have embarked on such a task.

I had chosen as the topic for the Encuentro: "Doing Business in a Changing World Environment." Joan Faber and the Board and I outlined sub-topics and conceived of seminars and discussion groups that would focus on the importance of building a good and lasting trade relationship between the United States and Argentina. I secured a commitment from former U.S. Secretary of State Henry Kissinger to be a luncheon speaker, and persuaded several prominent and influential members of the American business community to travel to Buenos Aires to be the speak-

---

3. One of the very few naysayers in Washington was Vice President George Bush, who with some obvious disbelief asked me if I really thought an *encuentro* would do anything to change the attitudes of the Alfonsín government toward the U.S. When I said I did, Mr. Bush merely shrugged, but he wished me well with the project. He turned out to be a better forecaster than I was.

ers and discussion leaders at our events.

I also made sure we had co-sponsoring organizations in Argentina, such as the Unión Industrial and the Cámara de Comercio. Congresos Internacionales, headed by George Castex, handled the on-the-ground logistics in Buenos Aries, while I continued to organize the U.S. participants and make their travel arrangements in New York. During this time, the U.S.-Argentine Chamber of Commerce had pulled itself out of the doldrums and its newly-activated membership supported the upcoming Encuentro enthusiastically. We were looking forward to a solid turnout and success.

The first blow came when, less than a month before the Encuentro was set to open, Henry Kissinger canceled out as a speaker. His stated reasons for not coming seemed flimsy, and I found myself rather angry as I scrambled to find another suitable speaker on such short notice.[4] In a way, the bad luck turned to good: Maureen Reagan, the smart and savvy daughter of President Ronald Reagan, accepted my sudden invitation to fly to Buenos Aires to replace Henry Kissinger. Although she had no official position in the Reagan White House, Ms. Reagan actually wielded considerable influence there and she had just been designated co-chairman of the Republican National Committee. I felt that her presence at the Encuentro would add unusual political value to the event, more so than Henry Kissinger, who had long been out of office.

Then, less than a few weeks before the opening session of the Encuentro, after a great deal of money and effort had been spent, President Alfonsín canceled his appearance without offering an explanation. He didn't even offer to send remarks that could be read in his absence. Receiving the news in New York, I was stunned and baffled. I heard through friends in Argentina that Alfonsín had been advised not to attend after learning that the U.S. ambassador to Argentina, Frank Ortiz, would not be there. Alfonsín was supposedly told that if the U.S. ambassador did not consider an *encuentro* important enough to attend, then

4. In his memoirs, Mr. Kissinger apologized to his readers for including so little about Argentina. He claimed that while he served as secretary of state, Argentine affairs simply did not occupy a large part of his agenda, and it wasn't until the 1990s, when Menem was in office, that he began traveling frequently to Argentina on business, and thus came to love this "fascinating and lively country." He might have arrived at that feeling sooner had he attended our *encuentro* in 1986.

surely it was not important for the president of Argentina to attend! I doubted that anyone had told Alfonsín that the only reason for Ortiz's absence was that the ambassador would be at the wedding of his son in Mexico City (the wedding plans were made before we decided on the date for the Encuentro). In addition, the ambassador was still recovering from recent surgery and had to limit his activities.

But what was really worrisome was that, apparently, Alfonsín's foreign minister didn't understand that we were not staging the Encuentro to improve the U.S Ambassador's profile in the world. It was being staged to improve Alfonsín's profile, and to help the business community in Argentina. Those business people and government officials who would be traveling twelve hours from the U.S. to Buenos Aires for the Encuentro weren't coming to see the American ambassador. They wanted to see the president of Argentina, and they would be looking for signs that the country was finally preparing to join the first world. If Alfonsín simply stood them up on this occasion for no apparent reason, it would certainly send the wrong message, and in capital letters to boot. And it did.

I was also told that Alfonsín had been shown polls which indicated that the public was wary of closer ties to the U.S., so he was advised that it would be to his political advantage not to be seen at the Encuentro. If that was true, it certainly didn't say much for Alfonsín's feeling for leadership. Still another theory for his sudden demurral was that the head of one of the Encuentro's co-sponsors, the Cámara de Comercio, was Ernest Grether, who allegedly had offended Alfonsín at a recent conference where they shared the speakers' platform. Alfonsín supposedly had made it plain to his aides that he simply never wanted to be anywhere near Grether again. If that was his reason for canceling, it was an unworthy one. It didn't hurt Grether. It hurt Argentina.

There was one final theory that I heard only months after the damage was done: It was that Alfonsín was advised not to come because he was told that the entire Encuentro was nothing but a fancy show to make me money and get me nominated as ambassador to Argentina. Had I any idea that Alfonsín might have been under that misimpression, I would have found a way to make sure he knew the truth. It was widely known that

Ambassador Ortiz would soon be leaving his post and it was certainly true that my name was being mentioned quite openly as his successor. There was a good chance I could have been nominated and I gave the matter the very serious consideration it deserved, but fully a month before the Encuentro was scheduled to open, I notified all those who had pledged to support my nomination that I wanted my name withdrawn from consideration, which it instantly was. The Alfonsín government should have been better informed about these events.

But even if I had wanted the post at that time, which I did not (in part because I had a medical problem), seeing the Encuentro through to its opening and its close was my obligation as the president of the Chamber of Commerce. It was a project I believed in, and I cared little for how it affected my reputation beyond wanting to make sure that I did a good job for the Chamber and for both countries. As for my personally making money on the Encuentro, I didn't need it and that wasn't my agenda.[5]

I was not prepared to accept Alfonsín's cancellation, so I sent telegrams not only to him, but to several members of his Cabinet and administration, including Dante Caputo and Ambassador del Solar. I pointed out in my very cordial text that the U.S.-Argentine Chamber of Commerce was the oldest and now the only remaining non-political entity in the U.S. dedicated to the support of Argentina; that we had spent time and money to bring down thirty-five speakers from the U.S., including five sub-cabinet members of the U.S. government. I didn't neglect to mention the myriad things that the Chamber had done for the Alfonsín administration since its inaugural in 1983, including the successful lunches we had hosted not only for the president but also for Dante Caputo. I cautioned in my letter that the president's sudden, unexplained refusal to honor his commitment to open the Encuentro would not serve him well abroad, and his reputation for being a new thinking and forward-looking Argentine leader would suffer in the eyes of the many important Americans who would be attending the event. I urged the president and his aides to reconsider, and my telex was backed up with letters from former Argentine ambassadors to the

5. In July of 1966, I joined with Barry Traub to purchase the San Francisco Merchandise Mart, the subsequent success of which made me independently wealthy. In 1981, we sold the Mart for $30 million.

United States, all of them reiterating the benefits a successful Encuentro could bring to Argentina.

But the president did not respond to these letters. Nor did anyone from his administration. The cancellation stood without any explanation whatsoever, and the administration neglected to offer anyone to stand in for Alfonsín at the event. Word soon got out that neither the president nor any member of his cabinet would be attending the Encuentro, and the effect was predictable. Close to five hundred people had responded positively to our initial invitation to attend. But the number who actually registered now dwindled to about one hundred and sixty. Official blessing was a key element in attracting Argentine participants, and the Alfonsín government now seemed to be going out of its way to advertise the fact that we did not have its blessing.[6]

WHY WAS THE PRESIDENT'S DAUGHTER SNUBBED?

Fortunately, nothing affected the quality of the event itself. The speakers were lively and the discussions were substantive, and the visiting Americans thoroughly enjoyed their stay in Buenos Aires. Maureen Reagan gave a wonderful speech which was much talked about, and she was our honored guest at the Encuentro's opening dinner at the Jockey Club and our reception at the American Embassy. I noted with pleasure that Ms. Reagan's picture appeared on the front page of every Argentine newspaper the day that she arrived.

Surely the Alfonsín government was aware of her presence, yet they failed to take advantage of the opportunities it presented to them. I had encouraged Maureen Reagan to stay an extra day in Argentina on the assumption that members of the Alfonsín administration would of course want to meet with her, and had expected Ambassador del Solar to make the arrangements. But not a single member of the Argentine government made any effort to invite this daughter of the United States president for

6. One of the few members of the Radical Party who made a point of attending the Encuentro was Fernando de la Rúa. At the event's close, he sought me out to thank me personally for the Chamber's efforts in promoting Argentine business abroad. In 1979, I had met de la Rua at a luncheon in the Harvard Club in New York City and was so impressed by him then that I spontaneously remarked to a companion: "This man will be president of Argentina one day." Twenty years later, he was.

Maureen Reagan (middle), the daughter of President Ronald Reagan, in Buenos Aires for the 1986 Encuentro, where she was the featured speaker.

so much as a cup of tea, nor did they pick up a telephone and call her hotel to say hello. Ms. Reagan, who has been around politics all her life, left Argentina wondering why on earth the men running the government were being so ostentatiously chilly. This was especially puzzling since Dante Caputo was scheduled to come to the White House the following week to talk about debt relief for Argentina. It was a moment when the Alfonsín government should have been putting its best foot forward. Instead they put their feet down their throat.

When Mr. Caputo arrived in Washington, I understand that he was greeted by questions from both the secretary of state, George Schultz, and the assistant secretary of state for Latin American affairs, Eliot Abrams, as to why Alfonsín had not kept his promise to speak at the Encuentro or at least sent a replacement. I later received a phone call from a very upset Ambassador Ortiz: he told me that Caputo's answer, as reported to him, was that Alfonsín had not been invited! Did Mr. Caputo really think these men who ran the State Department were so uninformed? They knew that Alfonsín had confirmed his intention to be at the Encuentro not once, but twice to Ambassador Ortiz. And of course, when I returned to the U.S. from the Encuentro in Buenos Aires, I had briefed officials in Washington about how events had transpired.

According to Ortiz, Caputo was also asked why no one in the government had met with President Reagan's daughter, to which Caputo reportedly replied: "She never called us." Needless to say, the White House was baffled by the suggestion that the courtesy was owed by the president's daughter, and not by the Argentine government. Furthermore, the snubbing of Maureen Reagan called Alfonsín's political skills into question. If Alfonsín did not know that President Reagan spoke often and at length with his very politically-active elder daughter, he should have known.[7] Ms. Reagan had flown ten-thousand miles to Argentina on short notice to improve the business climate between the United States and Argentina. She lent her prestige and her father's pres-

7. Even if Maureen Reagan had been totally apolitical and only in Buenos Aires for a shopping holiday, Alfonsín should have possessed the savvy to realize that inviting her to the Casa Rosada for a cup of tea would have bolstered his relationship with the leader of the free world. That he so completely ignored the president's daughter suggested to many people that Alfonsín was anti-American in a very personal, petty way.

tige to our enterprise, and Alfonsín and his advisers showed exceptionally poor judgment in not seeking her out.

Caputo's answers immediately became the gossip in Buenos Aires, New York and Washington. When I heard what he'd allegedly said, I could hardly believe my ears. That very same week, I was planning to attend a luncheon in New York, co-sponsored by the Council of the Americas and the Chamber, where Caputo was scheduled to make a speech. I resolved to get the answer directly from Caputo himself. During a question-and-answer session following his speech, I rose from my chair and identified myself to the foreign minister:

"How, Minister," I asked politely, "can I explain to the 150 members of the Chamber here, and the hundreds of people in the U.S. and Argentina who thought President Alfonsín was coming to our Encuentro, why he canceled at the last minute?"

Dante Caputo's face turned a deep red. He was so enraged he couldn't answer at first. Then he finally managed to say, between his teeth, that President Alfonsín had been "busy." He then added in an outburst that the telex I had sent to him and others in the Alfonsín government "was the most insulting one I have ever received!" (Since the telex was edited by former Argentine ambassadors before it was sent, I can guarantee it was both diplomatic and courteous.)

Undeterred, I asked Caputo to tell me why Maureen Reagan had not been invited to meet with the president and his administration while she was in Buenos Aires. "She never called us!" was his angry reply. With that, Caputo swiftly turned to another questioner, eager to change the subject. I sat down.

Alfonsín was justly admired around the world as the father of Argentine democracy, and I, too, believe that all of us who care about Argentina owe an incalculable debt to him. Without diminishing any of his triumph, it can nonetheless be said that Alfonsín's reputation as an economic savior came nowhere near his reputation as a political savior, and that the American financial community's confidence in Alfonsín was not strong. He was not well served by his aides and I felt certain that by associating himself visibly with the Encuentro, Alfonsín could have improved his image with financiers and businessmen in America. They might have felt that the most important man in Argentina was committed to modernizing Argentina economically, even if some of his political associates had agendas of their own.

Once again, it was a case of misfeasance, not malfeasance, on the part of Argentina's leadership, but one can't help but wonder why people didn't know better. Alfonsín's sudden cancellation did nothing to reassure the American business community that he was a reliable partner. Nor did it do anything to dispel the lingering suspicion that his administration, however forward-looking politically, was backward-looking when it came to its old-fashioned hostility toward the United States.

Set against his monumental achievements in bringing political stability and true democracy to Argentina, the failure of Raúl Alfonsín to appear at the Encuentro or to invite Maureen Reagan to tea perhaps appear very trivial indeed. But, unfortunately, even little mistakes can contribute to large and unhappy consequences. The truth is that Americans know very little about Argentina, and even the slightest impressions can be lasting ones. Alfonsín needed all the help he could get from the U.S. to promote foreign investment and to secure favorable treatment from the International Monetary Fund. He needed an organization like the U.S.-Argentine Chamber of Commerce to promote his interests in America and vouch for his trustworthiness. Unfortunately, within some of the most influential circles in the U.S., Alfonsín acquired a reputation for lacking political and economic sophistication—and the people who paid the price for that were the Argentines he was elected to serve.

"KING" ALFONSÍN IS TAUGHT A DEMOCRATIC LESSON

By 1986, people in Argentina were themselves becoming dissatisfied with Alfonsín. While they continued to support him as he faced a series of military threats to his government, the public sensed it could have better economic leadership. Surrounded by old cronies from the Radical Party, Alfonsín didn't seem to be getting good economic advice, so the econo-

*Luncheon at the U.S.-Argentine Chamber of Commerce in honor of
EduardoAngeloz, Governor of the province of Córdoba (sixth from left).
The author is standing to the immediate left of the Governor.*

my was deteriorating dangerously, and his popularity slipped at home. Like many politicians in political trouble, Alfonsín increasingly traveled abroad at the urging of his foreign minister. Alfonsín obviously reveled in the cheers and admiration he received in foreign countries as the champion of Argentine democracy, but he didn't attract sufficient foreign capital to improve the standard of living at home.

Argentina's local off-year elections of 1987 were a wonderful example of how firmly democracy had taken root in Argentina in such a short period of time. The candidates came from all across the political spectrum and voters freely cast millions of ballots to make their choices for the Senate and the provincial governors' seats. It was a tribute to Alfonsín's leadership that the election was so fiercely contested yet peaceful, but when all the votes were counted, the Radical Party had been defeated by a solid majority at the polls. Alfonsín had campaigned hard for his party and had hoped to celebrate the election as a personal vindication of his power, success and popularity, just as Frondizi had hoped in 1962. Just like Frondizi, Alfonsín was to be disappointed. He was reported to be in such a state of shock at the election results that it was rumored he would resign and call for a new election. (Personally, I never believed Alfonsín would do any such thing.)

All kinds of theories circulated in Buenos Aires about the causes of the Alfonsín's political defeat, but the one I found most likely was told to me by a member of the president's own party: "Alfonsín was beginning to believe his own publicity, that he was King Alfonsín. The Argentine people wanted to show him that they liked democracy but he was not God. His economic ideas were a disaster."

So Alfonsín was humanized and the Peronists now were in control of both legislatures and most of the provincial governments. The only real exception was in the province of Córdoba, where Eduardo César Angeloz, a Radical, was elected governor.[8] But this, too, was actually a defeat for Alfonsín, who had campaigned against Angeloz in the Radical Party's primaries. In a nation where appearances often mean more than

8. Alfonsín did not take a lot of comfort in the election of Angeloz, his fellow Radical. Alfonsín had been hoping to amend the Constitution to run for yet another presidential term, and Angeloz's singular victory in Córdoba threatened to break the lock that he had on the party's nomination.

reality, the appearance of a defeated president meant that Alfonsín actually did lose power. This excellent politician from rural Argentina, who had brought democracy back to his country, was now through as the national leader. It would be years before Alfonsín would be able to admit it, even to himself.

BEYOND ALFONSÍN: ARGENTINA
LOOKS FOR NEW LEADERSHIP

But as long as Alfonsín and his Radical Party still occupied the Casa Rosada, they had to be reckoned with. I felt that it was important for the Chamber to continue to work with the Alfonsín government, but that it was also important for Americans to learn about other leaders and ideas within the Radical Party. When Governor Angeloz expressed interest in coming to the United States, I helped arranged a lunch for him in New York co-hosted by the U.S.-Argentine Chamber of Commerce and the Council of Americas. In addition, I arranged for him to visit Henry Kissinger, David Rockefeller, His Eminence John Cardinal O'Connor, and Rabbi Morton Rosenthal of the Anti-Defamation League. I made sure that Governor Angeloz spent time with members of the Editorial Board of the *New York Times*, the *Wall Street Journal* and the small but influential *Journal of Commerce*. The foreign departments of Morgan Guaranty Bank, Citibank and Manufacturers Hanover Trust held breakfasts and dinners for Governor Angeloz at my suggestion.

The visit was a solid success, and shortly after Angeloz returned to Argentina, President Alfonsín held his fourth press conference in four years and announced that he thought Angeloz should be the Radical Party's candidate for president in 1989. As soon as Angeloz had left New York, I contacted the political advisers to the Peronist Party's Antonio Cafiero to offer to arrange a similar trip for Cafiero in the United States.[9] Everyone expected Cafiero to be the Peronist Party candidate for president in the next election, and those in the United States who had not

9. Carlos Grosso and Guido di Tella.

already met him were eager to do so.

Cafiero wanted to come to the United States in April of 1988, a month after my term as president of the U.S.-Argentine Chamber of Commerce would expire. Nonetheless, I arranged for the Chamber to hold a reception for Cafiero, and also got the Council of the Americas to agree to hold another reception for him in New York. Cafiero was scheduled to deliver a speech at the Center of American Studies of the Johns Hopkins Institute in Washington, where he would be formally introduced as the Peronist Party candidate for president.

But in February of 1988, Cafiero abruptly cancelled his plans to visit the U.S. Much to his and everyone else's surprise, he had been unable to nail down the Peronist Party's nomination. He was facing stiff opposition from the governor of La Rioja, Carlos Saúl Menem. Hardly anybody outside of Argentina had heard of Menem and when they first did, the reports were negative. With his sideburns and long hair, he was called a "wild man," and because of his Arab ancestry, he was equated with Muammar Qaddafi.

Interestingly, I had heard of Menem quite some time before, and I had received a positive portrait of the man. While on a trip to Argentina to plan for the Encuentro, I was having breakfast at the home of Robert Felder, a political minister in the U.S. embassy in Buenos Aires. Our conversation was interrupted by a phone call. I couldn't help but overhear Felder cheerfully saying in Spanish: "You know that we like you and respect you. It doesn't really matter if the ambassador doesn't invite you. He's away. I'm the political officer and I meet you all the time." Felder continued with similar reassurances. After he hung up the phone, he turned to me, smiled and said: "That was Carlos Saúl Menem, the governor of the poorest province of Argentina. I feel certain he will run in the Peronist primary and that he will beat Cafiero. In fact, I believe he will be the next president of Argentina, if there is no coup. And if he does become president, Menem will surprise everybody by being good at it." Since Felder was, in my opinion, one of the very brightest U.S. foreign service officers I have ever met, I took his prediction very seriously. (He later became a full-fledged U.S. ambassador and, in my view, he should be made U.S. ambassador to Argentina some day.)

THE ECONOMIC PICTURE DARKENS IN ARGENTINA

On the day that I retired as president of the U.S.-Argentine Chamber of Commerce, the *Financial Times* of London ran an article announcing that foreign investments were flowing into Portugal and China at enormous rates, and that the U.S. Chambers of Commerce affiliated with both countries were organizing visits to promote even more business. I couldn't help but think that such a story might have been written about Argentina had only Alfonsín been more willing to cooperate with the U.S.-Argentine Chamber of Commerce.

By April 1988, Argentina's currency had begun a massive slide and Alfonsín's diminished stature as a leader did little to inspire the kind of confidence it takes to turn such a situation around. To be fair to Alfonsín, he had inherited, right from the beginning, a rotting economic foundation, due to the policies of the preceding military junta and its economic minister, José Martínez de Hoz. As I mentioned in a previous chapter, I had a chance to discuss these matters with Martínez de Hoz himself when he visited Harvard University in the spring of 1988. Our conversation was cordial, and the former economy minister insisted he could not have acted otherwise during his tenure with respect to the closing of Banco de Intercambio Regional, as a matter of Argentine law. Without attempting to argue against his version of history, I informed Martínez de Hoz that on the very day we were having lunch, the Federal Deposit Insurance Corporation of the United States was injecting $2.5 billion into a Texas bank because we thought it was better to retain confidence in the system than to liquidate a bank, even an overextended one. I recalled how the U.S. government had, on various occasions, rescued Bank of America, Continental Bank, Citibank and Chase Manhattan. Even having the government take over a bank or sell it to someone else was preferable to closing it. Whether Martínez de Hoz had been powerless to stop the closing of BIR or not, the liquidation of one of Argentina's largest banks had been an admission of failure of his economic plan, as well as the entire banking system. Argentina would have needed only a few million dollars to save BIR.

Interestingly, Martínez de Hoz was more optimistic than I was about the future economy of Argentina. He said it might take time, but he thought that Alfonsín could stop the State from controlling industry, although he believed it would finally be up to the next generation of Argentines to get the country fully on track economically.[10]

But even Martínez de Hoz had to admit that, for the immediate future, Argentina was on a roller coaster, politically and economically. Carlos Saúl Menem defeated Antonio Cafiero in the Peronist presidential primaries—a real shocker to Argentines. Menem was now set to run against Governor Angeloz, who was not backed by Alfonsín but who nonetheless was stuck defending Alfonsín's poor economic policies. With confidence in the future now in a nosedive, capital began fleeing the country. In July of 1998, the government closed all the banks for three days, devalued Argentina's currency and announced a new economic plan. It was too little too late, and everyone knew it. The economy continued its massive slide. The following month, the *Wall Street Journal* summed up the situation in an article headlined: "Argentina's President Alfonsín Nears End of Term with Image of Failure."

Then Argentines were jolted by the sudden return of Isabelita Perón from her self-imposed exile in Madrid. No one knew what she wanted or was up to, but many Peronists suspected she had been invited back by Alfonsín to remind voters of her disastrous twenty-one-month rule, as a visible caution never to re-elect the Peronists again. Quite wisely, Governor Menem managed to be away on a two-week trip when Mrs. Perón made her re-entry into Argentina's political life, so he didn't have to meet her or greet her, or even be seen with her. Although Mrs. Perón was the talk of the town for several weeks, Argentines simply finally re-absorbed her without chaos—another sign that democracy had set down strong and healthy roots under Alfonsín's administration.

But no sooner had the hubbub over Mrs. Perón quieted down than Argentina was rocked by a three-day military rebellion—the third in Alfonsín's term. The president was away on a trip to the U.S. when a

10. When de Hoz returned to Argentina from his trip to the U.S. he was arrested and kept in jail without trial for four months. The Argentine Court of Appeals ordered his release.

The author opens the Encuentro in Buenos Aires in June 1986.

rebel colonel, Mohammed Ali Seineldin, staged the uprising, but Seineldin's timing was nonetheless very poor. Argentines were committed to civilian rule and peaceful elections, and they wanted to prove to the military they were no longer welcome to disrupt the political life of the country. Upon his return, Alfonsín was able to face down the military, only to turn around and find himself facing another violent crisis: a thirty-six-hour attack by an alleged guerilla group on a military base in the suburbs of Buenos Aires. It was a dramatic shootout, and armed battalions finally had to be called in to secure the area. Argentines everywhere were frightened that a new round of guerilla warfare might be about to begin. They began to worry they might not get to have another election.

Their jitters were reflected in the volatile economy. Inflation soared to an annual rate of three thousand percent! A clamor arose in the country for both the economic minister and the foreign minister to resign, but Alfonsín stubbornly resisted until his own Party's candidate for president, Governor Angeloz, insisted. Unable to accept the public's rejection of his policies, Alfonsín didn't lift a finger to help Angeloz's campaign. Those who might have voted for the Radicals became increasingly fed up with Alfonsín's attitude, and in my mind, it became perfectly clear that the Peronists were on their way to victory.

May 14, 1989, was Election Day, and it was a beautiful day in Argentina. Eighty-five percent of eligible voters came to the polls in one of the most orderly elections in Argentine history. Carlos Saúl Menem received forty-seven percent of their votes, more than enough to win the electoral college, and the Peronists were swept to victory in both houses of Congress. They even won in the province of Buenos Aires, traditionally a Radical stronghold. But as usual in Argentina, things would have to get far worse before they got even a little bit better.

ELEVEN

1989–2000
Carlos Saúl Menem
and the Future
of Argentina

Ambassador Terence A. Todman (left) is embraced by President Carlos Saúl Menem.

On May 15, 1989, Carlos Saúl Menem, a member of the Peronist party running with Perón's flag wrapped around him, won Argentina's presidential election with 47.3 three percent of the vote. Just a year earlier, Menem had not been predicted to be in the race, let alone win the election. When the governor of the poorest province of Argentina announced that he was running, many in Washington dismissed it as a joke. There was a great deal of laughter about the upstart candidacy of this short, mysterious man with long hair and sideburns, the "wild man" of Argentine politics.

The Peronist party had been expected to nominate Antonio Cafiero—and it was also expected that Cafiero would lose the general election to Eduardo Angeloz, the Radical Party nominee. (Angeloz eventually received thirty-seven percent of the vote against Menem.) Looking forward to the election, most Americans who are interested in Argentina were very comfortable with the prospect of an Angeloz victory. Angeloz was seen as the most popular, the most coherent and the most pragmatic leader on the Argentine scene. I personally thought Angeloz very astute and a good professional politician.

But by February 1989, the laughter that had greeted news of Menem's candidacy was beginning to subside. Knowledgeable people in the U.S. began to think that since the Argentina economy was such a disaster, Argentine voters would focus on what we in the U.S. call "pocketbook issues"—and thus were very likely to vote against a continuation of Radical rule. That meant Angeloz was in trouble.

The Conservative Party nominated as its candidate Álvaro Alsogaray, the last economy minister of President Arturo Frondizi. Everyone knew Alsogaray was in no position to win a majority of votes, so people began to suspect that the Peronists could actually win the presidency. The U.S. government decided it was in its interests to learn who Menem really was and, in doing so, it learned that Menem deserved respect.

Unlike some forty years earlier, this time the U.S. government made the correct decision to stay absolutely neutral in the Argentine election. Its neutrality went so far that in April 1989, when the Alfonsín government asked the U.S. for loans, the U.S government refused. It not only felt that the loans would be useless in turning around the Argentine economy, it also worried the loans might be taken as a sign of support for the Radical Party in the upcoming election. The response of the Alfonsín government was to tell the U.S., in so many words: "If you don't support us, then Menem will win." And the answer from the U.S. was, in so many words: "So?" At long last, Washington was willing to trust the judgment of Argentine voters.

Not all Argentines, however, were so relaxed about the prospect of a return of Peronist rule. In the weeks leading up to Menem's victory, a kind of panic ensued. People and dollars began vacating Argentina. Families sold their heirlooms and their estates. The elite worried that they could no longer afford to live under the Radicals, yet they hated the idea of living under another Peronist government. They feared a coup or a civil war— or both. Their one desperate hope was that the election results would be inconclusive, creating the likelihood that Álvaro Alsogaray and the Conservatives would be drawn into a ruling coalition with the Radicals— something I already knew that would never come to pass.

I was present at a lunch at the Harvard Club in New York City in late 1988 when María Julia Alsogaray, Álvaro's daughter, was asked if her father would be willing to form a coalition with the Radicals if Angeloz needed that to win. Ms. Alsogaray immediately bristled and asked: "Why not with Menem?" I concluded right then and there that most likely a deal had already been struck between the Conservatives and Menem, so that if neither the Radicals nor the Peronists won a convincing majority, the Conservatives were prepared to throw their support to the Peronists in a run-off. As it turned out, Menem won a clear-cut victory, but the

Conservatives reaped rewards, too. Álvaro Alsogaray became Menem's highly prominent economic adviser and his daughter was put in charge of the national phone company. In the course of privatizing it, she became the most powerful woman in Argentina. For the next several years, she and her father remained great allies to Menem.

But ultimately, Menem owed his victory less to allies like the Alsogarays than to widespread, popular revulsion against the economic policies of the Alfonsín government. The Radical Party candidate, Eduardo Angeloz, campaigned energetically but he was stuck with Alfonsín's economic legacy: Inflation was out of control. The currency was nearly worthless. Under Radical rule, investment and privatization had gone nowhere, but precious capital kept leaving the country.

Angeloz could neither defend his party's policies nor break free of them. Worst of all, during the campaign, it looked like Alfonsín was so reluctant to relinquish his status as leader of the Radical Party that he appeared to many Argentines to be doing nothing to help Angeloz win and everything to guarantee that he would lose. For example, just three days before the election, the Alfonsín government denied Japan's Honda Motor Company the chance to build a motorcycle factory in Argentina, giving the license to a domestic company instead. Honda's down payment alone would have pumped $20 million into Argentina's flailing economy, and Angeloz had campaigned publicly in favor Honda getting the deal. Yet Alfonsín said "no" to Honda at the last minute. Even to the voters it looked like Alfonsín did not respect the ideas of his own party's candidate, and they lost respect for Angeloz for failing to stand up to Alfonsín.

Unfortunately, even Menem's victory at the polls in mid-May of 1989 did nothing to reassure the country that better economic times might soon begin. Within a week of the election there was a financial panic, and by the middle of June 1989, inflation was running at four hundred thousand percent. With the economy now plunged into even deeper chaos and public weariness of Radical rule running at an all time high, pressure began to mount on Alfonsín to leave office early.

Menem had already announced his cabinet, and the nation was amazed by his boldness. Rather than stock his cabinet with aging, avenging Peronists, Menem reached into all corners of the Argentine political landscape to demonstrate that his administration intended to break free of the past to build broad political support (just as I had hoped). He named Miguel Roig, from the largest agribusiness entity in Argentina, to be the new minister of economy; he asked Álvaro Alsogaray, head of the Conservative Party, to be his principial economic adviser. Menem was poised to set the nation's finances on a new foundation, and the public did not want to wait. With the economic waters rising all around him and having lost the political authority necessary to govern, Alfonsín decided to depart without finishing his term. Menem's inauguration was moved up a full six months, from December to July 8, 1989.

MENEM TAKES THE HELM

Menem swept into office with energy and gusto, and the first months of his administration were filled with great beginnings and great uncertainties. He amazed everyone with his combination of daring and pragmatism. The international media began watching Argentina closely, sensing that history was in the making. Argentina's economy was still in a dizzying whirl, but Menem's team projected confidence and a willingness to break with the past. That—and a few autocratic, eyebrow-raising financial maneuvers by a rapid-fire succession of economy ministers—helped stabilize Argentina's currency.

Menem himself lost no time in traveling to the United States and Great Britain to give personal reassurances to the world financial community that he was serious about putting Argentina's economic house in order and about changing the way Argentina did business. In Washington, Menem was able to quickly establish a cordial personal rapport with President George Bush that served to facilitate better relations between the two countries at the bureaucratic level as well.[1]

I saw Menem in both Washington and New York, and was deeply

1. It is highly unorthodox for brand new heads of state to be granted meetings with U.S. presidents, who traditionally wait to see what policies new leaders will adopt. The bureaucracy in the State Department in Washington was therefore opposed to a Menem visit so soon, but the U.S ambassador to Argentina,

impressed by his political style. Wherever he went, Menem created an electric buzz around him. He made people believe that Argentina was headed in a new direction because of his unshakeable confidence. Speaking in private and in public to other heads of state and politicians, Menem projected a winning air, and in politics, domestic or international, looking and acting like a winner is always the best place to start. As Robert Felder had predicted to me, Menem was surprising everybody, and in a very favorable way.

Perhaps the biggest surprise of all was the pledge by this lifelong Peronist to privatize Argentina's state-owned industry. By all the standard measures, it looked like political suicide: The base of Menem's support came from the Peronists and their unions. So how could any elected Argentine politician, especially a Peronist, so openly embrace an economic agenda that replaced lifetime job security with the insecurities of the free market?

Yet I had always known that, paradoxically, only a Peronist president could and would free Argentina from the shackles of Juan Perón's outmoded ideas. Just as in the United States, where only a famous anti-communist like Richard Nixon could open business relations with communist China and get away with it politically, and where only a Kennedy-esque liberal like Bill Clinton could end America's federal welfare system and retain the loyalty of his party to win re-election, only a Peronist politician in Argentina could risk burying Perón's worst ideas, once and for all.

In many ways, Menem acted so quickly and with such agility, the would-be critics of his new economic agenda scarcely had time to react. But they quickly regained their balance and no one should forget how difficult Menem's first term really was. By the end of 1989, the unions were so worried by the pace of privatization that they staged a national strike. Menem refused to back down in the face of union pressure. By coincidence, the head of the army died on the very same day, and the public was seized with panic about domestic stability in Argentina and the fate of their still-infant democracy. The fact that Menem weathered both storms

Terence Todman, was able appeal directly to President Bush, who agreed to the meeting. Todman was also instrumental in arranging for Menem to address a joint session of the U.S. Congress, an honor only rarely accorded a foreign head of state.

and emerged looking stronger than ever seemed to break a spell that had haunted Argentina for forty years. It was finally seen that an elected leader could be his own man, neither the puppet of the military nor his political base.

It helped, too, that the Soviet Union and East European bloc were at the same time disintegrating dramatically, so that Argentines began to see a whole new, post-Cold War world taking shape. This time they wanted to be part of it. They began to like Menem's forward-looking, outgoing, strong leadership and they liked seeing his international savvy admired everywhere. It was also helpful that the U.S. had a good ambassador in Buenos Aires. Terence Todman, who had previously been our ambassador to Spain, is a professional who knows Argentine history and who became an extremely intelligent advocate of reinforcing shared values between the two countries. He made it easier for Argentines to rethink their view of the U.S., and was one of our more popular U.S. ambassadors to Argentina.

ARGENTINA REJOINS THE WORLD

Among the very smartest things that Menem did during his first years in office was cancel a secret missile project that was underway in the province of Córdoba. The U.S. feared that once Argentina completed work on the missiles (allegedly financed by money from Arab countries), the missiles would find their way into the hands of outlaw nations. At the urging of Washington, Menem stopped the project, and that single act went a long way to convincing the U.S. government that a new day had dawned in U.S.-Argentine relations.

It was also helpful that Menem issued a decree to send two Argentine frigates and six hundred soldiers to the Persian Gulf in support of the allied effort to reverse Saddam Hussein's invasion of Kuwait. Argentina had not openly allied itself with the winning side in World War II, and Menem's bold move in 1990 helped erase almost overnight fifty years of ill-will and isolation. It even helped heal some of the wounds caused by the Malvinas War. Menem's standing up to Saddam Hussein was especially welcomed because Menem is of Arab descent. It was not lost on anyone that Menem was very firmly endorsing the notion that an international principal was at stake in the Gulf war, not tribal loyalties.

The decision to participate in the Gulf military action was not thoroughly popular in Argentina. Some in the Peronist Party publicly disagreed with Menem, and most of the Radicals were outraged. Ex-President Alfonsín was a stiff opponent of Menem's action, and Menem's surprise presidential decree to send troops to the Gulf passed Congress by only two votes. But Menem stuck to his guns and said bluntly: "It is time for Argentina to be in tune with first world opinion." He was right.

To the great benefit of Argentina, Menem did more than just stay in tune with first world opinion. He positively danced with it at times, so closely that Menem's relations with the U.S. were jokingly described by his own foreign minister as "carnal relations." Fortunately, Argentina's strong desire for good relations was met with equal enthusiasm on the U.S. side. President George Bush's private enthusiasm and public support for Menem was so strong that Bush—against the opinion of some of his own U.S. advisors—went ahead with a planned visit to Buenos Aires in the face of an attempted military coup in Argentina. Such an open display of faith in Menem's ability by an American president did not go unnoticed by the international community.

In the U.S., the press admiringly called Menem "the Gorbachev of Argentina," recognizing and applauding his determination to see Argentina revamp its economic structure. But unlike Gorbachev, Menem was able to consolidate his political power at home and win democratic support from his people for reform. Although Argentines did not always happily dance along with Menem—they mostly were dragged along, grudgingly, through the throes of economic restructuring – they wanted political stability. Menem, despite his often autocratic and drastic leadership, was by and large giving them the stability they craved. [2]

Of course, the day-to-day mode of politics in Argentina continued to

2. There was a very tense moment during Menem's early years when the United States took a firm stand against corruption in Argentine trade and investment practices. The U.S. ambassador, Terence Todman, took the lead in making it plain that the U.S. expected the eradication of corruption to be part of modernizing Argentina and bringing her in line with first world economies. Faced with very damaging accusations of personal and administrative corruption, Menem initially tried to arouse anti-American sentiment

be crisis-oriented and scandal-ridden. There was trouble with Menem's wife and the exposure of corruption in the administration. There was endless political maneuvering on the part of Menem's enemies and rivals, and Argentina's highly partisan press and even cool-headed professional Argentina watchers continuously predicted Menem's imminent downfall. But each time, Menem surprised them by bouncing back, stronger than ever. In the vigorously contested midterm elections of 1991, Menem skillfully led his Peronist Party to a healthy victory, carrying most of the country.

THE MENEM-CAVALLO TEAM

The political maneuvering that really captivated the attention of Argentina watchers and foreign investors was the relationship between Menem and his longest-lasting economy minister, Domingo Cavallo. They were truly a fascinating pair. Cavallo had made his start in politics as a Radical in the province of Córdoba, where he worked for an internationally renowned candy company. The company was owned by a very politically active family named Pagani, who backed only two men: Eduardo Angeloz and Domingo Cavallo. For many years, these two ambitious men worked hand in hand to promote the Radical Party's interests in Córdoba.

When Angeloz was elected governor of Córdoba, Cavallo wanted to serve as his minister of economy—but Angeloz turned him down. Understanding that his ascendancy in the Radical Party was now blocked, Cavallo switched parties and became a Peronist. He also became a backer of Carlos Saúl Menem. At that time, very few people regarded Menem as having much of a future in national politics in Argentina.

Cavallo also worked politically to promote his own power base in the Peronist party. He, too, harbored dreams of becoming president. Nonetheless, he supported Menem's candidacy, and when Menem was

to defend himself, invoking the name of Spriulle Braden and accusing the U.S. of renewed meddling in Argentina affairs. When the public failed to take the bait and the Argentine press excoriated Menem in print, Menem did a stunning 180 degree about face, reshuffled his cabinet and made a point of drawing closer to the American ambassador. Although he did virtually nothing to end the corruption, the understanding by Menem that the days of U.S.-bashing were over for good in Argentina marked the end of an era.

elected president, Cavallo waited to be asked to be the minister of economy. Instead, Menem asked Cavallo to become his foreign minister—in no small part because Menem wasn't keen on having a political rival with his own ambitious agenda holding such a powerful position inside his administration. After all, a minister of economy can either make or break a presidency. A foreign minister, on the other hand, spends an awful lot of time out of the country.

So Menem asked Miguel Roig to be his minister of economy, and Cavallo had no choice but to accept the post of foreign minister, even though he would have preferred to stay at home and be the architect of a new economic plan for the nation. When Roig died of a sudden heart attack seven days after taking office, Menem once again bypassed Cavallo and named Roig's deputy to the top job. That new minister of economy didn't last, either: he shortly resigned after being indicted by the Venezuelan government for activities he'd undertaken while still in the private sector.

Yet Cavallo had to stand by and watch as Menem named someone else yet again as his third choice for minister of economy, a man named Antonio Erman González, who quickly pleased the public by keeping the currency values stable month after month. The international community was just beginning to take notice of González's accomplishment when a brief military uprising caused a panic in the money markets nearly bringing the Argentine economy to its knees. To restore confidence, Menem abruptly got rid of González and, at last, asked Cavallo to become the minister of economy. One of the great working partnerships in modern Argentine political history had now officially begun.

During Cavallo's tenure as minister of economy, the Argentine economy came to maturity. But it should never be forgotten that it was Menem who had the grand vision and the political charisma needed to raise Argentina to such heights: He wanted Argentina to join the first world and restore good relations with the United States. He wanted to get the nation moving toward privatization. But it was Cavallo who had the technical brain to come up with a detailed, workable, bureaucratic agenda for stabilizing the currency and restructuring the economy that was believable to the international community, and thus capable of generating investment. But that was only half the battle. It took Menem, the consummate politician, to win the necessary domestic backing for Cavallo's plan. The popularity Menem won in his own country demonstrated to the world that finally, for the first time in forty years, Argentines were ready to back a president who was neither a prisoner of the military, the labor unions, nor even his own party. So the world financial community, also for the first time in forty years, felt comfortable signing on to the economic dreams of an Argentine government.

Through self-promotion, Cavallo gained most of the credit for keeping the country moving forward economically, to the point where Menem could often be heard complaining to the media that it was the "Menem Plan," not some non-existent "Cavallo Plan," that deserved the credit for Argentina doing so well. Menem no doubt wanted all the credit, but the international financial community perceived Cavallo as indispensible to Argentina's future success, which only encouraged Cavallo's long-simmering political dream of becoming the most powerful politician in the country.

It is not international financiers, however, who vote in Argentina's elections but Argentines themselves, and they never warmed up to Minister Cavallo's personal style. In the bi-elections of 1991, Cavallo's political ambitions suffered a severe setback in the province of Córdoba, where the Peronist candidate for governor that Cavallo had personally groomed and backed lost to the Radical opponent, none other than Menem's archrival, Eduardo Angeloz. However acute Cavallo's disappointment, people throughout the country, and abroad, let out a huge sigh of relief. People liked the Menem-Cavallo team, and they wanted it to continue as a team. They didn't want Cavallo to spend his time maneuvering in electoral politics and they were rather glad to see his political hopes dashed. Even though Argentines had trouble with Menem's flamboyant, rule-breaking way of governing, they recognized the fact that only Menem had the national political clout to make the Argentines swallow the sacrifices necessary for making Cavallo's ideas work. Neither of them could do it alone—and even Menem and Cavallo must have realized that at some level. While their relations were obviously tense, competitive and even backstabbing at times, the Menem-Cavallo partnership was, despite it all, a remarkably creative and productive relationship, and Argentines were lucky to have them both.

U.S.-ARGENTINE RELATIONS IN TIMES OF TRANSITION

During fifty years of representing Argentine interests, I never once saw a reason to take sides in Argentine politics. Menem didn't turn me into a Peronist, yet during the 1990s, I was happy to see so many of the things I had hoped for coming to pass in Argentina.[3] Democracy was now thriving: it was rough-and-tumble, but it was peaceful, and at last the country seemed to have the political leadership it needed to come to grips with the modern world. Argentina's economy was stabilized and dollarized. Its biggest state-run industries and utilities were being privatized, and although not everything went smoothly, things often went better than expected. Relations with the U.S. were so good that the American ambassador to Argentina, Terence Todman, had become one of the most popular and respected men in the country. When the Argentines dubbed him "El Virrey"—Spanish for "viceroy"—it was in recognition of the new and, at times, overwhelming importance of U.S.-Argentine relations. One writer said that the days of "Perón o Braden" had now been replaced with "¡Menem, sí! ¡Todman, sí!"

Because President George Bush and President Menem enjoyed an especially strong personal rapport, most everyone in the Argentine government was hoping (to the point of self-deception) that President Bush would be reelected to a second term in 1992. The Argentines wanted to continue their speedy motion forward in good relations with the U.S. and they were especially keen on having Ambassador Todman, a Bush appointee, remain in Buenos Aires. So I, along with most everyone politically aware in Argentina, was thoroughly dismayed when, months before the U.S. election, George

3. I even had the pleasure of seeing a very modest idea of mine adopted by the Argentine government. I had suggested to Domingo Cavallo that Argentina initiate a program of awarding medals to outstanding Americans who had made significant contributions to improving U.S.-Argentine relations. The first awards were given in 1992 and have continued yearly to this day.

Bush's State Department opted to reassign Todman as part of a regular rotation of duties. Although I am generally in favor of rotating U.S. ambassadors every few years, it seemed to me that in this instance, the timing was wrong.

Accordingly, I wrote letters to President Bush, the secretary of state, and the leading Republicans on the Senate Foreign Relations committee, suggesting they make an exception to the rotation rules. They seemed disinclined to do so but, as things turned out, the Democrats who controlled Congress were in no hurry to confirm a replacement for Todman, since it was an election year. So Todman was still in place when President Bush lost the election to Bill Clinton in November of 1992.

Unlike other famously ill-fated appointments made by the new president, Bill Clinton's choice of James Cheek to serve as ambassador to Argentina was swiftly confirmed by the Senate. Terence Todman, who had been ordered by his new superiors in the State Department to pack up and leave Buenos Aires within two weeks, requested an extension because President Menem was scheduled to soon travel to Washington to meet President Clinton. Argentina was also in the midst of changing ambassadors to the U.S., but they intended to have both their old and new ambassadors present during the upcoming meeting of the two presidents. Todman advised the U.S. to do likewise, but the State Department stubbornly refused. It was a very dumb move by the Clinton administration.

The Argentines were both mystified and miffed: They thought very highly of Todman and worried that the Clinton administration's unceremonious dismissal of him boded ill for continued progress in U.S.-Argentine relations. Cheek was not known in Argentina and he was thought to be uninformed about Argentine affairs; Argentines viewed Todman's removal as unfortunate and untimely. Matters were not improved when it got around that Cheek refused to be briefed by Todman before coming down to assume his new post. Worse still, upon arriving in Buenos Aires, Cheek declared: "I did not come here to be 'the viceroy' of the Clinton administration." Argentines took that as a direct rebuke to the way they had pursued good relations with the U.S.[4]

Despite this glitch in understanding at the ambassadorial level, rela-

4. Ambassador Cheek left Argentina in 1996 after serving his full term.

tions between Presidents Menem and Clinton were positive. Although the two didn't "click" in the same personal way Menem and Bush did, the two presidents, both of whom had come from the poorest regions of their respective countries, and both of whom were reinventing their party's ideologies, had an intuitive understanding of each other. They admired each other's prodigious political talents, personal audacity and survivor skills. So relations between Argentina and Washington during the Clinton years remained productive, something I believe was very necessary for the well-being of both countries and will serve the hemisphere well for many decades to come.

MENEM'S LEGACY

By law, Menem was only entitled to serve six years as president. But with his political strength at its peak, Menem was hardly going to sit by and let himself be retired from office simply because the Argentine Constitution called for it. Very craftily, Menem engineered a deal with Ex-President Alfonsín to change the Constitution so that a president could succeed himself for a second term. Even Alfonsín knew that Menem was certain to run and that no Radical was likely beat him, so the deal virtually ensured that Alfonsín, as the last Radical to hold the office of president of Argentina, would remain the leader-of-record of the Radical Party for many years to come.

Much to the relief of the international community, Menem did win re-election.[5] His second term was not as dramatic as his first, although his rule continued to be marked by surprising successes, sudden tragedies, constant drama and occasional comedy. With Cavallo initially staying on as economic minister, the country's finances remained stable, and relations with the U.S. continued to improve. As only a Peronist could do, Menem was able to privatize a great many companies that had been created as state companies during the first term of Juan Perón. By

5. I found it remarkable during the election that Menem was so often seen on the campaign trail with his minister of economy at his side. In all previous Argentine campaigns that I can recall, the economy minister was usually sent to a kind of political Siberia prior to the election, to avoid reminding the voters of the always dismal state of the Argentine economy.

Menem's second term, business communities throughout the world had accepted the economic revolution in Argentina as real.

Menem had his run-ins with the military, but by giving in a little here and taking away a little there, he kept things under control. In an odd way, Menem was perhaps the only beneficiary of the Malvinas War, since it was Menem who was most able to take advantage of the loss of prestige that the military suffered as a result of losing that war. At the same time, Menem worked hard to reclaim the Falkland Islands for Argentina, and probably got closer to making that a reality than Argentina's generals ever did.

Menem, like Alfonsín before him, never completely satisfied human rights advocates that he was doing enough to redress the horrors of the past, and continuing revelations about the behavior of men in uniform, even beyond the years of the "the dirty war," shadowed Menem's administration and could shadow future administrations as well.

But by the end of Menem's second term, the Argentine people were ready for a change in government. Unemployment, never much publicized during Menem's rule, had been steadily creeping upward into double-digit rates. In a bold move, Menem had pegged the peso to the U.S. dollar, and while that substantially helped the Argentine economy in many areas, it also left it terribly vulnerable in other areas. A major problem occurred when Brazil devalued its currency thirty percent against the U.S. dollar, and many Argentine businesses simply moved across the border because it cost that much less to do business there.

Like so many strong politicians, Menem made the mistake of failing to listen to his critics as well as his friends. Much of his legacy will be marred by accusations of corruption, and he will be remembered as a man who undeniably had an insatiable appetite for power.[6] It is not surprising that, in October of 1999, voters in Argentina rejected continued Peronist rule and instead gave the Radical Party a new chance to govern. Although the voters knew that prior Radical presidents had failed, they saw in Fernando de la Rúa a willingness to bring in new people with

6. Having changed the Argentine Constitution once to allow himself to run for re-election, Menem made an effort to change it twice to allow himself to run for yet a third term. It was not permitted.

modern ideas. And they also saw, in solid contrast to Menem, a quiet, dig-nified man who was well-prepared to tackle the more subtle and com-plex problems Argentina faced now that democracy and a free market economy had been secured.

But despite all his personal faults and political mistakes, I have no doubt that future historians will give Menem high marks for the path-breaking contributions he made to modernizing his country. Menem set Argentina on an irreversible course of economic rationality and credibil-ity in the world of economic powers. The foundation for continued sta-bility and prosperity has been firmly laid, and it will be up to future gen-erations of Argentines to preserve what was created for them.

ARGENTINA'S CONNECTION TO THE REST OF THE WORLD

Aerolíneas Argentinas was responsible for first bringing me to Argentina and hence shaping my personal and professional life. I therefore feel this book would not be complete without briefly summing up something of what I have learned in forty years working as the American lawyer for Argentina's national carrier.

After sixty years of operating Aerolíneas Argentinas as a state-owned industry, the government of Argentina, under President Menem, decid-ed to privatize Aerolíneas, although the corporation that bought it, SEPI, is actually owned by the government of Spain. As of this writing, there is an ongoing debate about what the future of Aerolíneas should be. There are questions about the size of its fleets, the extent of its air routes and whether or not it is too vulnerable to an "open skies" policy. The chal-lenges of operating a profitable airline are enormous, and a nation's flag-ship carrier always involves special considerations and complexities.

There is no one single model a government should follow in setting a nation's air policies, because each country has different needs. Thus, as one looks around the world today, one sees that some countries retain national air carriers that are operated or subsidized by the state, whereas other nations rely solely on privately-owned airlines to serve their nations' needs. Similarly, some nations sign "open sky" treaties, while others do not. This variety in policy has little to do with the size of nations or even the health of their economies. The decision whether to maintain a national air carrier is a political one, involving a combination of national pride, national ideology, national air service needs, and national employment needs. This is true of both democracies and dictatorships. In the modern world, air service is a special kind of public utility, so no government can responsibly allow all the answers to be dictated by the private market.

As the lawyer for Argentine Airlines, it would be unwise of me to express an opinion here as to what air policies the Argentine government should pursue. The issues are fascinating and complex, but they are beyond the scope of this book. But I do feel quite comfortable in advocating that all governments of Argentina, present and future, do the most they can to promote tourism to Argentina. With only thirty-seven million people, Argentina has a difficult time supporting frequent and convenient air service in and out of the country. By cultivating tourism, Argentina will more rapidly increase the volume of travelers using Argentina's airports and air carriers. It will also increase the number of flights leaving Argentina for foreign destinations, thereby expanding air service and lowering the price of tickets for Argentine citizens.

Needless to say, a healthier air transport system and consumer savings is not the only benefit that increased tourism would bring to Argentina. Tourism is a great modern phenomenon that serves as a way of distributing the globe's wealth. Tourism brings money into a country quickly without foreign investment. It generates interest in a country, which is then transfered over to the investment sector. There is no reason why Argentina cannot compete internationally for tourist dollars: Argentina offers both modern cities that have a high standard of service and natural wonders comparable to Switzerland's. Argentina has the additional advantage of offering absolutely uncrowded, pristine places for relaxation and outdoor recreation, and the novelty of getting off the beaten track.

Foreign visitors freely spend money and thereby create employment in the service industries. Even in places with very robust and diversified economies, like New York City, where I live, the government has learned that promoting tourism is an extremely good way to boost revenues, and now New York teems with tourists from all over the globe. The new private businesses that have been created to serve tourists pay taxes to the city, as do the tourists themselves (on hotel beds, restaurant meals, tours and admissions to local museums).

Tourism also helps a nation bear the costs of protecting and preserving its natural wonders, of which Argentina has many. It helps a nation preserve its heritage, as foreigners often prize the history and indigenous culture that modern young people neglect. Argentina has a wealth of riches—natural, cultural and recreational—to offer the world, and in my opinion it does not do enough to advertise itself around the globe.

I believe that Argentines should work more actively to overcome the poor image their country acquired during the years of terrorism and military repression. This is not an impossible task: As of the writing of this book, South Africa had about 4.5 million visitors each year, even though it was only recently considered a pariah nation (and it is not easy to get to). By contrast, Argentina had only 260,000 visitors. As a beginning, it would help if tour operators began organizing attractive package tours to Argentina for large and small groups.

It is also true that tourism works very subtle and positive changes in a country. As Argentines come into greater contact with people from every part of the globe, and foreigners come to know Argentina first-hand, many of the foolish prejudices people have about each other will disappear. The more people come to know personally the beauty and grandeur of Argentina, its unusual landscape and wildlife, and its wonderful culture and people, the more Argentines will find acceptance in their political and economic relations with the rest of the world.

THE FUTURE OF ARGENTINA:
THE CHALLENGE AND THE HOPE

In the end, the credit and the responsibility for all of Argentina's success and failures rests squarely with the Argentine people, and for the past fifteen years, they have performed admirably. It was the Argentine people themselves who finally recognized that changes needed to be made if they were to become a democratic nation and move forward into a new era of prosperity. It is they who have recognized, even more deeply than some of their political leaders, that Washington and New York City are, in reality, the center of the world in terms of power and finance. Argentine voters have clearly embraced leaders who recognize this and they have rejected those who could not see it.

In the 1999 presidential election, for instance, the Peronist candidate, Eduardo Duhalde, suggested a forgiveness of the Argentine debt and that helped cost him the election. Young Argentines know they have to pay those bills if they are to be part of the new world. They are willing to work hard to be included in the first world economy and want to be accepted on equal footing. Young and ambitious Argentines want to go to school in the United States; they want to be associated with U.S. companies. America is a model for their hoped-for success. They are still learning, of course, but they are learning very quickly.

Needless to say, however, it is not economic success alone that will determine the future well-being of Argentina. What is most important is that she continue to grow and deepen as a democracy. Argentina now has a steady track record of peaceful elections. The last presidential campaign saw two worthy candidates oppose each other, and the victor, Fernando de la Rúa, is a professional who has worked his way up the ladder of experience. He knows the art of politics and how to negotiate. He exemplifies the new generation of Radical Party members who understand that the old philosophies of the past don't work. I believe all Argentines and the international community wish him well.

I think it is unlikely that anything or anyone could persuade Argentines to tolerate anything less than democracy for the foreseeable future. But while there are no longer predictions of a return to military rule, the real future test for Argentine democracy will be whether Argentines can control those who abuse power who aren't in uniform. During the Menem years, there arose a tendency for those in office to consolidate their personal power; it is possible, even in a democracy, for single politicians to have too much power, and Argentines are learning to distrust charismatic government.

Argentina must also develop the kind of cultural and civic institutions and mechanisms that promote and guarantee open government. It is through open government that Argentines will best put a brake on corruption and favoritism in high places. Politics everywhere to some extent depends on forging alliances by "rewarding" one's friends, but neither business nor democracy can thrive unless there is a fair and level playing field, and the game is legally played. As Argentina restructures itself economically and increasingly turns to privatization, more open procedures need to be in place to ensure that public servants do not enrich themselves at the public's expense, or allow unwise economic policies flourish for purely selfish and hidden political reasons.

Argentines would also do well to study how the governments of other countries avoid the bankruptcy of large and important domestic corporations. Recently the Japanese government intervened to prevent the collapse of its nation's largest department store chain, and the United States judiciously will provide loans and other relief to large corporations whose collapse would trigger a panic in the markets or put too many people out of work. We call this concept "too big to fail," and it recognizes that some businesses are too fundamental to the overall health of the economy to be allowed to slide into bankruptcy. The major political parties have to be willing to work together to make this happen, and Argentine politicians have been too slow to realize that everybody stands to lose when large and important enterprises are threatened with ruin. As the case of the collapse of Banco de Intercambio Regional proved, there are times when the national economic interest transcends party politics, and the failure to see that and act appropriately can send a nation into a downward spiral from which it may not recover for many years. Argentina simply cannot afford such costly mistakes.

The very largest challenge facing Argentina today is to educate a new generation of business leaders and economic thinkers who will wisely and profitably chart Argentina's future course. Because of its fifty years of political turmoil, Argentina failed to develop a sufficiently large pool of people who have hands on experience dealing with foreign investment, the global markets, international banking, and creating incentives for business growth. At the same time, Argentina today, like every other nation in the world, must cope with a communications revolution, which is upending traditional business practices and whose ultimate direction and effect no one can predict. Fortunately, Argentina has one of the very best and most generous educational systems on the planet, and its youth have a global outlook. Argentina needs to recognize now that these talented, bright young people need room to develop as entrepreneurs.

But on every score, I am optimistic. The Argentine electorate is more mature than it has ever been. Argentina's interest in reaching out to the rest of the world has never been stronger. Argentines are still blessed with an abundance of natural resources, the greatest of which is the Argentine people themselves. If the people of Argentina throw their support behind leaders who possess character, integrity and common sense, then there is nothing that this nation cannot do.

ACKNOWLEDGEMENTS

T his book could not have reached completion without the aid of some very generous and able people. In particular I would like to thank United States ambassadors to Argentina Frank Ortiz, Terence Todman and Raul Castro for reading draft versions of this manuscript and offering invaluable suggestions and words of praise. I would also like to take this occasion to thank them for their many years of wise counsel as U.S. ambassadors to Argentina, and in other positions of enormous responsibility. I also want to thank them for the warm friendship they have given me over the years.

My editor, Kathleen Quinn, worked hard in making this book thoroughly accessible to my readers. Laura S. Rozenberg, a talented Argentine journalist, brought her considerable wealth of knowledge to patiently fact-checking the manuscript. I am immensely grateful to Mary Filiatrault, Trudy Diamond and Angela Maloney, all of whom loyally worked for me on Argentine matters for a number or years. Elba Rodríguez typed successive drafts of the manuscript and kept me organized throughout the process. Barbara Bartels and Miriam Marks provided able assistance in diverse areas. Kenneth Wainer organized decades of correspondence, files and records to make the writing of this book possible. I am deeply grateful to them all.

I remain grateful to the late Ambassador Robert C. Hill, who played such a large role in my coming to understand Argentina in depth. Likewise I am grateful to Robert Felder, once a U.S. foreign service minister in Buenos Aires and now a U.S. ambassador; to ministers John Bushnell and Wayne Smith, and to Robert Zimmerman, who was head of the Argentine desk at the U.S. State Department at a very active time in our relations with Argentina.

I want to thank Thomas K. Finletter, former secretary of the air force and John J.B. Shea, who hired me to be the New York office manager of the Stevenson for President Campaign of 1956; to Congressman Samuel S. Stratton of New York with whom I worked until his untimely death (and who, in my opinion, would have won the Senate nomination in 1964 if Robert Kennedy had not intervened!); to Senators Fritz Hollings and Jesse Helms, who have shown an enormous amount of interest in international affairs and interest in Argentina, and particularly Senator Helms, who as chairman of the Senate Foreign Relations Committee has encouraged United States support for a successful Argentina.

To Frank Coates, Jr., a roommate at Harvard Law School and to his father Frank Coates, Sr., the executive vice president of Northeast Airlines, who gave me my first job there; to James W. Austin, the president of Northeast Airlines, and Ralph Starkey, the official of ICAO who introduced me to Brig. Miguel A. Moragues, the president of Aerolíneas Argentinas.

To all of the employees of the Export Import Bank of the United States whom I worked with over the years but particularly to Marvin Solomon, who formerly headed the legal section; to Warren Glick, general counsel; to President Henry Kearns and to John Clark and Hobart Taylor, directors; Robert Morin, vice president of the Aircraft Division; to Thomas Doughty, Clem Miller, Bill Crafton, Arthur Pilzer and other officials at the Bank who assisted Argentina and Argentine Airlines.

To the officers and counsel of the New York State Banking Department, particularly commissioners James Bolster, John Heimann, Muriel Siebert and Vincent Tese; to Ernest Kohn, Larry Fine and Spiro Donas. I also wish to thank Robert Gray and Lawrence Merthan of the public relations firm Hill Knowlton.

I am grateful to many distinguished Argentines who personally gave me so much insight into Argentina and who did so much for their country: President Fernando De la Rúa, Ambassadors Rafael Vázquez, Alejandro Orfila, Jorge Aja Espil, Carlos M. Muñiz, Arnoldo T. Musich,

Carlos Ortiz de Rozas, Raúl Quijano, Esteban Takacs, Arnoldo M. Listre, Carlos Keller Sarmiento; to the other Argentine ministers I met, namely, Rogelio Frigerio, Alvaro Alsogaray, Adelbert Krieger Vasena, Conrad Storani, Alfredo Gómez Morales, Mariano Grondona, José María Dagnino Pastore, Oscar Camillon, Bernardo Grinspun, Domingo Cavallo and Jorge Wehbe.

I wish to thank Saúl Rotsztain for the years he assisted the Argentine Chamber of Commerce in the United States and to George Castex for the enormous help he gave me, especially in preparing the Encuentro. I also owe thanks to Governor Eduardo Angeloz of Córdoba, a good friend who was also a Radical Party candidate for president of Argentina; Horacio Roitman, the attorney general of Córdoba; José Bemet, José Romero Feris and Senator Ricardo Arrechea; Armando Blasco, Jorge Domínguez and their fine families. All these people increased my understanding of Argentine politics during the long years I have known them.

I am grateful to the officials of Banco de la Nación with whom I worked: Mario Nosiglia, Hillaire Chanteon, Jorge Hernández and David Cash (who was assassinated by Argentine terrorists); to the president of Banco Nacional de Desarollo, Luis F.A.J. Gottheil, and to Antonio Frogone, Luis Mey and Eduardo Pérez Alen, all of whom contributed to our victory in the case of *Mirabella vs. Banco Nacional de Desarollo*.

I owe a special debt of gratitude, since 1958, to the very fine law firm of Severgnini, Robiola, Larrechea, Quijano & Grinberg in Buenos Aires, whose founders and present-day partners have been, unfailingly, professional and intelligent lawyers. They provided me with my professional introduction to Buenos Aires and I will be forever grateful. I especially wish to thank, individually, Alberto Severgnini, Mario Robiola, Juan Francisco de Larrechea, Bruno Quijano, and Mauricio and Hector Grinberg.

I wish also to express my deep gratitude to the many hardworking people of Aerolíneas Argentinas, whom it has been my privilege to represent in the U.S. for more than forty years. In particular I would like to thank the general counsels with whom I worked: Roberto Forn, Martín Barrantes and Gabriel Pérez Junqueira; the Argentine managers of

Aerolíneas in the United States: Alberto Smart, Paul Hildebrandt, Romani Del Val, Bernardo Bolatti, Manuel Basaldúa, Miguel and Edgardo Abadía, Santiago Curchitser, Diego A. Hohmann, Walter Bohl and Arturo Muzzio. I also want to thank Liliana Bechara and Marcelo Moscheni, in New York and Buenos Aires respectively; and the presidents of Aerolíneas Argentinas I have known: Brig. Miguel Moragues, Juan Carlos Pellegrini, Brig. Arnoldo Tesselhoff, Brig. Luis María Klix, Brig. Fernando Toscano, Brig. Roberto Baltar, Brig. Amílcar M. San Juan. I wish to thank the long-time comptrollers of Aerolíneas Argentinas, Carlos Scherpa and Carlos Negri; and the financial vice president and comptroller, Silvio Becher. I am grateful to Ing. Manuel Morán, the president of Aerolíneas under SEPI, and to the two fine women who have made the running of the New York office possible all these forty years, Olga Belén and Ebe de Panciroli de Oroza.

A number of other Argentine citizens from all walks of life have been of immeasurable help to me over the years, and I would like to thank them now: Dante Simone, Mariano Grondona, Carlos Diz, Menegazzo Cane, A.M. Acassusso Capurro, Néstor Errecart, Antonio P. Frogone, Guido Jontza, Jorge A. Monteferrario, Eduardo Pablo Setti, Nancy and Lawrence Smith, Atilio Alterini, Eduardo Barbier, Andrés Cisneros, Juan Carlos Brandan, Ricardo Cairoli, Fred Chaoul, José Chalen, Jaimie Cotton, Judith Evans, Claudio Escribano, Horacio Fargosi, Buey Fernández, Gustavo Figueroa, Rafael E. Fondevila, Octavio O. Frigerio and Luis M. Gottheil. Ernesto E. Grether and Robert Favelevic; Jorge E. Hernández, Pablo Wagner Kildegaard, Gustavo Leguizamón, Brig. Ezequiel Martínez, Mario Raúl Nosiglia and Archibold B. Norman, the publisher of the Argentine magazine *Review of the River Plate*, which published many of my articles over twenty years and helped promote U.S. and Argentine relations. Rafael H. Saiegh, Brig. Roberto Temporini, Brig. Roberto Fermín Aguirre Champeau, Federico A. Dodds, Rafael Trozzo, Richard Hessert and Ricardo Zinn.

To the officers and directors of the Argentine American Chamber of Commerce I owe a great deal of thanks for helping me and other Americans draw closer to Argentina. I particularly want to thank former presidents Fred Vinton, Jr., Ogden White, Jr., Félix Uno and Enrique Bledel. The following directors were also particularly helpful to me: Ricardo A. Bunge, Héctor Caram Andruet, Alfredo Weiner, Byron G. Tosi, Maurice Acoca, Jonathan Green, Francis N. Cahn, Ezequiel A. Camerini, David H. Drewberg, Perla M. Kuhn, Arturo Muzzio, Bruce A. Olson, Margaret E. Sayers, Frederick D. Seeley, Jacques F. Trevillyan and Julián Magdaleno (who worked very hard as the managing director of the chamber for many years). Joan Faber worked for a year organizing the Encuentro for the Chamber, and I owe her many thanks.

I want to also thank my friends Barry and Marjorie Traub, two of my most cherished friends, and Martin Project, who also assisted me greatly and founded the New York Venture Fund, of which I am a director.

I want to give special thanks to Paul Ambos, who started as a young lawyer in our firm and rose to a partner quickly. He is a superb professional lawyer with great character and integrity.

Last and most importantly, I want to thank the most intelligent and hard working lawyer and friend I have ever known, a man whose character equals his intelligence and integrity, my brother and partner, Jay Henry Levine. Without his dedication this book could not have been written at all, and in our partnership, his brilliant academic and practical ability has made everything possible.

More people than I can mention in this space contributed to my understanding of the events described in this book. I hope they forgive the omission of their names and understand that I am grateful to them beyond words.

As to any errors in judgment or fact that may have slipped into this book despite my best efforts, I take full responsibility.

Laurence W. Levine
New York City,
August 2000

INDEX

CREDITS

1/20?